Five miles a pint!

Walking the South West Coast Path

Tim Newing

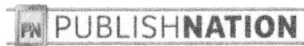

PUBLISHNATION

www.publishnation.co.uk

Table of Contents

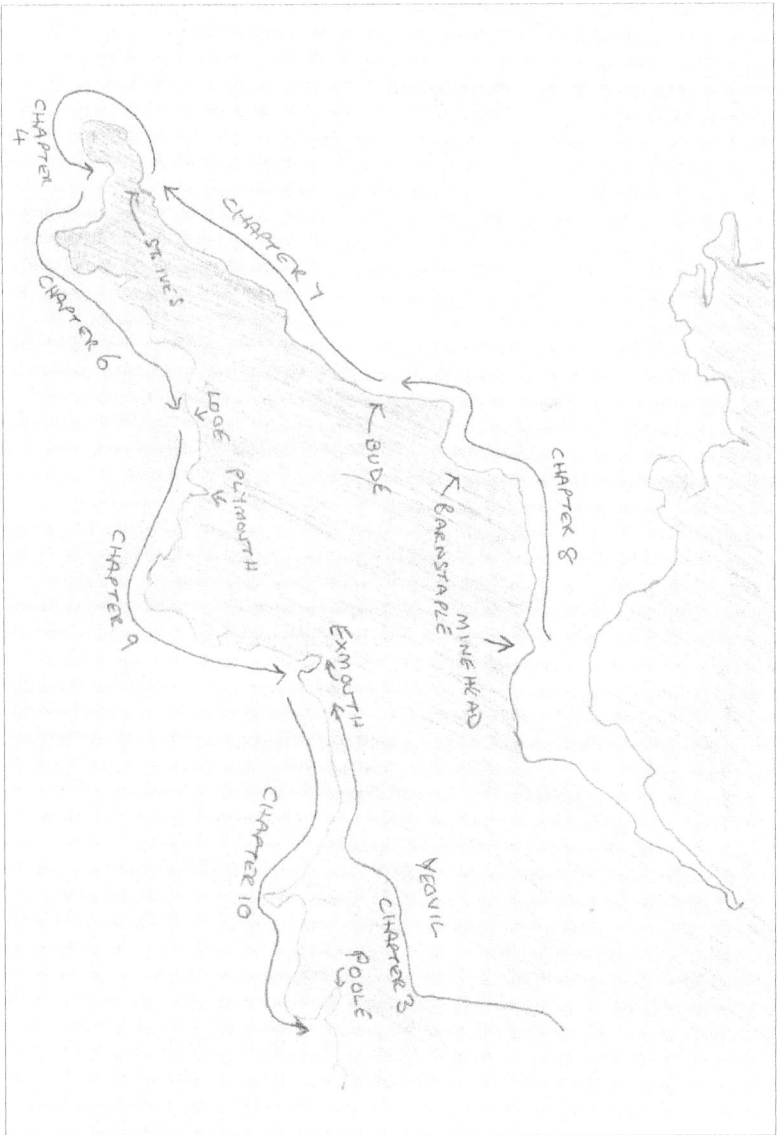

(Chapters 2 and 5 are not on The Path and have their own maps).

2

1. How did we get ourselves into this mess anyway?

On a bright and sunny March afternoon, the view from the little two carriage train from Lancaster to St Bees was superb. Sea and bird-rich mudflats stretched out to one side with small villages and fields to the other. In the distance the mountains of the Lake District provided a backdrop and the train progressed slowly stopping at almost every Victorian station on the way. An announcement reminded passengers that if they wanted to alight at one of the others, they needed to make a special request to the conductor. At one point it crossed an estuary or inlet with the track so narrow and so close to the water that it seemed like we were actually on a boat, albeit a strange long thin one. With time to sit and relax I reflected on what had brought us here to follow in the footsteps of Alfred Wainwright and make our attempt on the long distance 'Coast to Coast' Walk.

OK, so I know that you thought that this book was going to be all about our EPIC journey along the South West Coast Path (SWCP) and what, I hear you ask, am I doing going on about Cumbria and the Coast to Coast. Well, bear with me for a while, because walking the SWCP was never part of a plan; it sort of started by accident and then got a life of its own. And, of course we didn't start our hiking career by intentionally taking on England's longest waymarked footpath. Oh no, apart from day walks and walking holidays abroad, we started with the Coast to Coast. Graded medium-hard and almost two hundred miles long, I'd long wanted to give it a try. I'd started to research and plan. I'd even bought a guide book by Terry Marsh (TM). '*Not a walk on which to cut one's teeth as a backpacker,*' it said on page one of the introduction.

I checked the diary. The last two weeks of March 2011 were free and I mentioned it in passing to our friend Paul.

"I've always wanted to do that." he said. "I've never done anything like it before but I've got lots of holiday to use up before the end of March."

3

A few days later he received an email from me:

"Were you serious? Do you want to come? I'll be booking the B&Bs this week so make your mind up." Poor chap; no time to back-out elegantly, so he came.

Then I let on that the people who run the 'transport your baggage' service along the length of the walk don't start until April and so, in TM's parlance, we'd be 'teeth-cutting'. Lesley and I, fresh back from almost four weeks in Nepal with a minute luggage allowance, were pretty confident that we could get away with not too much baggage. We sent Paul a packing list and the name of a place that sold cheap gear. He bought some, tested it, and went back and bought more. It all seemed to have come from a single manufacturer. The Karrimor Kid (KK) was born.

Oh, the Karrimor Kid - just hear him wheeze
The Karrimor Kid has knackered knees
The shiniest kit, the brightest star
But can he move without a car?

He did about 90 miles practice in the six weeks left before we started and in hilly Devon too. We did a bit less, with rucksacks full of bottles of water and bubble-wrap to simulate the real thing and we all 'rested' on the last weekend. Monday came and with it an email from the KK:

"Not sure if I'm going to make it. Did my knee in mowing the lawn. Am off to the physio to see if he can put it right".

The Kiwi physio showed no mercy:

"You won't make it any worse. Just strap it up like this and take some painkillers. But remember to put the strapping on before your sun-cream."

Sun-cream? On knees? In March?

And so, started what turned out to be bouts of periodic madness in the form of long-distance hiking. The middle-aged protagonists, were me (Tim), my wife Lesley and of course Paul. The formula was set: Walk each day carrying all our luggage, Paul and Lesley with smaller rucksacks (the 'Berghaus Bags') and me with a larger one christened 'the walking wardrobe'. We would stop each night in a B&B or pub somewhere close to the route and where we could find the all-important hikers' supplies: food and beer. As you read on, you will most probably notice that

4

the B&Bs and their owners made quite an impact; the quirkier the better so far as we were concerned! Perhaps unfortunately, but probably for the best, I have changed their names to make finding them again more 'interesting'.

We were so enamoured by the Coast to Coast walk and Wainwright's plea that people made up their own routes that, soon after, we madly embarked on our own version, The Hare-Brained Hike: a walk from our house in Wing, Buckinghamshire to Paul's house in Kennford just South of Exeter in Devon. The route we took by chance included part of the SWCP, the first part we attempted: the stretch from Lyme Regis to Starcross.

Yes, I know that's East to West and the wrong way compared to the 'norm' and so we had to do it all again later on, but it was still the first part. Therefore, The Coast to Coast and the Hare-Brained Hike are the first chapters of this book and I'm sorry, but you just have to read about our EPIC adventures in Northern England and then on the Southern chalk hills of the Ridgeway and Wessex Ridgeway before you get to the real SWCP part. Think of it as a necessary evil that makes the rest so much better.

Even then, there was still no intention of walking the whole of the SWCP. After all it's 650 miles for goodness sake. And we'd noticed that, due to the pressing need to find places to stay, places to eat and, of course, those all-important British cultural centres, pubs, we did tend to walk further on each section than officialdom recognises. In the end the Coast Path was, for us, not to be a mere 650 miles, but 720!

We'd also learned one important lesson, or so we thought: the need for practice i.e. getting out there and doing some hiking in advance of the trip and with the actual gear that is to be taken. And so, when Lesley and I booked a walking holiday to the mountains of Turkey the following year we needed somewhere hilly to practice on. An email went to Paul entitled 'Another Hare-Brained offer'.

Hello fellow Hare,

I'm calling this one 'The Penzance Practice' - A long weekend walking round Land's End on the coastal path. See attached outline. Any interest? If not, you could be missing out on sore feet and several pints of Cornish Ale! We could do an earlier date but have picked 31 March because that's still the Mad Hare month

5

and because it would get your day off into your next leave year (just).

How could he resist? And of course, once we had done that, we wanted more. Paul found traces of a walk known as 'The Alternative Coast to Coast' going from Walney Island in the Irish sea off Cumbria to Holy Island in the North Sea off Northumberland. Having completed that, in just about the worst possible weather, we still weren't satisfied for some reason. That's when we started to do sections of the SWCP for its own sake. Sorry again, but I've included a chapter on the Alternative Coast to Coast so that you can get the full idea of the background to what happened next (and, of course, because it expands the total mileage walked in this story to an amazing, or perhaps stupid, 1,400). Eventually we had done enough of the SWCP to make the challenge to finish it just too tempting to resist.

This journal is unlike most of the other 'walking The Path' reports. They, rather sensibly, start at the beginning, progress to the middle and finish at the end. Usually the walk seems to be tackled in one 'hit', which is fine if you can spare the 8 weeks or so needed to do it this way. However, our story is not like that. It follows what we actually did chronologically rather than geographically. Snatching time off from work, usually once per year, and always in the spring or in the autumn when accommodation is cheaper and more available, we would start somewhere we could get to by public transport and finish somewhere where public transport could rescue us again.

After a while it became easier to plan because we discovered that whatever the terrain, whatever the weather, the presence of 'killer steps' or otherwise and regardless of whether we stopped for a pint at lunchtime or not, we always seemed to manage an average of two miles per hour over a whole day's hiking.

Was ours the best way to walk 'The Path'? I've no idea, but I'm told by Paul and Lesley that we had 'fun!' Oh, and by the way, we managed to sample over 100 different beers and ales en-route (174 if you include the 'pre-Coast Path' walks).

Tim Newing 2019

2.   In the footsteps of Alfred Wainwright: The Coast to Coast (March 2011)

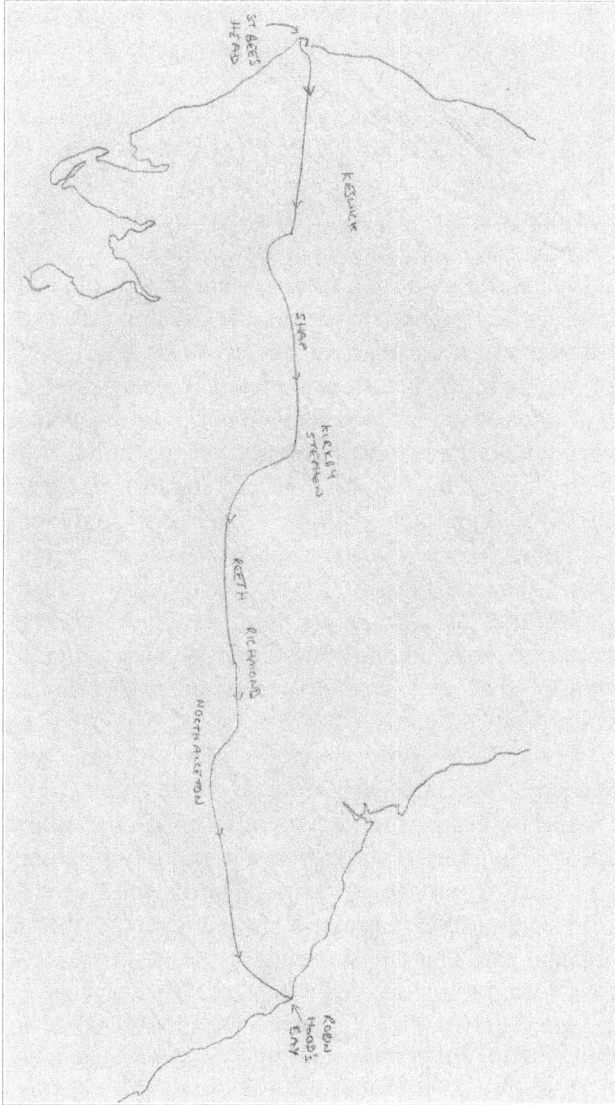

The little train from Lancaster to St Bees passed Windscale; St Bees next stop. We started pulling our heavy rucksacks from the overhead luggage racks. The lady opposite looked at Lesley.

"You're like a rose between two thorns," she said.

Surely, she couldn't have been referring to Paul and me? Did we really look that bad already? She was on a day trip to Maryport.

"What's there?" we asked.

"I don't know," she said. "But I'll get off and find out and then I'll go home again."

Our B&B was about three houses up from the station at St Bees. It was early afternoon when we knocked on the door. Helen's husband opened it, releasing an aroma of fried bacon and sausages, and ushered us into the kitchen. He turned his attention to the frying pan.

"It's my lunch," he claimed, as Helen arrived.

"Oh good, you're on time then," she said to us. "I've put you right on the upper floor where you have views of the start of the walk at St Bees Head. Would you like some milk for tea? and are you going to sit and watch the rugby this afternoon? We're off to a horse meeting early tomorrow and have lots to get ready and my friend Janet will look after your breakfast. You're our first Coast to Coast walkers this year. You are early in the season aren't you, I do hope that you get good weather."

I suppose that she must have stopped to breathe at some point but it wasn't obvious.

We managed to escape the rugby offer on the basis of the lovely sunshine outside and went for a wander round the old red sandstone buildings of the village, nestling in the valley out of harm's way. The church was especially inviting doubling up as a kind of local history museum rich on the legend of St Bega (précis: Irish princess runs away to escape marriage to Scandinavian prince, shipwrecked on Cumbrian coast and decides to found a nunnery), the St Bees Man (précis: mummy of man buried between 1300 and 1500 and discovered in 1981) and the local shipwrecks (providing enough timber to construct the church roof).

Before long we found ourselves lured to the coast and the sandy beach where the usual winter Saturday afternoon things were happening: excited dogs rushing around, excited kids playing with the sand and not noticing the cold and wet, and not excited at all frozen parents wandering about looking miserable. We officially started the walk by performing the two required rituals: boots dipped in the salt seawater and the selection of a (very small) pebble each to carry across the country to Robin Hood's Bay.

The next morning were woken by the traditional Cumbrian weather pounding against the Velux roof-windows, the rain trying to get at us before we'd even set off. St Bees Head had become invisible, and, looking the other way, there was no sign of the Cumbrian hills; the buildings on the other side of the street were about as far as we could see. Janet served up a huge breakfast and helped delay the inevitable by chatting almost as much as Helen.

"People come from all over the world to do this walk." she told us, "But the funniest are those that set off and are back ten minutes later asking which way they should be going – and they expect to be able to walk across England."

Feeling faintly relieved that we'd found the first signpost in the sunshine yesterday, we left, dressed in full waterproofs, closed the garden gate behind us and almost bumped into a chap on a quad-bike with three dogs on the back.

"Nasty weather," he offered sympathetically.

The dogs wagged their tails enthusiastically. We were all unreasonably fresh and keen so we gave him an optimistic, "Could be worse." and walked strongly off down the street past the statue of St Bega and her rather rain-filled coracle and a second man out walking his dog.

"Just off? Are you going the whole way? Oh, good luck!"

And thus, with this inauspicious start, began our long-distance hiking careers that would eventually lead us to complete the South West Coast Path (SWCP).

Down at the deserted beach the sea was grey and angry with huge rollers. Up on the cliffs the wind and spray were joined by thick mist and we could see nothing, not even the lighthouse when we passed it. The route follows the coast around for a few

9

miles before turning inland and, as we did so, the wind dropped, the rain relented to a persistent wet drizzle and we found ourselves crossing a flat agricultural section between villages. Some of the paths seemed to have been replaced by rivers, lakes or just muddy bogs.

Paul quickly came to the conclusion that his waterproof boots weren't and started singing The Hippopotamus Song. As soon as we could, we picked up a stony track leading out of the fields and onto a road via a gate bearing a helpful notice saying that if we reached this point, we'd gone wrong but to turn left up the road to pick up the Coast to Coast route once more.

One o'clock saw us sitting on a long stone bench in the shelter of the covered entrance to St Leonard's Church in Cleator drinking our flasks of coffee. I'd waited until Lesley and Paul had practised with heavy packs before floating the idea that, with a big breakfast and huge pub meal every day, we wouldn't need to carry heavy sandwiches. I wasn't so sure that it was such a great idea now!

On the edge of Cleator we crossed the river Ehen thus entering the Lake District National Park and facing our first real climb. The two guide books we were carrying had different opinions on this section. Alfred Wainwright (AW) relishes it, whilst Terry Marsh (TM) talks about the need to collapse in a heap upon reaching the top and before admiring the vast panoramic view.

As we climbed through the cloud the rain finally stopped but our 'vast panorama' extended about ten metres. I took a photo of Paul on the cairn at the top, by which time Lesley had wandered on and disappeared in the mist and hadn't collapsed in a heap at all. We rapidly set off after her, having found out by now that she was the only one with good enough eyesight to read the grid reference numbers on the GPS machine without resorting to reading glasses. They, of course, were pretty useless in these conditions.

We reached a point where Wainwright's original route went straight on and more or less fell off the other side of the fell while the more reasonable TM's circled round on tracks through a pine forest with weird eerie lighting in the mist. As we consulted the map a chap with a backpack appeared from behind and overtook us going at a rate of knots.

"Are you enjoying it?" we asked.

"No," was his simple reply, as the mist enveloped him again.

The track led round the end of the fell and then by a river into Nannycatch gorge. We followed a little path between the crags as it criss-crossed the brook on bridges. We were supposed to come out by a fake stone circle but, in the mist, we carried on too far missing the road by about twenty metres and walking parallel to it for a while, only realising our mistake when we heard a car driving along it.

The road took us down to Ennerdale Bridge and our stop for the night. The door of the hotel was locked but the bar seemed open and inside they were expecting us. Do all walkers go to the bar before their rooms? Paul assured us that this was the tradition. We settled in by the fire and a short, round girl in her early thirties, who was running the bar, came over to chat. After a while she told us that when she was eighteen, she had actually done the Coast to Coast walk, but with some of the local squaddies. It had taken them four and a half days. We were impressed! Her main complaint seemed to be that they'd spurred her on for the last fifteen miles or so by the promise of a beer at the end and when she arrived all she found was an ambulance. She spent the next three days in hospital. It wasn't a reassuring story!

You could tell we were in a hotel rather than a B&B. We didn't get the chatty welcome on arrival, and in the morning instead of chat there was a CD player in the dining room. That's why, when we left along empty tarmac lanes under a cloudy sky, Paul and I were singing fifties rock and roll, and Lesley was trying to pretend that she wasn't with us. But soon we came to our first lake, Ennerdale Water. The route ran along its Southern edge via a narrow, rocky path. It was Lake District views as I remembered; spectacular scenery that stopped part way up where a ceiling of grey cloud obscured any high bits. Paul's knees were holding out, strapped up strongly, and everyone was rested and ready for day two.

At the end of the lake there was a flat green bit, I suppose it might almost be called a field. Anyway, there were sheep on it and a farmer, out with his dog. We had a long chat and the farmer seemed very keen that we continued on his land on the South side of the valley rather than take the forest track on the North. Yes really, a farmer encouraging people to walk across his land. Unkindly we speculated that perhaps he'd laid land mines, or wanted to do a bit of shooting later on. We opted for the 'traditional' Northern route which took us through pine woods for several miles along the valley. Gaps through the trees revealed lovely views back the way we'd come but mostly it was rather boring. It earned a whole paragraph of wrath from AW. TM tries to maintain the interest by talking about the discovery of a Neolithic hand axe factory in the valley and the legend of a marauding giant dog.

Finally, the track led us, and an approaching Land Rover, to Black Sail Hut. As Youth Hostels go it was tiny. A couple got out of the Landy and started to open up, releasing a whole flock of waiting balloons that scuttered off across the scenery.

"We're cleaning up after the people who rented it this weekend," the girl said, "Would you like to look inside? it only sleeps sixteen, in two eight berth dormitories and this small common room gets very crowded."

We peered in. It looked small and very dark in there with big open fireplaces. I bet it can be cold and horrible up there but it turned out that the hut was already fully booked for the rest of the year so we didn't have to stay and see.

There was a small rickety bench outside, and the chap sitting on it got up and made to set off back down the valley the way we'd come. We thanked him for giving up his lunch spot, but did we really look so bad that people felt the need to show us beds and give us their seats? Nothing that a spot of coffee and a celebratory Mars bar wouldn't fix, maybe.

There'd been a notice on the counter in the hotel this morning, warning us to be careful not to miss the invisible path leading away from the Youth Hostel and making the mistake of taking the better path leading to a bridge over the river Liza. Clearly, one major feature of an 'invisible path' is its invisibility, so we took the only path available for fifty metres or so and then, looking up at a different angle, spotted the invisible one. Now, would a signpost have been a good idea?

12

Anyway, it took us to the side of a little brook tumbling down a pretty sheer bit of hill and up we went, climbing into the mist and stopping as instructed by TM to admire the views. Well, for us the inside of the cloud looked pretty much the same as the inside of the one yesterday, but as we gained the ridge and paused to check the map there was a call from in front of us:

"Do you know where you are?" A figure emerged.

"Well, yes, thanks, we do actually."

"Oh good, could you show me?"

He opened a big scale map, much better than the one we were using and Lesley, demonstrating her superior eyesight, read the grid reference from the GPS to convince him. He was about seven hundred metres from where he thought he was, and heading South instead of West. A second figure, his mate, emerged.

"OK then, on a scale of one to ten how embarrassed should we be?"

Lesley uncharitably suggested a nine and, as the mist swirled around, we caught sight of a boundary fence behind them, which if they followed it would take them back to the right place.

We climbed across the top of the pass, the mist swirling about us now and not quite so thick, so that we could just about see the next cairn from the previous one, and as we went further it seemed to clear even more. We even started to get some patches of blue sky as we approached the workings of Honister slate mine. We found walls, we found old roads, we found great tablets of stone that Paul threw around a bit. No-one else was up here today. Even down at the main quarry buildings on Honister Pass everything was shut (yes, even the tea room!) The owner/manager had been killed in a helicopter accident a few days earlier. It had been all over the local news when we were in St Bees and today was his funeral.

Tea-less we carried on all the way down the old toll road (now a bridleway) to Seatoller and the next closed tea shop. Still without a beverage, but with very tired legs, down we went again to emerge on the road at Stonethwaite to find our B&B. The door was opened by Wendy with long grey hair tied in a ponytail and who, I guess, was around seventy. We lowered our packs to take our boots off and she grabbed them and hauled them inside. Yes, even mine. Now I'd spent the last three days trying to convince Lesley and Paul how massively heavy it was and wasn't I a hero for carrying all this stuff. My story was rather ruined. But then she picked up both their packs together and headed off up the stairs with them. I felt a bit better.

A quick look at our rooms and then it was straight back down for tea and biscuits. Ah, at last! Tea!

A lone chap arrived on the bus from (H)uddersfield and was taking tea. With slow speech and a tendency not to bother with all the letters in his words it turned out that he'd come for a few days walking and planned to go up '(h)aystacks in t(he)'mornin(g)'.

As I emerged from the shower, there was Wendy. She had a large parrot on her shoulder (yes really, and this was *before* we'd been to the pub) and apologised for not having chatted to us over tea. The funeral had been of her nephew but she hadn't attended as she never goes to these sorts of things, but the lady vicar had popped round to make sure she was all right. She recommended the food in the riverside bar half a mile away in Rosthwaite and when we got there, we found it to have an enormous real fire, enormous dogs and to serve one of our favourite beers, Old Peculiar.

Day three and this was the one that we'd all been worried about. On a map of the profile of the whole Coast to Coast walk this bit looks like a section of dragon's teeth, all sharp and pointy, and we know from long walks in the past that day three is when the legs are at their most tired. Paul started the day by taking photos through his window without even getting out of bed, so that didn't bode well, but out there the weather had cleared and we could see mountains.

Wendy served breakfast and as soon as it was done the parrot was back on her shoulder, even when she went outside.

"I'm off to help my brother with the lambing today," she told us. "He does rare breeds. Isn't the weather going to be lovely? You're going to Patterdale? You know, you really should stay on the top and not drop down into Grasmere. You'll see all the views and I've done it that way twice now, look here, on the map, you just follow this boundary and it takes you all round."

The parrot seemed to approve. It was tempting, and AW does encourage people to find their own routes.

We decided to experiment with a bit of initiative straight away and, leaving Wendy, the parrot and her bird-table, occupied at that point by three woodpeckers, we went down the lane to Stonethwaite rather than to Rosthwaite on the basis that we'd done that bit on our trip to the pub the previous night. The path follows the river up into the high fells, past waterfalls, and to a small green hanging valley beneath a rather dramatic rock outcrop known as Lining Crag.

It took a while to plod up the hill, but it was rather gorgeous. Progress wasn't helped by the very young lambs, looking cute and shouting loudly for their mothers as we passed. We took a short rest on the edge of the hanging valley and then a climb up round the side of the crag and onto its top. From here there was a fantastic panorama, the highest peaks still wearing patches of snow. We set off across the top on a compass bearing, aided in places by the odd cairn. It was flatter now but still climbing and we came across our first really serious bit of black peat bog that needed to be detoured around. Finally, we were at the top of the pass, Greenup Edge, and stopped on some rocks for coffee and the now familiar Mars bar. In front there was a broad heather-covered bowl and beyond mountains, coming and going as the tantalising mist swirled around.

As we dropped into the bowl and walked to the pass in the distance the mist gradually cleared so that, by the time we got there, it was a truly gorgeous day. Decision time. AW's route went straight over and down to Grasmere, although he did offer some alternatives entitled *Let's do a ridge walk* and L*et's climb a mountain* that turned out to be Helvellyn and Striding Edge!

Wendy's route turned right and kept to the high ground past some lovely blue tarns, following a line of old fence posts across the heather and bogs. We took a vote. Unanimous. Stay High. It was lovely but pretty tough going. Eventually it reached the Dead Pike high point and then set off along the edge of a craggy steep edge with the A591 in the valley far below. A while later we reached the point which Wendy had

15

described as 'a bit steep'. The line of old posts seemed to jump off the edge of the cliff towards the road in a suicidal bid. We might have guessed that this would have been the choice of a parrot-wearing iron-man granny. Fortunately, she'd also mentioned a second, less-dramatic route, for wimps she'd seemed to imply, not marked on the map and along another of those 'invisible' paths. We took it anyway and before long had managed to lose over 300m in height and get safely down to the road.

Now we were getting really tired, but still had lots of the walk left to do. We sat for a rest and another Mars bar. Paul changed his socks and examined the blisters - growing nicely. The sun came fully out and so did the shorts. Next, we had to climb up a gully alongside a small brook to regain all that lost altitude. It was really hot. Paul washed his head in a waterfall and spent the rest of the day with bits of moss in his hair.

We'd drunk everything we were carrying and so, at the highest waterfall we could find, we re-filled the coffee flask. Just beyond, where the river turned into a flat boggy bit there was a rather sick looking sheep standing right in the middle. Still, the 'sheep-wee coffee' in the flask, while tasting 'unusual', did see us through the rest of the day.

At the top of the pass was a lovely little lake, Grisedale Tarn. The water overflowed to create a river heading down the opposite side. We followed it along a long, spectacular valley with a rocky track underfoot. Some other people were out walking and, rounding a corner, we suddenly found a hut with a group of University students hanging around outside eating biscuits. Sadly, they had none for sale!

Eventually we reached a rough road and stopped for a rest and, for Lesley, her third Mars bar of the day! Seldom in the history of this country has one so thin eaten so much chocolate. But, supplied with extra energy she led the route march into Patterdale, through the village and down the road beyond. We turned up a track where the map marked the farm we were to stay in. As we approached sheep bounced out of our way, off the track and over drainage ditches looking like someone had put springs on their legs. We certainly didn't feel like bouncing anywhere.

"Have you come all the way from Rosthwaite?" Mrs I. asked, as we thankfully took off the boots and rucksacks in her hall. "You've had a lovely day and done well to get here so early."

It was about six and just starting to think about getting dark. We hobbled up the stairs.

"There was a gentleman from Reading here last night doing the Coast to Coast but he arrived by taxi. He'd only got as far as Grasmere and then this morning he caught a taxi back there to do the second half today."

And then she became our favourite person of the day:

"I'm going out in an hour. Would you like a lift to the pub?"

The public rooms in the farm were immaculate and at breakfast there was a fire lit in the dining room. Outside was a light frost and clear blue skies. When I went to pay and ventured into the big farmhouse kitchen, I found the real home. Things all over a big table and a TV on the wall in front of a big and obviously well used squishy sofa. Mrs I. wanted to talk. I got the family history, the local news from the village, the funeral details and the holiday report; they'd just got back from Australia and New Zealand. Outside I found Mr I deep in conversation with Lesley and Paul. They were fending off four rather bouncy dogs looking a bit like slim, athletic Dobermanns who seemed to be trying to lick them to death and he, waving a bottle for feeding lambs, was trying to convince Lesley and Paul that they were Australian sheep dogs of some sort.

When we finally left and detoured back up the road to the village shop opposite the pub, we debated the motivation of B&B hosts and came to the conclusion that they all need to have people to talk at. As we progressed, we gained more and more evidence for this theory, the hotel at Ennerdale Bridge being the only place on the entire route where we didn't get a major talking to.

The shop turned out to be just what we needed. Half village convenience store (more Mars bars required) and the other half everything a Coast to Coast walker might need: new Thermos and blister plasters for Paul and special stick-the-sole-back-on-the-boots glue for Lesley.

17

The route then crossed the river and went for a massive climb up a wall of mountainside opposite. With not a cloud in sight and all the mountain-tops in clear view we set off up the steep path in shorts and t-shirts. The views looking back were fabulous. When we finally reached the pass, it wasn't obvious which way to go. A number of tracks set off across the bog each heading for a different bit of high ground. With map, GPS and compass we picked a promising one but soon found it wasn't right, so off we set on a bearing through the heather and bog. Looking back, we still couldn't work out where the path started from but in front, across a ravine, it was in clear view with two people wearing backpacks walking determinedly along it.

We followed them for a while and then they appeared to have a tiff with one setting off left up the nearest summit and the other continuing. We soon caught up with him sitting on a rock at Angle Tarn. "Are you doing the Coast to Coast?" he asked. "Oh great. Do you mind if I come along with you for a while?"

It turned out that this was Sean, the 'gentleman from Reading'. Yesterday he had walked the 'missing' section and stayed in the pub in Patterdale. This morning he'd climbed the hill but missed the same path we did, only to meet someone he'd had breakfast with who'd walked with him for a while to show him the way (so no tiff after all). In retrospect coming with us may not have been his best decision of the day. We even confessed to our little detour this morning, but he was not to be put off.

Now as a party of four (and trying not to think of Shawn the sheep) we followed the clear path across the hills with the most fantastic scenery in all directions. In places the going became boggy and the path indistinct but almost never horizontal. Our undoing was to leave the path to detour to a small crag overlooking a particularly special view for a coffee stop because, when we set off again, we picked up the end of a wall and followed it to the nearest summit and missed the path that went through the wall and not to the summit at all.

Once we were on top of the wrong mountain and looked at the map, the mistake was obvious of course. Unfortunately, between Rest Dodd and the Knot there was a drop of well over

100m but no real choice, so we marched all the way down, and marched all the way back up again. Exhausting! Strangely Sean didn't make an excuse and leave us. In due course we safely reached Kidsey Pike, more coffee and decision time. The 'proper' route is down the spur that stretches out in front and round the side of the lake in the valley far below. We pointed it out to Sean. Mrs I. had been adamant that, given the weather, it would be much better to stay high and follow the line of the old Roman Road along the top for several miles and cut down to the dam at the far end of the lake later on avoiding the difficult rocky path as well as enjoying all those rare high views. The vote was taken. We all opted for Mrs I.'s suggestion over AW's – yes, even Sean.

The way was well walked, mostly on short turf and all along the high ridge, and was lovely. After a few miles there was no sign of the crossing path we needed to take to get back to the lake. Not even when the GPS said we were in the right place and the map clearly showed it. We went on a bit further. Still no sign, but not wishing to damage my 'never go back' reputation, it was time to set off on a bearing across the landscape to try and intersect it. The going deteriorated, first into heather and then peat bog with deep black gullies that we had to circle round. We were being pushed lower and lower down the mountainside and now the problem was deep river gullies that we needed to cross. All the way down, and all the way up again. With no paths the going was slow and very tough indeed but eventually we got to a small rise and there, right in front of us was the path, a broad track, once more in short turf.

We followed it for a mile or so to another point where the GPS and map said that there should be a cross roads and we could descend to the lake, but on the ground of course there was no such thing. How frustrating! We carried on, and after a while spotted a farmer's track below that seemed to be heading roughly the right way. More cross country and now Paul and Sean were beginning to get really tired, while the recent expedition to Nepal started to pay off for Lesley and me.

This track did go some of the way and we had a couple more 'linking' bits to do before we found a sheep trod that finally took us down to the water. We'd dropped a huge amount, over 500m from the summit, and it felt like it. But it was getting rather late and we still had a long way to go.

All of a sudden, we'd come to a much flatter area, with limestone walls and lowland vegetation. The Lake district seemed to have just stopped suddenly with that huge descent and there was no more ahead. Very soon we came to Coast to Coast diversion signs to avoid a missing bridge. Unfortunately, the diversion appeared to go around in circles so once more we chose our own way and set off for a route march to try and arrive in daylight. Sean, although limping was still cheerful, and determined to keep up.

We passed some nice bits as we went down lanes and through fields, especially the ruins of Shap Abbey, but we didn't stop much. Had we done so we might never have got going again. Finally, we came into the Northern end of Shap but it was one of those long thin towns that seems to go on for ever, especially at the end of a long hard day, and Mrs I. had warned us that our next B&B was right down the far end, next to the Greyhound pub. Sean made it to the pub and went in to get a room.

It was dark when we knocked on the B&B door but inside Mary was waiting for us. Her thing is to provide cream tea on arrival, so that's what she did. At seven at night we had tea, scones, jam and clotted cream before a set of quick showers and a stagger back to the pub. Sean was there, sitting on a bar stool with stockinged feet hanging down not touching anything. He bought us all a drink to say thank you:

"I'd never have found that route and made it here if it wasn't for you."

Hmm, maybe not; maybe he'd have just stuck with the proper path and arrived hours ago instead.

Fortunately, Mary offered us no route suggestions over breakfast and we were all a bit crotchety when we set off down the lane alongside her house. Paul had released his knees from their strapping; the walking seemed to have mended them, but his blisters were maturing nicely. We'd all developed colds and Lesley's was so bad that she'd lost her voice. None of our legs seem to move the way they used to.

Our first task was to take the footpath to the pedestrian bridge over the M6, which marks the completion of the first third of the walk. Lesley spotted Sean on the other side, but when we got there there were only footprints. We walked across green fields, now with cows as well as sheep, and to the 'hidden' village of Oddendale lurking behind a band of trees. Here the fields gave way to the heather moorland and the outcrops of limestone pavements of Crosby Ravensworth fell. We picked up the route of an old Roman road, detouring only as instructed to inspect a rather inconspicuous double stone circle. As we started to drop into a valley, we stopped to look at the map and compass and a half naked jogger came past.

"Aim to the right of the tree on the horizon," he shouted and then he was gone.

We started crossing a large expanse of undulating moorland, cut by incised river valleys with large rounded granite boulders dumped all over the place by retreating glaciers, pleasant and very different from what had come before, but not photogenic, dramatic or exciting. A grouse popped up to look at us, peering intently until we got the binoculars out when, of course, it took fright. It was to be the first of a very great number.

About lunchtime we entered the village of Orton with its old church, old cottages, Quaker history and closed shop. A man getting out of a Land Rover saw us looking sadly at the very shut pub and said, "Have you tried the chocolate factory? They have a tea shop."

What? A factory for chocolate? Here of all places? But indeed, it was true. From the tea shop there were windows looking into the area where women clad in white overalls were doing things with brown and white 'water wheels' of molten chocolate. As we sat, we watched a video showing how they make white chocolate mice, but all too soon it was time to move on and take the road out of the village and to the fields of cows and ponies that lead onto open moorland once again.

Our stops were becoming rather more frequent now and we sat for a while by Sunbiggin Tarn on the edge of a rare road through the area. We moved on when a number of cars turned up and disgorged their human cargo. Most of the afternoon was spent negotiating the wild moorland, but Lesley started lagging badly. We stopped and fed her another Mars bar and the transformation was astonishing. Off she shot, leaving Paul and me way behind.

Finally, we came to a disused railway line and a bridge over Scandal Beck and then we had the first real climb of the day, all the way up Smardale Fell. It was lovely, but did seem to go on for a very long time on tired legs. So much so that we even checked the GPS to see if we had missed a turn or something. But no, we were in the right place. It eventually crossed the summit and emerged onto a road, with the last couple of miles of fields dropping down to the market town of Kirkby Stephen in the valley below.

We arrived at the B&B just before dark. It used to be a pub and still even had the bar in one corner. Carol allowed us to collapse in the lounge and fed us tea and hot cross buns until we felt we could manage the stairs.

"There's another Coast to Coast walker coming to stay tonight," she said. "He phoned earlier and asked me to say 'hi' to you. You all walked together yesterday he said, but he got lost this morning and is running a bit late."

Sean! What could have happened to him?

Upstairs the rooms were big, and contained an amazing number of beds. We had three doubles in ours. Lesley soon found out that there were chocolates hidden all around. Her childhood Easter egg hunt training started to show.

There was still no sign of Sean when we were ready to go out, so we told Carol that we were off to the Kings Arms and would love to see him and buy him a beer when he arrived. In fact, what we did was go to the Spar and buy tissues, Lemsip, throat lozenges and any other cold remedies we could get our hands on, before doing more work on the beer log.

The Kings Arms turned out to be a family run hotel out of season, with a few people in the bar and the chatty owner serving. When we asked for food, he dashed off only to return a few minutes later.

"The chef was just going home but he's staying for a while now."

We felt bad: never a good idea to upset the chef, but he seemed happy enough when he appeared to ask us how we wanted things cooked a bit later on.

Just as we were being asked to go through to the deserted dining room (they'd rustled up a waitress for us from somewhere as well), Sean stumbled in. He looked bad: dirty sweaty t-shirt and muddy trousers. It was about 8.30. He'd knocked on the door of the B&B and Carol had given his pack to her daughter to take to his room and sent him straight round to the pub to find us. He looked a bit better after a beer or two and some food, and told us that he'd done the last few miles using his torch to find the paths and stiles and thought that maybe he should have a rest day tomorrow.

The last entry of my diary for the day read 'I wonder how we'll all be in the morning. At least we've done the last of the really hard walks for a while.' How wrong can you be?

Sean joined us for breakfast and we compared notes. The three of us had all slept badly, owing to a bug-induced inability to breathe. Paul's blisters were now pretty impressive, especially one on the top of a big toe, or, more basically, the one that was the top of his big toe. Lesley's voice, which had recovered after some alcohol last night, had gone again and all our legs were tired. Sean seemed even worse. Cold free but with a definite lack of desire to ever see any footwear again. He asked Carol (rather pathetically we thought) if he could possibly stay another night and we last saw him scantily clad heading back up to bed having delivered just about all his clothing for her to wash. We never did see or hear from him again and the next section turned out to be one of the toughest of all.

Just up from the B&B was an enormous old church, almost like a cathedral. We popped in for a look leaving Paul on the seats in the entrance changing his footwear. Those few hundred yards were the last he ever did in those boots. They'd started to wear from the inside out, with the cavities thus created accommodating the growing blisters.

In the village of Hartley, we came across an old bloke with a stick, walking his dog. He pointed out the big grand house on the hill above the town and told us it was a rest home and then

23

he insisted on holding open a gate for us. We must have looked very bad!

A track took us past a quarry that went up, up, up, passing llamas on the way (hang on, they live in the high Andes, don't they?) and onto open fell. Here there was more up to do, initially on a track but then on paths across peat bog. Once again, the weather was fantastic and the views great and, in the distance, we could see the Nine Standards Cairns. There was more up and then the path followed a gully (up of course) with a tall cairn on either side looking like sentry boxes and framing the Nine Standards still in the distance. A bit more up and just as everyone was about to collapse, we were finally there: The Nine Standards Rigg and the watershed of the country. Rain that falls on one side ends up in the Irish sea, and that that falls on the other in the North Sea.

Just beyond, there was a trig point and then we were into serious open bog-land, dancing around the very worst bits to find something less than over-the-top-of-the-boots deep. Finally, a rough gravel track by a small shed-like building at the top of a small stream turned up and we had lunch (the Mars bars had finally given way to a biscuit alternative), sitting on a grassy bank in the hot sunshine listening to grouse shouting "go away, go away". It must have been almost exactly on the boundary of the Yorkshire Dales National Park.

The stream took us down the valley, growing as it went into the top end of Swaledale and to the remote farm of Ravenseat. As we approached, there was a lot of ferocious barking and it was only when we got quite close that we could see a very tiny white fluffy dog standing in the middle of a small humpback bridge guarding the way in. We called to him when we were close and he came rushing down and rolled over at our feet.

The path turned to follow the valley and the scenery had changed completely. Lots of dry-stone walls, green grassy enclosures, a deep river gorge and noisy sheep with their noisy young lambs everywhere. Paul went camera crazy. He'd been brought up in Yorkshire and this seemed like home even after thirty or more years away. In the warm sunshine reminiscent of a really good June day it was indeed really lovely. If only those legs would work that is.

Keld is the half way point for the whole walk and the 'official' overnight stop for this section but it was the one place where I hadn't been able to get any accommodation. Before reaching the buildings, we turned off to take the path through the fields on the other side of the river. When I'd planned this section, I hadn't looked too hard at the map and was expecting a gentle riverside stroll the four miles extra to Muker. But not a bit of it. The way was rocky and uneven and had no qualms about climbing and then dropping an alarming amount. Paul's emergency footwear had soles so thin that he was feeling every pebble.

We joined the Pennine Way for a couple of hundred metres and then the two long distance paths went their separate ways near a nice waterfall. Ours climbed, fell and climbed some more and we could see Muker so far along the valley that Lesley didn't want to believe it was our destination. We stopped for a rest at the turn-off to Crackpot Hall, a ruined farmhouse high up on the valley and where AW takes you up onto high moorland again to go and look at the old lead mines, but we carried on as the path turned into a track and gently dropped to the valley floor. It followed the river to a pedestrian bridge and on to the village.

A rather large Mr K. was sitting outside his Farm on a bench in the sunshine, looking like he was waiting for us. Well, we were a bit late and he probably recognised us from the big packs and slow limping motion. In almost every other place we stayed, we were shown through a spotless entrance designed to impress. This one was different. We went straight into the working kitchen. Overstuffed ancient armchairs were on one side of a big table and kitchen surfaces on the other. Mrs K. (also fairly large) was there, ironing their underwear (large) most of which was spread out all over the place. No problems, no embarrassment. She simply stopped to chat to us and then let Mr K. take us through some rambling corridors and upstairs to a couple of large and immaculate bedrooms. Ours had a bay window looking out along the length of the valley and was equipped with a coffee table and a couple of rocking chairs. Marvellous! They'd obviously had new showers installed as well - nail you to the floor with hot water. Double marvellous!

The pub was just around the corner and one of the only two places we found that served giant Yorkshire puddings. It also did Old Peculiar again. It was Friday night and busy, but the young landlord took time to talk to us.

"Ah, Mr and Mrs K," he said. "They work here in the pub on our days off and so far, they've outlasted three landlords. I'm their fourth."

Now, when we'd arrived, we'd been asked what we wanted for breakfast and Paul had decided to make a stand against the ubiquitous Full English. Worried about gaining weight with massive pub meals as well, he'd said that he'd just have cereal and toast.

"Oh, you get those anyway," said Mr K. "What do you want for breakfast?".

"Well, what have you got?" tried our hero.

"You're the guest, you can have what you like," came the expansive, generous, but not especially helpful reply.

The conversation went on in this vein for a short while until Paul tried,

"How about a bacon sandwich?" which seemed to be acceptable.

In retrospect, perhaps it was a mistake to try and be different in a farm, and especially one run by amply proportioned people. Once we'd attempted to make an impression on the fruit and then the yoghurt and cereal, two huge fried breakfasts were brought in and Mr K. went back to fetch Paul's bacon sandwich. He came back with what appeared to be little short of a small loaf filled with most of a piglet, and then hung around for a chat and to make sure that Paul didn't leave anything.

We tried some diversionary conversation while Paul got to work.

"Lovely valley. We walked past Crackpot Hall yesterday and what a great position that's in."

"Oh yes," said Mr K. "My Uncle and Aunt used to live there. I remember visiting as a child and there was a slope inside from the front door to the back of the house where the front was falling into the mine-workings below."

"So, have you always lived here?"

"I was born in a farm about a mile away. This was my Grandmother's house and we moved here about five years ago when she died aged 104."

It turned out that the Grandmother (or maybe her mother, I guess) had started doing B&Bs in 1922 for people who used to come out of the towns by train and then go round the dales on bicycles, and Mr and Mrs K. have just carried on with the tradition.

Eventually Paul seemed to have managed the impossible, but maybe we'd need to check his pockets later on. We were allowed to leave although Mr K. tried to persuade us to take some fruit away to eat as we walked.

Outside it was slightly misty and much cooler than yesterday and there was a definite sense of hobbling as we went back to the bridge across the river until the legs woke up again. Paul had abandoned his worn-out boots but was still going. He reported that each night he was reaching the B&B not knowing if he could continue the next day but somehow, after a night's rest, he felt he could do a bit more. Today was the shortest walk of the entire route and with no big hills either. It followed the river gently down the valley through fields and a few woods.

Whilst pleasant, the route was a bit 'samey' and the most memorable features were the very narrow squeeze stiles, which every self-respecting stone wall (and there were an awful lot of these) came armed with. Never easy, and especially when wearing big rucksacks, these ones were particularly difficult as each was guarded by a spring-loaded gate covering the gap. So, it was a fairly acrobatic art to get through. The technique seemed to be to pull the gate open and try and get one foot part way up the wall to where the gap started. Then you had to be fast. The second leg had to be moved in behind the first and the body lent forwards to get the rucksack into a sensible place as you needed to let go of the gate to free up the arms. The gate of course now came crashing back into place, clobbering the back of your legs if you weren't far enough forwards. Then your arms are on top of the walls to lift the body up to a suitable height where there was enough width for the rucksack to pass.

So now you are suspended above a narrow gap above a stone wall. What next? Well, you have to throw yourself forwards in a kind of ungainly leap. If all goes well you end up landing with both feet on the ground on the other side of the wall, but if you don't get enough horizontal motion there's that embarrassing bit where the body and feet are through, but suspended in mid-air as the wretched rucksack comes down and gets wedged in the gap - not good, and especially not good just after a big breakfast. Good job we didn't eat the fruit.

We arrived in Reeth around two and knocked on the door of our B&B. Robert opened it and suddenly looked panic stricken.

"Ruth's out and I don't know which rooms she wants you in. She won't be long, I'll give her a call."

Ruth wasn't answering her mobile and Robert looked even more stressed. It didn't matter to us, we just wanted to drop off our bags, get out of our boots and go for a look around.

Reeth turned out to be big, compared to the places we'd been through and a bit of a tourist trap. It had a large but 'on-a-hillside' sort of village green with buildings all around: some craft shops, four cafés, three pubs, a bakery and even a tourist information place. Even in March there were quite a number of day-trippers and cars parked all over the place. The lady in the tourist place seemed to find it hard to believe that we were doing the Coast to Coast,

"You're so early in the season, even the museum is shut."

Oh well, with no museum to see we'd better go back to the B&B then. We knocked on the door and this time Ruth answered.

"Sorry my husband panicked," she said. "We're doing some decorating and he didn't know what to do with you."

It turned out that he's a builder and was supposed to be installing a new bathroom just as soon as we were out of the way, and then she was painting before the next guests turn up. She showed us some nice bedrooms, with perfectly good bathrooms, and the most incredibly thick fluffy towels (maybe they were sheep in disguise), and gave us tea and cake. So, for the first time since St Bees we had time enough to sit and relax for a while.

Later we walked up to one of the pubs. They had notices about 'Swansong' and we had to ask the barman what it was about. It turned out to be a band that were performing in the pub that night, due to start at 8:30. Well, what with the early mornings and all that fresh air we hadn't been managing to stay up very late but we thought we might just do it. By 8:30 they were still setting up. 8:45 and no music, and we were all nodding off into our now empty beer glasses. Nine O'clock and we could do no more. We went home and never did find out what they were like. Pathetic!

When we looked out of our window in the morning it was to see Ruth go and fetch something from her car and get accosted by a very loud boy next door who rushed out shouting "Happy Birthday!". We checked later and it was. Paul was back on the Full English again. Nobody risked anything else for the rest of the trip.

The early morning mist cleared and we went out into another hot, sunny, shorts-wearing day that started with a walk along the riverbank and then went up through fields, with more of those stone walls and squeeze stiles. Soon we were being pursued by another walker, a lone chap, and coming towards us was a lone woman. She stopped to talk to Lesley,

"Have you seen my 'lost flock'? A group of four girls doing their Duke of Edinburgh walk?"

Nope, we hadn't. It turned out that the lone woman and the lone chap were the teachers executing a pincer movement and the girls had set off from a camp-site at Keld but had not been seen since. We carried on. The two met. The words 'b****y kids' floated towards us on the breeze.

Soon we came to the site of Marrick Priory but not much is left now except for a bit of a ruined tower and a new outdoor centre with rows and rows of wetsuits hanging up to dry. The teachers caught up with us. The girls had been spotted. Somehow, they'd got ahead by taking a different path. We climbed steeply up through a lovely wood, the teachers following and us at high speed to impress, but at the top of the rise we needed to take a breather. The teachers hurried on trying to get to a point where they could see the girls but not vice-versa. In due course we followed.

The village of Marrick was small but with some substantial buildings and the path seemed to have been diverted around the back of a farm. Suddenly, and, with no sign of the teachers, we came across the girls looking at their map.

"Hello," we said.

But they didn't seem to want to talk. We carried on across fields and down the side of a broad green valley with extensive views along its length. Hutton's Monument, a twenty-metre obelisk, was visible on the skyline.

The next challenge came near a farm with a steeply sloping field, slimy with recent muck-spreading activity. They'd even managed to slime one of those gate-guarded squeeze stiles. Soon after we stopped on a grassy rise in the sun for a coffee, and the girls caught up with us. They rested nearby and did seem a bit more prepared to talk. No, they hadn't liked the slimy field, and yes, the squeeze stiles were hard, and yes, they were going to Richmond. They set off before us but we caught up again on the steeply dropping tarmac road into Marsk. Two were walking normally but the other two were going backwards.

"Sore feet," they explained.

It seemed like the balls of their feet hurt so they were trying to take the pressure off in an unusual way.

We took a look into the 12th Century church of St Edmund, where the box pews were still in place, and tried not to think of Black Adder. A little further on there was a small grassy patch and the girls seemed to have sat down for lunch. They didn't talk to us this time as the female teacher was there standing over them and looking unimpressed. We never saw them again. I wonder if they made it.

Now our route headed across some fields and joined a track high up, just below a ridge of a limestone outcrop. The scenery was, as AW puts it *'of high quality'* and it was nice, gentle walking with plenty of young lambs to admire along an easy track for a few miles until, eventually, just about where the National Park ends, we could see Richmond in the distance, the houses all grouped around the castle with its tall tower.

There was a sign here as well, telling us we'd reached Richmond and that Robin Hood's Bay was only (only?) seventy-six miles away, which caused an outbreak of singing. Not altogether successful though, as it turned out that Lesley had never heard of the 'Seventy-six Trombones' song and Paul and I didn't really know the words. Furthermore, the tune doesn't do anything very interesting, especially when we sing it. We passed through a wood (lumberjack song) and came out onto a lane dropping into the town (desperate now, we'd moved onto the 'Always Look on the Bright Side' number from Life of Brian).

Our guest house turned out to be only a few minutes from the main centre of town and Joan, a small, roundish, bouncy woman answered the door. She reminded Paul of a fierce seaside landlady and inside were lots of 'Thou Shalt Not' notices. She made it clear that he was not to wash his boots in the sink – which was exactly what he'd been planning. However, she looked after us well, did all our laundry and gave us some good ideas of where to do emergency shopping and to eat,

"Most people have had enough of pub food by the time they get here." Dead right! We went to the Thai.

I'd planned a day of rest into the itinerary, and we'd reached it: a day off in Richmond. But that didn't mean a day off from the Full English, or the B&B hostess chat. Joan told us stories of how crippled many of the Coast to Coast hopefuls are by the time they get here and how, in the season, the chemist en-route always has a window display full of bandages, blister plasters, sun cream and painkillers. She told us of the American lady who'd got stuck in a squeeze stile and then fallen forwards out of it, bashing her face on the rocks as she fell, and how terrible she looked.

It was Monday. There were shops. They were open. Richmond market square was lovely. All cobbles and Tardis-like stores, with small frontages but incredibly long and thin inside. Emergency retail therapy followed. First was the cobbler. We'd been gluing Lesley's sole back onto her boot each night and it would last until about lunchtime and then start to come apart again. We found a man who would glue and nail it back together for £2.50 and it lasted the rest of the trip. Next a tour of all the outdoor shops looking for boots for Paul and then a celebratory visit to a coffee shop and a look at the castle. Finally, we sat on a bench in the market square, wondering if we were old enough to be permitted to do that. We ate buns for lunch.

We had a long rest in the B&B for the second part of the afternoon and then set out again to the nearest pub. It was having a beer festival and so it needed to be investigated for the sake of the log. Paul unwisely chose 'Ginger Tom-cat'. We've got one of those at home and know what he smells like! But by the time we'd gone on for a curry it was only a distant memory.

So now, after our rest day, we faced the longest single stretch of our journey, nearly 23 miles, the crossing of the almost completely flat Vale of Mowbray. We lingered over breakfast putting off the evil moment until Joan tactfully more or less said,

"Isn't it time you should be going?" We took the hint.

The route was quite pretty for a while. It went through the centre of Richmond and around the castle, and then through fields and woods with at least some contours to make things interesting. Okay, so the bit past the enormous and rather whiffy sewage works wasn't the best, but soon after that Paul and Lesley almost got mugged by a flock of ewes with tiny lambs which livened things up a bit.

After a while we did get into what AW describes as 'those interminable flat fields' and passed under the noisy A1. This marks the two-thirds point of the walk and we found ourselves in the somewhat litter-strewn bottom end of the race-course car park. Lesley couldn't believe her lucky find of a whole posh-looking china dinner service, but common-sense prevailed when she thought about how heavy it would be to carry and we managed to leave it behind.

We had to wait a while at Catterick Bridge. I believe it is normal, and indeed sensible, for rather slow heavy-laden pedestrians to give way to a somewhat faster, and indisputably heavier but with significantly less all-round vision, army tank. Most of the cars seemed to be treating it with respect as well and followed at a safe distance in a long procession.

We did some more flat stuff, and after a while came across an old spaniel attached to someone peering at a flock of swans in the distance.

"Most have gone now," he told us "But last week there were perhaps 200 on that marsh. Those left are all Mute except for that one third from the right, which is the last of the Bewick's." He passed over the binoculars, so we could confirm his analysis. Yup, they all looked like swans to us!

We stopped for coffee on a bench in the churchyard at Bolton-on-Swale. The skies clouded over, the temperature dropped, we got some spots of rain. We admired the memorial to Henry Jenkins: born 1500 and died 1670 aged 169. As we went into the church, a small, elderly, but clearly very active lady rushed forward to show us how to work the light switches (we do have some at home you know) and then rushed to the other end of the church (much faster than we could follow) to make sure we knew where the Henry Jenkins plaque was, and then brought us the Henry Jenkins history laminated cards. I'm amazed that she didn't try and sell us Henry Jenkins t-shirts on the way out - an opportunity missed.

More flat fields followed, but we'd looked ahead and spotted that four or five miles further on we got to another village and this one had a pub. Lunch stop, we thought and put on a spurt. AW had managed a bag of crisps and a pint and still described this section as 'a slough of despond'. We weren't so lucky. It was a Tuesday and therefore the pub was shut! We found out later that it was also shut when the tired Julia Bradbury and her BBC film crew got there. We made a point of sitting provocatively at the picnic table by the pub door drinking OUR coffee and eating OUR Mars bars but no-one went past to see our little protest. Even the weather gave it up as a bad job and the clouds started to clear.

We had trouble getting started again. The underneaths of our feet were sore and tingling, and strange muscles in the legs were complaining. Amazingly Paul's feet in his new boots were holding out − just about. Although today's walk wasn't much longer than several of the others, it was the flattest by far and turned out to be the hardest on the bodies. Our theory was that this was because you didn't get the same variety of gradient and underfoot terrain, and therefore the change of muscle use, but whatever the reason there wasn't much point hanging about there; we still had nine miles or so of dull, flat fields to do.

In the distance we could now see the wall of the Cleveland Hills rising up in a blue-haze and we knew that our stop for the night was right at their feet. They seemed a long way away.

The BBC filmed Julia sprinting between the cars as she crossed the A19, a busy dual carriageway, but I'm afraid we only managed a bit of a fast hobble and got hooted at. However, once across, a little lane took us through the few houses of Ingleby Arncliffe and down the short way to Ingleby Cross and the Bluebell Inn. It was five to six. We'd done almost 23 miles in ten hours. The pub was shut but a blackboard in the porch announced 'Newing – rooms 2 and 3. Keys are in the doors. Re-open at 6'. Aha! We were expected.

In a separate block, to the side of the car park, was a line of rooms, probably the most characterless we got on the whole trip, but we were just pleased to see them! Each was equipped with an electric foot spa! Never seen that before. Unfortunately, we only discovered it the next morning, just as we were leaving.

We dropped our packs, removed the boots and headed for the bar. Well, Lesley and I did. As Paul limped through his door, still in his brand-new footwear he said,

"Don't worry if I don't appear in the bar. I may be some time."

But later, he did. After all, there was food in there. The landlord walked with a limp. Real or just empathetic, we wondered. He asked about the crossing of the dual carriageway,

"We keep asking them to build a bridge but they won't do it, you know. Not until someone gets killed anyway". The place was full of off-duty farmers who nodded in agreement.

Amazingly, we all managed to set off again the next morning, immediately crossing the boundary into the North York Moors National Park. We were all stiff and the underneath of the feet felt well used. It was more of a hobble than a walk for the first mile or so. Clearly someone had had a word with AW and he was feeling much better as well. He called the next section 'splendid'. Meanwhile TM was back to normal too, telling dodgy legends about the places nearby: the village of Osmotherley: précis: princess dreams that her son Os would drown on a certain day so sends nurse with child up mountain away from water. Nurse falls asleep, son drowns in a spring, princess dies of grief and is buried by the side of her son. Hence Os-by-his-mother-lay. Uurgh!

Remember that blue-haze wall of hills we saw yesterday? Well, straight away we were climbing up it, on a forest track, and joining the route of the long-distance Cleveland Way path to the summit of Beacon Hill and out onto open heather moorland.

It was a bit misty up there, but much better than the heavy rain that the BBC had been promising for several days. As we continued, the clouds rose. We dropped down through woods and into fields where the path vanished and two ladies with backpacks asked if we knew the way. They were doing three days of the Coast to Coast, eleven miles a day because that's all they could manage, and, they said, looking a bit guilty, with a G&T at the end of each stage. We failed to mention the beer log. Rather cheekily Lesley asked what their husbands did while they walked. One worked and the other was 'useless' but did seem to drop them off at the start and pick them up again at the end. She said that the family joke was that if she died, then he'd have to re-marry by lunchtime in order to survive.

We climbed the next hill. More open moorland with noisy grouse everywhere and then, along beside an 'edge', moor to the right, cliff to the left, with great views down into the flat plain below. A small shower caught us here, so on with all the gear and then down a dip, up to a trig. point and a lunch stop in a sheltered hollow.

The ladies caught up and overtook us here, and we never saw them again. We suspect that the café that suddenly appeared in the next valley about half a mile on had something to do with that. But the roller-coaster-like progress continued via a steep climb up Cringle Moor to a stone seat and another great viewpoint.

From here the path dropped once more and the official end of the day is a short distance and one more climb away at Clay Bank Top, but with nowhere to stay. Paul had developed a limp and we were all pretty exhausted. We cut down a steep bridleway off the high ground and onto the flat fields of the plain below, where footpaths on the map, but rather more imaginary trails on the ground, led us to Great Broughton. Paul must have been feeling bad. Normally he has super-acute pub sensors, but we'd almost passed the Bay Horse before he noticed it. The Jet Miners came up soon after and just beyond was a cross roads and a very welcome B&B.

Ann opened the door into the porch, strewn with posh uncomfortable looking high-heeled shoes. She was younger than our other hostesses and skinny and, apart from the fluffy slippers, smartly dressed. We were too tired to care that our worn muddy boots just didn't fit in. Inside our bedroom one of the wardrobes was full of fancy party frocks. 'Chardonnay drinker' Lesley called her, summoning up all sorts of 'Essex girl' images. Paul's single room turned out to be two rooms, four beds and an en-suite bathroom as well, but even better there was a high ledge at the bottom of one of the beds just right for putting the feet up onto. He was suffering from swollen ankles.

Lesley and I even had time, once we had finally managed to extract ourselves from the hot power-shower, to sit in the lounge (without footwear) and watch TV. It hadn't improved! We asked Ann which pub we should eat in. She gave us a précis of each and they all sounded good so we asked about the beer,

"Oh, I don't know about that," she said.

"Chardonnay drinker!" Lesley announced again, once she was gone. We settled on the closest.

Ann was super-chatty at breakfast. She and her husband (away working on oil rigs) had done the last section of the Coast to Coast, the bit we were heading for. She told us how easy it was and how nice the Lion Inn high on the moor is, and by the time we were ready to go, the rain had stopped.

We must all have been feeling better. Last night, perhaps seeing the state we were in, she'd offered us a lift back up to Clay Bank Top this morning. Now, we thought this might happen so I'd been coaching Lesley on how to politely refuse, but when the offer came there was a distinctly long gap before any reply was made. This morning, though, the suggestion that some could take a lift with the rucksacks while others could complete the walk properly, without cheating, and all meet up at Clay Bank Top was also refused. We set off towards the hills hidden by low cloud with Lesley setting a cracking pace on the tarmac.

Unfortunately, we turned off the road slightly too early, on the left side of a stone wall instead of the right. Our nice forest track contoured round for a bit and then threatened to drop. The 'proper path' had headed off steeply uphill at an angle so by the time I got worried we were about 500m adrift. It doesn't sound much, but did we go back? No! We hacked steeply up through pine-woods, over a couple of walls and across peat bog and heather - exhausting, but finally reaching a spot height, our broad and obvious path, and gale-force winds.

As we went the wind got stronger but the clouds started to blow about and lift and we were left with great views in all directions. We joined the line of an old miners' railway track that wound across the moor and AW suggests that our walking speed should increase to five miles per hour. Not likely!

Of course, we blamed the wind. It was fine in the cuttings of course, but on the elevated sections, where the natural landscape falls away on both sides, it was all we could do to stand up at times. Eventually we rounded a corner and the wind attacked again, from a different direction. It actually picked Lesley up and dumped her in the heather. Not enough breakfast, clearly!

We could see the isolated buildings of the Lion Inn, up a rise ahead of us. The gale pushed us up, the gradient offering no resistance, but at the top a right turn was needed. We all got blown over attempting the manoeuvre and it was a matter of waiting (or in Lesley's case, sitting) and then lurching forwards between the gusts to the shelter of a stone wall and on into the pub car park.

Inside it was lovely, a real haven: warm, with open fires strategically located, and busy with people lunching. We started unwrapping. By the time we were down to about the same amount of clothing as everyone else, bowls of chips arrived, our first and only 'proper' lunch of the trip. A very shaken elderly couple came in and sat down. They'd just lost their caravan. As they were driving across the moor the wind had taken it and blown it over and away, ripping the tow bar off the car in the process. They'd come in to wait for the AA. As we dressed to leave:

"Be careful!" they said and we opened the door and went back out into the gale.

We noticed, as we staggered unevenly along the wide verges of the unfenced roads, that any motorists gave us an unusually generous berth, and we opted to keep with the roads and avoid the rough short-cut paths through peat bogs. Eventually we were off the absolute summit and in a slight lee took a track along a spur with a lovely valley stretched out below. It relishes in the great name of Great Fryup Head but instead of giving us the legend of the Norse goddess of beauty, TM starts talking about goblins in Glaisdale! Eventually we came to a gate onto a road and, far ahead, our first view of the North Sea.

The road led us to a wide-open grassy track that dropped gently and steadily the couple of miles into Glaisdale and our next B&B. It was quite different - a big, solid, old farmhouse with tall ceilings and large, dark rooms with big fireplaces, and packed full of antiques. The owners sounded like their homeland was on the other side of the North Sea. Unfortunately, it also had lots of display crockery on the walls and fluffy stuff. For example, in our room, the tissue box had been captured by a knitted fairy-tale cottage. The tissues could only escape through the chimney! Also, unfortunately, the pub was some way away and down a steep hill to boot. But you know what? With the walk to the pub and back we were only half a mile short of the Vale of Eden marathon and all felt reasonably okay. One more day and maybe we *were* going to make it after all.

A rare thing at breakfast: other guests in the B&B - an oddly matched couple, the chap stocky, broad and bald and the girl heavily made up and as skinny as anything. She wouldn't have made it across the moor yesterday! They'd come to Yorkshire for a long weekend and went fly-fishing for trout yesterday.

"Where did you learn that?" we asked. Apparently, his father and uncle had done it for years so it was instilled in him from an early age.

"And you?" we asked the stick-insect.

"Oh, it was my first time yesterday."

And guess who'd caught the one and only fish. She told him that he'd hidden his embarrassment well.

Our last walk took us back through the village, past the pub and a railway station to a very photogenic bridge across the river. Handy, except that we didn't want to cross but instead to climb steeply up through a wood, with paving stones that were worn down in the centres through use over the years. We emerged on a road that dropped once more to a second railway station. From here an old toll road ran along the valley bottom, where Lesley made friends with a dog on a quad-bike, before we emerged again at Grosmont.

This village had two stations. One for real trains and one for the modern ones. Unfortunately, we were a day too early in the season for the steam locomotives to have emerged from hibernation. The very steep climb up out of the valley and onto the open moor, and into the wind once again, gave us our first clear view of the sea and of the ruined abbey at Whitby on the cliffs. It was to haunt us all day. Always in the distance and gradually getting closer, but whenever it appeared the route seemed to head off in a different direction, almost as though it was scared of getting to the end of the walk. Indeed, a look at a map will show that the route takes a steep drop off the moor to the little village of Daisy Bank and then a big 'V' South and back North, while there is a perfectly good road cutting straight from West to East.

But, like the obedient people we are, we did what we were told and found ourselves in a lovely wooded nature reserve in a sheltered valley. A river ran through it, creating a spectacular waterfall at one point and there was even an open tea shop, but we were going well now and keen to make progress so I'm afraid that it had no custom.

Soon we were out on the moors once again and crossing peat bog. At the very last stage, the last half mile of the last bog, the path became indistinct. In retrospect it's probably because the land drops into a shallow little basin that looks okay but is really a giant trap, and so people either find their own way or get sucked in, never to be seen again. Having got so far, without once getting wet feet, I was mortified when, leading our little procession, I put one foot forward and the black goo came straight up and over the top of my boot with a noisy suck. Instinctively I put my other foot forward to stop myself falling and the damage was symmetrical. After that I ploughed on. Lesley and Paul took a longer, higher, and drier detour.

Lanes now took us down to a couple of villages, Low and High Hawsker, and the eagle-eye of the map reader had spotted a PH marked at the latter. The anticipation buoyed our spirits in the sunshine over this section, until our hopes were dashed on arrival. The latest owner has most inconsiderately turned it into a private dwelling. We went on un-refreshed down lanes and through the first caravan park, through the second with its closed tea shop (what's wrong with these people?) and finally out onto the coast path. We were tired, and our feet hurt, but this was the final section to Robin Hood's Bay.

The coast path did what all coast paths seem to do - undulate up, down, up, down. There was no sign of the bay until, suddenly, rounding a promontory, there it was, no distance at all. Our B&B was right at the top of the village, only about 50m off the route and so, as suggested by the chap when I'd booked, we checked in, dropped our bags, ate the biscuits in the rooms and carried on to complete the walk at the sea at the bottom of the steep main street.

The tide was in, so it saved us some distance to comply with AW's final instruction: 'Go forward and put your boot in the first salt water puddle.' I went a bit far. Wet feet for the second time. Julia had done the same.

We also observed the other rituals. Our three pebbles from the beach at St Bees were released and placed at the edge of the water to be lovingly taken on their next adventure by the next wave. We had our photograph taken outside Wainwright's bar by the plaque marking the end of the walk and then we went inside for a beer and to sign the book. Not many entries yet this year, and last year looked like a history of bad weather, bad knees, bad feet (the comment 'is it normal for your toenails to fall off' was a little alarming) and what a great time everyone had had.

We climbed back up the hill to the B&B to get changed and showered and then didn't have the energy to go far for dinner. The closest pub had a birthday party going on and was rapidly filled up with young things wearing little clothing and older ones wearing more. A band was due to start playing at 8:30. By 8:30 they were still setting up. 8:45 and no music, and we were all nodding off into our now empty beer glasses. Nine O'clock and we could manage no more. We surrendered our table to the masses and worked our way to the exit. Just as we got there the first chords were struck – blues. We stayed to listen to the first number, and then, pathetically, but strangely satisfied, limped the short distance home.

The next morning, we had the most massive breakfast yet: fruit, then cereal and yoghurt, then a fry up with two eggs, two sausages, two bacons. Big slabs of black pudding for Paul and me, and special fried bread for Lesley. Mushrooms, beans and then toast, four different types of marmalade and then home-made muffins. But we were okay. We'd had some practice! A couple turned up and asked if they could have a small breakfast. The owner looked shocked and then to us for support. We tried to explain as best we could and last saw them contemplating their groaning platefuls.

As we walked the few hundred metres to the bus stop, Paul was on painkillers for swollen ankles and had feet that looked somewhat agricultural underneath. Lesley's feet had returned from a ghostly white to a more normal pink colour and it was feeling rather strange and sad not to be setting off for another twenty miles or so.

Our friend Jane met us when we got off the train at Kings Cross and bought us all a beer to celebrate our achievement. She'd planned to come for at least part of the time but didn't make it. And when we got off the train at Leighton Buzzard much later on and I suggested a taxi back up the hill to Wing, I was treated with scorn. We walked of course! That last section took our total to just over 200 miles.

As the months passed the memories faded of course, leaving us all with the impression that we'd had FUN. The bodies healed and we soon forgot about some of the wetter sections. The Autumn season was approaching. How could we follow Wainwright's epic walk…?

3. The Hare-brained hike (Wing, Buckinghamshire to Kennford, Devon October 2011)

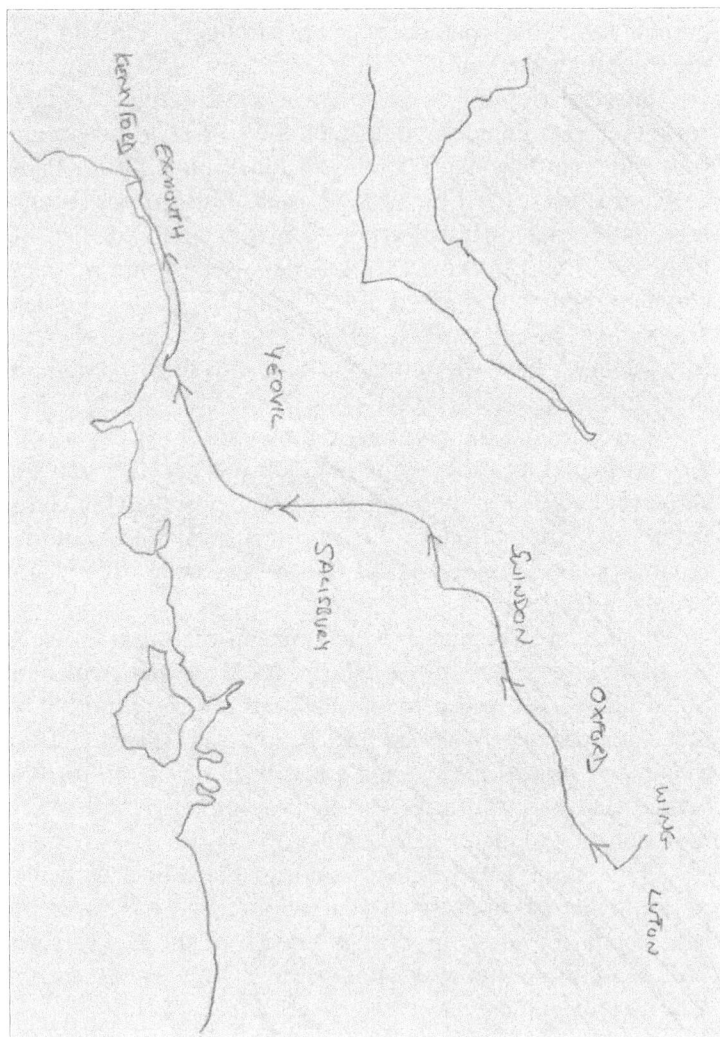

Paul, the long-term BT employee entered the disabled loo. Perhaps there was a shortage of phone-boxes at BT, or perhaps the transformation was more traumatic than that from Clark Kent to Superman. After a few minutes out popped the Karrimor Kid (KK). Older and more experienced after the Coast to Coast walk but perhaps not wiser. The purity of the branding had been diluted by the addition of a Regatta jacket. He set forth to enter the British railway network at Exeter.

His journey by train through the landscape that was to occupy us for the next two weeks provided time for reflection on our apparently quixotic intention: to walk from our house in Wing, Buckinghamshire to his, in Kennford, Devon according to the following principles:

1.   No Camping!

2.   Make maximum use of official long-distance footpaths (to stand a chance that the paths really did exist and that we would be able to find them)

3.   To keep to the high ground wherever possible (inherited from Wainwright's principles on his Coast to Coast path)

4.   To avoid towns wherever possible (another of Wainwright's)

5.   Definitely no camping! (Lesley was very keen on this one)

The straight-line distance is a 'mere' 149 miles, driving almost exactly 200, but the footpaths, meandering across the countryside as they do, gave us a target of 260 miles. And we had just 16 days to complete it. Lesley's work colleagues were bordering on the enthusiastic, and so were some of Paul's although they'd christened it the 'Hare-Brained Hike' and had then gone off to research whether it was Hare or Hair.

Some four hours later, Paul was in Wing and he and I went for a curry. The new restaurant owners told us of the latest lack of developments in their attempts to get plans through the town council for changes to their listed building and in response we told them about the Hare-Brained Hike. At first, they were nonplussed but soon settled on a consensus response: pity. They gave us each a very large complimentary brandy to see whether we came to our senses and wished us good luck as we left.

We found Lesley back home from her orchestra rehearsal, contemplating the need to average over 16 miles per day on the one hand and a large glass of wine in the other.

There was no backing out now.

It started just before eight on a Friday morning under clear blue skies and with mist hanging in the valleys that make up the great cabbage fields that surround Wing in deepest, darkest Buckinghamshire (well they did this October and rather smelly they were too). We headed straight towards the rising sun. An hour later we'd reached the local canal and our first long distance footpath, the 145-mile-long Grand Union Canal Walk. There was not a single person to be seen and no boats moving on the still blue water, all very pretty. The fleeces were off, the shorts were on and Paul was concerned.

"Round our way the sun normally rises in the East," he said. "And our plan is to go to the South West. We seem to be going the wrong way."

Do you get that when you go out walking; people questioning your navigational skills? And if so, how do you respond? I had to admit to myself that Paul did have something of a point and tried to make reassuring noises but after a couple of miles along the tow-path when it bent round to the right it seemed that the sun moved across the sky to match, remaining right ahead of us. Where the canal made another turn, South-West, which would have been rather helpful, we didn't. Instead we continued down lanes through the village of Ivinghoe and beyond. At the chalk scarp of Pitstone Hill the acorns of the eighty-five-mile-long Ridgeway National Trail indicated that we'd reached our second long-distance footpath. We'd covered eight miles in three hours which was to be the fastest on our entire journey.

The views from Pitstone Hill with Ivinghoe Beacon, where the Ridgeway starts, just a mile and a half away were great. The restored Pitstone windmill was visible near the new housing estate that marked the site of old cement quarries. In the distance, the big fancy Rothschild house, Mentmore Towers, could be seen. The sun once again matched our turn as we joined the path.

"Look, are we going around in circles or what?" asked Paul.

"This is supposed to be a one-way journey, not a circular walk you know."

We headed into beech woods where the sun was less obvious and overtook two ladies from Southampton with daysacks. They had been walking the Ridgeway in day trip sections and this was their last one.

We crossed the railway at Tring station (ten minutes back to Leighton Buzzard, anyone forgotten anything?) and the canal and then the bypass, and headed on into Tring Park. We and the sun curved round to head South West at last. Paul was not convinced, but look, we were following acorn markers, and then met a single chap with a Ridgeway book in hand going the other way. He'd cycled the first half of the path and was walking the rest. It was his last day. Paul was slightly mollified, until that is Mentmore towers, only a couple of miles from our start point, became visible again.

When we set off after stopping for lunch in a large, sunny field, Paul's knees had seized up. For about five minutes he hobbled along stiff legged until he'd managed to talk them into bending. Fortunately, this happened before we came across the two ladies again, who'd overtaken us and were now sitting on a log having a rest.

The small town of Wendover seemed to take forever to get to. The track wound through more woodland and then down past some posh houses with great avenues of beech trees. It morphed into narrow lanes, as though the planners were trying to keep the scruffy hikers away from their nice clean residents. Not surprisingly really, if Robert Louis Stevenson is typical of the kind of visitor that they get here. Mind you, he is reputed to have described Wendover as 'a struggling purposeless sort of place'. The other gem from the guide book was that the nursery rhyme 'Jack be nimble, Jack be quick' comes from Wendover, where lace-makers celebrating the feast of St Catherine jumped over a lighted candlestick for good luck. No lace-makers there now. Perhaps they all caught fire.

Suddenly we emerged right in the centre of the town by the clock tower, once a jail but now a tourist information office. There were no shops that we could see selling candlesticks, only clocks, but there was a tea shop! It wasn't in either the itinerary or the guide book, but it would have been rude to have simply passed by, so, cakes for three then. The two ladies popped out by the clock tower soon after and headed for the bus stop. We pretended that we'd been there for hours.

The onward route was West into the dropping sun and, unfortunately, straight up Coombe Hill, one of the highest points of the Chilterns. It's topped by a large monument to the soldiers of the Boer War. The large quantity of delicious sickly carrot cake I'd just consumed proved something of a handicap and, vowing to remember to be more abstemious in the future, I admired the views back to Mentmore towers, that at least had the decency to appear to be little further away than before. The opening ceremony for the Ridgeway National Trail had taken place here in 1973 and, after declaring the path open, the good and the great showed their commitment to it by strolling the 1.8 miles back into Wendover, presumably to a pub.

Ahead, we could also admire the distant cooling towers of Didcot Power station. They were to haunt us for days to come. However, if you go there now you won't have this problem. The demolition started in 2014.

We were getting tired now (or perhaps it was just too much cake) but continued along the ridge and dropped to cross the entrance to Chequers, the Prime Ministers' official country residence. It was well populated with CCTV cameras mounted in trees and we just had to wave at them as we crossed the Victory Drive and before we climbed up and over the next wooded ridge. Finally, just as it was getting dark enough to make map reading difficult we emerged within fifty metres of our destination: The Red Lion at Whiteleaf.

There were people sitting in the last of the sunshine at the tables outside the pub, having a beer at the end of the week. They seemed impressed by the Hare-Brained Hike, and that we'd just covered twenty-three miles, but less so when they found out that we'd gone around in a big loop and were only twelve miles, as the crow flies, from home. Paul manfully managed not to voice the 'I told you so' thought and Lesley managed not to ask for a review of the rest of our planned route. Perhaps they were just both too tired.

Inside there was a big log fire, flagstones on the floor and a large landlady, who immediately got us started on our beer log. She had no problems with boots and rucksacks littering the place up as we collapsed untidily onto any furniture that enabled the feet to be suspended in some way. She warned us that she'd just had a visit from her grandson and things may not be as clean and tidy as usual. Do you think we cared at this stage?

Upstairs, the carpet outside the rooms was rather covered in porridge, an unusual feature that added to the character of the place. Thanks, grandson. When we came back down, she'd reserved us a table right by the fire. She'd obviously had a lot of Ridgeway hikers staying through the season. The rest of the bar filled up with locals and their assorted dogs through the evening, as we tried not to stand up too often.

Breakfast had to be early. The Welsh chef wanted to watch the Rugby World Cup semi-final. Don't upset the chef! It suited us; we had eighteen miles to go and the weather was unbelievably good for October.

Our broad straight track (a Ridgeway and Icknield Way combo) went between lines of trees and bushes (planted to keep the flocks from straying when used as a drover's path, apparently), with occasional open patches and views down across the Vale of Aylesbury, and over to guess what? Oh yes, Didcot power station. Paul was happy at last, we were steadily heading South-West. It seemed that we were not so much walking a ridge, that was away to our left, but in no-man's land between it and the line of villages to our right.

We were in Red Kite country. Reintroduced from Spain in 1989 near Watlington, we saw them all day and they stayed with us, in gradually diminishing numbers, all the way down to Avebury. We'd also entered the land of apples. 2011 was a bumper year and boxes of them sat by many garden gates decorated with signs: 'please, please help yourself'. Happy to oblige.

There were no more Ridgeway long-distance path walkers even though it was Saturday. Just people out with dogs. As we lay in the grass by the track in the roasting sun, a very posh elderly lady slowly approached us with her small elderly and even slower dog.

"This morning I've watched the rugger, had a flu jab and now I'm out with the dog," she told us.

"How did Wales get on?" we asked.

"No good," was the simple response. We found out later that they'd lost by one point. Upset chef!

The flint-built St Botolph's church at Swyncombe was nice with a simple rectangular design, rather than the usual cruciform one. Eleventh century it said on the signpost but a biplane in one of the stained-glass windows suggested some more recent intervention. After that we tackled the only meaningful climb of the day and almost immediately deviated off the long-distance path through fields to get to Nettlebed and our B&B.

So, how would you feel about choosing to stay overnight in a place called 'Nettlebed'? Doesn't exactly conjure up the right ambience does it? And, as Paul pointed out, 'Norfolk', the name of the B&B, rather indicated either a dodgy sense of geography or some form of teleport in operation. Worse, we had all been reading Terry Pratchett, in which the witch Nanny Ogg has an important part, and the door was opened by a very active, switched-on lady who looked to be in her seventies and introduced herself as Nanny.

The house had a small frontage right on the main street but seemed to go on and on, Tardis-like, inside. It was deep and quiet, and full of books, half-finished paintings 'good deed' certificates and memories of a husband, lost just a few months ago to cancer, who had been in the Grenadiers and was halfway through writing a book on one of the battles of the First World War. To be fair, no sign of a tall, pointy black hat though.

Nanny gave us tea and four slices of cake. Odd, as there were three of us, but welcome after all those apples. We sat in her living room talking to her and she said that she kept going with the B&B because she liked the company. Then Lesley went upstairs, accompanied by Nanny, for a shower but left no trail of breadcrumbs. Paul and I were a bit worried. Not so worried though that we didn't split the last piece of cake as soon as they were gone! Nanny came back alone and made us more tea. Eventually I went in search of Lesley, leaving Paul with Nanny. Lesley had been transformed into......well, a clean one.

She'd showered and put on clean clothes. Nanny had booked us a table in the rather posh steak restaurant across the road.

An important day dawned: Lesley's birthday. Cards were duly produced at breakfast and Paul presented her with a Marmite branded water-bottle that was to accompany us all round the South West Coast Path in due course. Nanny said that she would have made cake, or at least found a candle had she known. Instead she gave us a good breakfast. We decided that Nanny had been great and lovely, just like some of the best characters in the Pratchett books.

We had a couple of miles to do before regaining the path at Nuffield, at first alongside the A road and then through fields, wet with heavy dew. But our first stop was at the petrol station at the edge of Nettlebed to buy biscuits. In we went with our boots and our big packs, and the bored Asian girl behind the counter perked up and asked,

"Where are you walking to?"

We told her about the Hare-Brained Hike and the plan to walk to Exeter. She looked bemused and went straight for the killer question:

"Why?" What would you have said? Eh? We didn't have a suitable reply until much, much later we thought of 'Have you seen the price of your petrol?'

There was a flint church at Nuffield, the Holy Trinity. We were told that its walls dated from AD 634 and contained Roman Tiles but inside, what we noticed most was the harvest tribute: apples, straw and some rather nice wreaths made from bread. In a simple but very well-tended grave near the doorway was William Morris of motor car fame. I bet he wouldn't have walked all the way to Exeter from there.

We came to Grim's Ditch. In the 3rd or 4th century BC it was a tribal frontier that ran for about fifty miles. Now it's a tree-covered high bank and deep ditch with, on this Sunday morning, the occasional cyclist, plenty of squirrels and more pheasants than you'd believe. Not Grim at all. It took us to the Thames. Well, on the map it looked like it did and we'd promised ourselves a stop by the river, but when we arrived all we got was a golf course, with the footpath channelled firmly between two hedges - no stopping there. We carried on until

North Stoke and a very convenient bench, right by the entrance to a large church. After a while the congregation came out, yes, all three of them, closely followed by the vicar and organist.

"Nice to see the bench in use," said one, before asking what we were up to.

Another mile or so and we did reach the riverside, with dogs walking their owners in fields on our side and massive posh houses on the opposite bank. A bossy woman with a megaphone in a motor-launch was berating a team of oarsmen in a skiff as they shot past at high speed. We went under Brunel's 'Four Arches' bridge, a magnificent example of 'a skew bridge with impressively slanting brickwork'. Unfortunately, as we didn't know what a skew bridge was at the time, its cleverness was rather lost on us and the brickwork not properly appreciated.

Where the bridge connects Goring to Streatley, the Ridgeway crosses the Thames. This is also the location of the nicely named Great Goring Gap, where the Chilterns end and the Berkshire Downs start. Once again, the planners seemed to want to keep us away from the beautiful people in their nice expensive homes. We were channelled down lanes to emerge right by the bridge and a tea shop. It had been a long stretch, the feet were complaining and the tea shop was full. We hobbled on into Streatley, and the feet went straight for the Beer Garden of the Bull and discarded the boots. Birthday girl demanded chips and something to enter into the beer log.

Just outside Streatley, a wide chalk path led us past a signpost showing that we'd done just over half of the Ridgeway National Trail. Paul was feeling much better about the general direction we were taking now. Some people out for Sunday afternoon walks were struggling up the gentle inclines and so, feeling rather superior (and fuelled by beer and chips), we strode past them and out onto the open tops of the hills. Beyond the racehorse gallops were good views of the Oxfordshire plain. Didcot Power station was much closer now.

Now, at this point the Ridgeway is pretty much what the name suggests: A ridge. The wide grassy and sometimes muddy path kept to the top and the land dropped away on either side. But the problem is that there aren't many, or in some places, *any* buildings up here. Places to stay tend to be in the villages lower down in the landscape. What I'm trying to say is that I'd had trouble finding B&B's on this part of the walk. Camping would have been easy on the ridge, except that water tends to run downhill and so all the places to get it were also lower down. Either way we had no alternative - leave the path and go downhill to a village some way off. Blewbury was our choice.

Sam, our fake-tan hostess in her fifties, didn't seem entirely organised. Mind you, we probably gave her the same impression! We seemed to have the guest room, while Paul was in the main living room where they'd installed a bed for the night. While Lesley dived straight into a hot bath, Sam worried that she hadn't stocked the rooms with biscuits (clearly vital), that the TV's didn't work (digital switch-over occurred a few weeks earlier) and about where we were going to eat? She started 'phoning around. We liked Sam!

There are two pubs in the village but neither do food on Sunday nights. Same with the pub in the next village, but fourth call lucky, so long as we could be there by seven. Lesley's soak, now enhanced by the presence of coffee and chocolate biscuits, was cut short.

We were about to set off when Mr Sam offered us a lift and to show us the start of the footpath back from the pub. Having three daughters (Paul had counted 14 different bottles of hair products in the shower), he seemed to be used to this sort of thing. We asked about their thatched house and the strange object on the roof.

"The original was a dragon, but we think this one's more like Basil Brush," he said.

The pub was fine, the food was good, and the footpath back only a mile and a half and not too dark, even when my torch gave out. But when we got back to Blewbury could we find the B&B? Nope. We unexpectedly found the church several times instead!

As we climbed the hill back to the Ridgeway in the morning, admiring the towers of Didcot once more, a jogger in her twenties seemed to double-up as we passed. Was it just the sight of us as we laboured under our loads? The state of our clothing

51

perhaps? Lesley and Paul thought she was clinging to a spaniel. Perhaps a heart attack? We did the British thing and ignored her.

Paul's GPS had recorded 2.9 miles from the B&B by the time we hit the broad white track of the Ridgeway, or 3.0 after he'd done a little dance to move it on a bit. The track soon went under the busy A34 - nice murals on the walls of the tunnel. So, imagine yourself here, on a long-distance footpath, miles from anywhere and in a tunnel going under the main road. You have paint and artistic tendencies. What would you leave here for posterity? Or at least until the Council came to clean it off. Perhaps political slogans, rude images or some sport-related art?

Nope, the individual who had found themselves in this position seemed to have a passion for......you'll never guess.... goldfish! And, as we continued pondering the possible events that could have led to this, what did we find in the next parking area? A goldfish transport lorry. Yes, really!

Then we did summits: Scutchamer Knob (what a name!) with the Wantage monument, a replica of a fifteenth century cross in Florence on the top, and Segsbury Hill, our very first hill-fort, and started looking for somewhere to stop for lunch. After stopping, the feet were sore and Paul didn't seem entirely right,

"C'mon right boot, why can't you behave, like left boot?" we heard him say.

Hill-fort number two was Uffington. We didn't see the bronze age white horse because we were standing above it but did admire the extensive earthworks, although mainly in a sitting down out of the strong cold wind and drinking coffee kind of a way. Soon after this we came to the Neolithic long barrow of Wayland's Smithy, with its lovely legends1.

---

1 Wayland was imprisoned on an island and lamed to prevent him from escaping, by a king who prized his work highly. Eventually Wayland killed the King's two sons and made goblets from their skulls. He then raped the King's daughter and made wings so he

When I'd phoned the Rose and Crown a few weeks earlier to book rooms, I'd asked if they wanted a deposit. "Oh no," the chap said. "We're a sixteenth century coaching inn. We don't go in for that sort of thing."

As we struggled through the car park, there he was, carrying a big load of logs inside for the fire. It was warm in there with flag-stone floors, wooden beams and posts everywhere, and places to scatter the boots and packs and to suspend the feet. Work started on the beer log. After the first sips both Lesley and Paul decided that they'd vote to stay there for the rest of the holiday and not bother with any more walking!

That night the pub was busy, even though it was Monday, with one heroic girl manning the bar and also acting as a waitress. She asked what we were up to and got the Hare-Brained Hike story.

"Oh, that sounds so exciting. I do wish I could come with you," she exclaimed. "We never do anything like that. All my boyfriend wants to do is to get drunk on a Saturday night and then lie in bed on Sunday morning."

Silently we all came to the same conclusion: time for a new boyfriend! In the morning Lesley and Paul, perhaps inspired by the barmaid, voted to continue and so, under bright blue skies, we returned to the ridge.

Hedges along another wide chalk track gave us some protection from the cold strong wind but after a while it dropped down to a road by what was marked on the map as a pub, but now seemed to be called The Borg. Perhaps it had been

---

could fly away, just pausing to land on an archway of the palace and let everyone know what he had done. Or, how about this one about Wayland's apprentice, Flibbertigibbet (what a name!). He was sent to buy nails but searched for birds' eggs on the way back and finally returned to the furious Wayland hours later. Wayland picked up one of the giant sarsen stones and threw it at Flibbertigibbet trapping him by the heel. Flibbertigibbet sat crying on the stone in the area of the burial chamber now known as snivelling corner.

assimilated by an Indian restaurant civilisation (or maybe I just misread the squirly Indian sign, or watched too many episodes of Star Trek when I was young).

A mile or so of road walking saw us across the M4 and into a field for a climb to hill-fort number three, Liddington, where Arthur is supposed to have defeated the Saxons. What a surprise, a broad grassy track with great views over the surrounding countryside, well, err, Swindon that is, with Didcot still in the background. A couple in their sixties(ish) were there. They were walking the entire Ridgeway Path as day trips and were on their penultimate one.

The path dropped again to go around Ogbourne St George then rose up onto the Downs once more to the Country Park at Barbury Castle. This had more great views (yes, really this time) and was the site of the battle of Barbury Hill in 556, when the Saxons beat the Romanised British to create the kingdom of Wessex. Guess what? It was a hill fort.

Here, at last, the acorns of the Ridgeway National Trail bend round to head South and we were nearing its end. Time to 'jump ship' to the 137-mile-long Wessex Ridgeway, exchanging acorns for Wyverns. We planned to follow these two-legged dragons all the way down to Lyme Regis on the South coast. But we'd been warned that although the path is there, Wiltshire is an almost completely Wyvern-free zone. Dorset is where they occur in numbers. Indeed, where the Wessex Ridgeway crossed the Ridgeway the only sign was that for a bridleway to Avebury.

Still, that was handy as it was where we needed to go next and the thinking was that a stone circle would make a nice and welcome change from all those hill forts. The path didn't muck about. It went straight through the circle of stones. Lesley was about all done-in by now, but she still managed to summon up enough enthusiasm to point a camera at the stones and thatched cottages, and shuffle the extra 'mile' into Avebury Trusloe and our B&B.

I was worried about this one. This seemed to be the only reasonably-priced place for miles around. Do you think that we found the following message on the website reassuring? Our sort of place? It read: *A place where we aim to produce a calm, caring atmosphere to balance, heal and to recharge body, mind and spirit. Humanity experience their truth in sharing and this is the purpose for opening my home.* The 'heal and recharge' part seemed right though.

I had called Claudette.

"Oh," she said, "I'm in Germany that week so I'm not sure (pause) but my ex-husband Peter did say that he would help me with the B&B (pause). I'm sure that would be fine."

Then, two nights before we left home, she'd called and left a message on our answer-phone with instructions to collect a key from next door, as Peter would be at work when we arrived and could we have an early breakfast so that he could get to work on-time?

We knocked on the door with some trepidation but Peter, in casual clothes and with a black woolly mop of hair, seemed to be expecting us. He had come home early from work especially, in fact, and had the kettle on. The dining room was full of crystals, geodes, books on strange healing practices, a guitar and a map on the wall showing nearby crop circles and Ley Lines. However, the tea was just what we needed, the rooms were fine, he didn't try and 'heal' our feet but did show us the way on the map to the nearest pub. Then he retreated to his home: the shed at the bottom of the garden.

It was a big pub and we were almost the only people in it. We started chatting to the Australian landlady, while we celebrated the completion of the Ridgeway National Trail. She admitted that she didn't trust the weather forecast much, but went off and checked it for us anyway. When she came back, the news was good: guaranteed zero precipitation.

We left Avebury Trusloe (early, as instructed, and after Peter had received a call from his ex-wife to make sure that he was doing things properly) via some more standing stones, lovely in the early morning light. The path climbed up through beech trees to a grassy ridge alongside racehorse gallops. We could see the Lansdowne Monument, a huge obelisk, far away in the distance and for much of the morning we headed towards it.

As we got close, we lost sight of it amongst the high ditches and ramparts of Oldbury hill-fort; yes, yet another one! But it was especially huge and impressive. What was inside all those earthworks? We'd got this close, we needed to see! Paul and I climbed the nearest rampart and then I headed straight towards it, up and down, up and down across the earthworks, while he attempted a flanking manoeuvre. Lesley of course did the sensible thing and stuck with the Wessex Ridgeway until she found a nice flat path through the main entrance of the fort. We all arrived at the same time. But what was in there?? A huge anti-climax. The Egyptian obelisk-like monument was absolutely enormous and with a skirt of scaffolding and netting to catch the falling down bits.

On the way out we came across our very first Wessex Ridgeway sign: a white wyvern on a green background. Later, in Dorset this was to become reversed, a green wyvern on a white background, and sometimes even a black wyvern carved into a wooden post. Maybe they were chameleon wyverns.

We headed South to pick up an old, grassy Roman Road and then dropped to do some wiggly bits, finally climbing to, you've guessed it, our second hill-fort of the day. This one, Oliver's Castle, was much smaller but sticking out on a promontory overlooking the vast plains to the West. An information board told of the Civil War battle that had culminated in a Royalist victory, and of the Roundhead cavalry trying to escape over the fort and coming to grief on the steep scarp slope. On the way down into the valley we looked back to see our first White Horse, a new one located on the side of Roundway Hill, cut in 1999 to celebrate the Millennium. It looked like it was trying to trot away.

Our plan was to bypass Devizes to the East but this meant some hard-on-the-feet tarmac along quiet lanes. We duly emerged into an industrial estate. The car dealerships, plumbers' merchants and office buildings weren't of much interest but then we spotted a Subway shop. None of us had ever been inside one before but there were people in there, drinking tea, eating sandwiches but most of all <u>sitting down!</u> We joined them. When it was time to leave, the place had filled up with smart office workers, policemen and a fire engine crew. We looked so out of place. Fortunately, no representatives of the third emergency service were in attendance as we might not have been allowed out, so pathetic was our hobbling exit on seized up legs and sore feet. We tried to remember that we were having 'FUN'.

We saw the rain as it approached us from behind over Oliver's Castle; broad brush-strokes of grey dropping down from heavy black clouds. We vowed never to trust an Australian woman in a pub again. The heavy but short-lived shower had stopped by the time we arrived at the lovely village of Urchfont. It had a shop selling ice-creams and treacle tarts and possibly other things too. We sat on the bench outside, being entertained by the comings and goings of the mums in their oversized 4x4's. When the rain came again the landlady of the (closed) pub opposite kindly offered us the shelter of her smoking area.

The last stretch of the day proved to be up to the edge of Salisbury Plain, passing unexploded bomb signs and around the perimeter of a firing range. They were just taking down the red flags when we arrived. A mile and a half later we dropped down to the pub in Market Lavington, where we were staying. When Paul took off his muddy boots on the pavement outside, they steamed in the cold air, just like those of a recently-demised Terry Pratchett Wizard.

In the dining room there was a certificate up on the wall. 'Breakfast Award' it said. When we came down in the morning we could see why! Huge, and not just the full English, but lots of extras and a big, friendly soppy dog to talk to as well. We spent rather longer there than we should have before setting off along tracks, with the feet still complaining, to the nearby village of West Lavington.

The book told us to look at the church which 'has seen so many additions over the centuries that it's difficult to make sense of the plan'. We tried to look. The door was locked and was as impenetrable for the two church cleaners hanging about as it was for us.

"It's lovely inside," they said. "And we have a Whistler window. You can see it from round the end."

So, what is a Whistler Window? We hadn't a clue. Did it make some sort of noise? Trying to seem knowledgeable we went, as instructed, round the end, and there, instead of the usual stained-glass effort, was a huge elaborately engraved window. Very nice!

Then it was up onto the top of Salisbury Plain again for a walk along a broad grass ride before picking up a hard army track around the edge of the firing range. I hadn't really thought much about this when planning the walk, but if I had I think I may have guessed that we might come across military areas on Salisbury Plain. Not that that would be a problem in itself, but what I hadn't thought about was their love of concrete. We were to discover the perils of this the hard way (no pun intended!).

The signs up here were not wyverns, but those of the Imber Range Path, a thirty-mile circular route which we were to follow for the rest of the day. We could see for miles over the flat agricultural plain with little villages tucked in just below the drop-off. There was a point where we should have turned off the main path, but we got distracted by half a dozen trail-bikers having lessons. They were not having a good time. They actually seemed to believe that our walking looked a better option than their muddy motorised transport. Our reward for our little detour was the sight of a man out walking his sheep (it turned out to be a big white dog) and of three boys jogging along a track closely followed by a large white (child-catchers?) van.

A couple of miles of bad-for-the-feet tarmac brought us to a big car park and picnic site on top of Westbury Hill, the highest point on Salisbury Plain, and hill-fort number seven, Bratton Camp. To the side was another white horse; white, concrete, and horse-like. We stopped for lunch, well, coffee but no food owing to too much breakfast, and watched two para-gliders practising take-off, landing and just floating about. It looked effortless. The view below, extensive though it was, was dominated by the chimney of a cement factory.

I swapped my boots for 'emergency footwear' (running shoes), which seemed to help a bit, and we carried on past the edge of the quarry. A large security guard ambled along doing his patrol but didn't seem to speak much English. We overtook and went along the ridge to pass a trig. point before turning to drop straight down a valley, climb the other side and find ourselves on the edge of Warminster Golf Course. As I was returning from a brief inspection of rather dry bush, I could hear Lesley and Paul singing loudly; a very odd song composed entirely of the names of Harry Potter characters. It stopped abruptly. Some poor chap out walking his dog had materialised behind them. They'd thought it was I who had returned! Both man and dog gave them a wide berth.

The army barracks in the valley below had lots of fit-looking people who jogged past us individually, or in herds. It looked like no effort at all. We tried not to hobble and to seem like we were having FUN. We admired the helpful signs for terrorists. Here was the HQ, there the officers' mess and further out the ammunition dump. We turned up a thin path through trees to climb out of this area before anyone challenged us. The top of Battleship Hill and its trig point was our reward. Yet another spectacular hill-fort of course.

Unfortunately, some dodgy map reading (okay I'll own up to that!) took us straight over the fortifications and down an 'almost path' through a wood to join a clear track towards Boreham the almost-suburb-of-Warminster in the valley below. But it didn't matter. The farm we were staying in soon appeared. Our hostess was waiting on the steps to welcome us. Inside it was lovely; big, tall, clean, recently decorated, and best of all it had much needed tea and huge slices of home-made coffee and walnut cake. Neither Paul nor Lesley liked coffee and walnut, but as I polished off my hunk and looked around expecting to be asked to 'help out', there they both were, tucking in as though breakfast had been hours ago! They promised it had been a one-off exception and wouldn't do it again!

I'd built a 'rest day' into the itinerary. After all, by now we'd done almost a hundred and forty miles. My feet hurt. Lesley's feet hurt and her shin had swollen to thigh-like proportions. Paul had expanding ankles and was all out of clean clothes. And then came the big problem What to do on our rest day? Any suggestions? Rest maybe? The centre of Warminster was close, only about a mile and a half away. We could probably make it that far.

We started the day slowly, lingering over breakfast. Our hostess took the bait beautifully when we asked innocently at breakfast if there was a laundrette in town. How could we possibly ignore an instruction to hand over our washing? She also said that if we went to Warminster and didn't like it, we could come back and spend the day in her house. We went to look. There was a town crier advertising a concert for the evening, a small museum in the library, and all the usual shops, which provided some cushioned innersoles for my boots and hot-cross buns. We seemed to need mince pies for some reason but they were unavailable. Surely October is closer to Christmas than to Easter? We almost bought a Christmas pudding instead.

Back at the B&B we sat in the garden to eat the buns and relax for the afternoon but Lesley decided that she needed innersoles as well, so after a brief period of unsuccessful negotiation back we went into town.

Do you think that we felt any better after our day off? No! As we tackled the first two hill-forts of the next day, our stiff joints didn't want to know. Sadly, they hadn't made the hill forts semi-detached and so there was a big drop between. And as well as the forts there were round-barrows and tumuli aplenty. We were getting pretty good at spotting such things by now!

Soon we dropped into the village of Heytesbury. At last we were free of Salisbury Plain. It made a nice change to be doing thatched cottages, rivers and ponds rather than hard army roads. We had coffee on a bench under a big beech tree in Corton, and Lesley and Paul started singing again. The tree responded by showering us with nuts. Time to move on; a climb up into an enormous mature wood, and, for the first time, serious mud. Clay mud, not the slippery chalky stuff, but deeper than boot-height in places. The book had kept warning us that the whole length of the Ridgeway could be like this; how lucky we'd been. Fortunately, we came out into long wet grass, which removed most of the goo.

Our next challenge was to cross the A303. It was Saturday lunchtime at the start of the half term week. The road was packed with a steady stream of cars and caravans full of luggage, kids and stressed parents. It took us a good ten minutes of patience before there was a gap big enough to rush across. The map suggested that Hindon, only a mile or so distant, had a pub. Off we marched!

People, the Saturday lunch in a village pub type of people,

came to talk to us as we sat in the sun outside the Angel. Our story was getting more credible now,

"You've walked from where?"

The reply provoked a range of reactions, a few even bordering on envy, but sitting there talking about it wasn't getting the miles done. We'd left the safety of the chalk plateau now and were tending across the grain of the land with distinctly more ups and downs, more woodlands and more fields full of pigs. Unfortunately, we'd also lost the wyvern markers and at one point almost lost the route. The GPS assured us that we were on a minor road, while we were clearly wandering around aimlessly in a grassy field. A car came past just the other side of a thick hedge. Aha!

Wardour has two castles, a new one and an old one. The book describes the latter, a hexagonal fortified house, as 'dramatic' and the new one as 'dull'. We came across the new one first. An absolutely massive Palladium eighteenth-century pile. But unfriendly. On the imposing entrance was a large notice with 'NO ENTRY' in big letters, and then in small print underneath 'except for footpaths'. The map showed the path going around the front of the building and then away heading South East and everywhere there were 'NO PUBLIC ACCESS' signs, but nothing to indicate where the path did go. Now why hadn't they gone to the same trouble and expense and told us where we *were* allowed to go instead of where we couldn't? You'd have thought it would be less difficult!

But the ruins of the old castle were indeed dramatic in the late afternoon sun. Set by a lake nestling in the curve of wooded hills it was impressive. And it was only a short way from here to our B&B in the small, mainly thatched hamlet of Donhead St. Andrew. We weren't in good shape. Lesley was in running shoes now, my feet ached and my knee hurt from where I'd landed on it after being lassoed by a trailing bramble. Paul's ankles were swelling well. When we knocked on the door, two tiny, hairy energetic sausage dogs came to greet us. They helped show us to the rooms although it wasn't clear how they negotiated the staircase being longer but much lower than the steps. Paul's room seemed to be already occupied by a swarm of flies.

"Oh," said our hostess. "I thought I'd got rid of them" and off she went to make some tea, leaving Paul with a large can of fly-spray.

As we walked the short distance to the pub Paul and Lesley speculated unkindly,

"She must breed flies for a living."

"No, she's buried her husband under the floorboards. She won't trouble us though, we're half dead already!"

When we got back, there was a bridge session going on in the living room (no husband we noticed). The flies had gone, but Paul reported a hornet the size of a small jump jet circling the place. Fortunately, it succumbed to the anti-aircraft fly-spray.

Mrs McFly (as she'd become known) hadn't done well at bridge last night. Perhaps there'd be an extra body under the floorboards. We ate breakfast in a room where the walls were hidden by books. The sausages seemed very large and very meaty. Outside the front door, her oak tree threw acorns at us as we left.

Our feet hurt! We were all wearing running shoes: emergency footwear. Paul had started on drugs, anti-inflammatory ones. Fields of new crops with no footpath signs or tracks on the ground lay in wait. We did the best we could, mostly finding the stiles and gates and, eventually, a good track through a small wood. Paul and I turned back aiming for a tree that had just been designated 'the gents' to see a roe deer standing on the path watching us. Further up there was a chap on a quad bike.

"It's not raining yet," he observed, and then he also observed the embarrassing footwear with disapproval.

It was a stiff climb up to Win Green, Wiltshire's highest point. It was topped with a trig. point, topograph and clump of trees around a barrow. The topograph suggested that we should be able to see the Isle of Wight and the Needles, but even with some imagination it seemed a bit extreme. On the steep way down the other side, the running shoes got out of control and Lesley and I were observed jogging down to the bottom where there was a Sunday rambling group. We tried to hide our feet beneath fallen leaves as they passed. Soon we met a couple with rucksacks coming the other way. They were only a few yards off, but when we opened the gate and they saw us they turned to the side desperately looking for a different route. "It's all right," we said. "We're not that bad." Immediately, Paul, who was in front, was asked,

"Where did you wash this morning?" What an odd question! They were sympathetic to the Hare-Brained Hike, the chap having once walked coast to coast along the Pyrenees. He was also sympathetic to the running shoes. In turn we decided to be sympathetic to their strange behaviour. It was not, in fact, an evasive manoeuvre but simply a map-reading error: looking early for a right turn. Does that sound reasonable to you? Well it didn't to us but we were being sympathetic after all.

The steep valley of Ashcombe Bottom now led us into the centre of Tollard Royal. On the way we passed quad-bike man again, this time just mounting a big motorbike.

"When I was younger," he said rather wistfully. "I rode from here to Delhi in five weeks."

We sat on a bench by the pond and were soon entertained by the antics of seven teenage girls with big rucksacks, who turned up, threw them down on the other side of the pond and collapsed onto the grass. There was the bossy one who knew what she was doing, the pathetic one who didn't and the ones in between. Our sympathy though, was with the poor chap in a white minibus who obviously had the difficult task of being 'in charge'.

'Benches Lane' went up a spur back onto the high ground and very disappointing it was too. Not a single bench. 'No benches lane' would have been a better description. Then we had 'No Way-mark' fields, planted with young crops and with stiles hidden in hedges. Suddenly, at the bottom of a slight dip we came across Dorset. We knew it was the county boundary because there was our first finger-post, carved as a stylised wyvern head (or tail, we couldn't decide). For the rest of the Wessex Ridgeway, all the way to the coast, except for a little part where it strays into walker-unfriendly Devon, these were our companions.

Ashmore had a big village pond, village green and thatched cottages. Lovely. Not so lovely were the GPS readings, which

63

suggested that our rate of progress was dismal and that we still had a long way to go. Lesley's attempt to drink from her water-bottle while on the move, as we attempted to pick up speed, left her rather damp. And the countryside entered switchback mode again. Steeply down off Cranborne Chase to cross the River Stour and to Irwine Courtney, and straight up the chalk outcrop of Hambledon Hill. Oh no! Another hill-fort! The book told us that in 1645 the local people, fed-up with being fought over by both Roundheads and Cavaliers, refused to let either army near. Armed with clubs they retreated up this hill (and probably admired the panoramic views) before Cromwell sent in a group of dragoons who locked them in the local church before deciding that 'they were mostly harmless and had them sent home under strict orders to behave'.

Once again, we had to leave the Ridgeway at this point and drop gently off the hill to go to a village, but then had a rather nasty road-walk to Shillingstone and our B&B. Bill and Mary were organised. They knew about pubs not serving food on a Sunday. Bill immediately offered to take us to the Saxon Inn, about three miles away. It was busy with people eating and talking about the result of the rugby World Cup final; somehow, we'd missed that!

You might sense that, although the scenery and walking were really quite lovely, we'd really had about enough by now. We were tired. Our feet and legs were hurting. We were getting slower and slower and we still had a very long way to go. Phrases like 'whose stupid idea was this anyway' were starting to be voiced. Could it really get worse?

The BBC promised rain for the next day. Lots of it. We had a brilliant red sunrise at breakfast. This might have been the point where we gave up, but all the B&B's were booked and somehow it just seemed easier to carry on. Bill said that we'd be OK until lunchtime but would get four inches of the wet stuff in the afternoon. Cornwall was already having a bad time. We set off in walking boots with waterproofs at the ready and everything wrapped in waterproof bags. It motivated us to get a move on.

The first challenge was a long steep climb back up onto the ridge again. It felt like we were doing the entire days quota of up, all in one go. A bridleway between hedges that turned into an almost deserted tarmac lane took us past fields full of Alpaca with fancy fringes, a trig point, a couple of radio masts and onto Barrow Hill. You've guessed it: a hill-fort! In the lee of one of its earthworks we stopped and along came a family with kids who rushed about shouting and screaming. Clearly Dad was on half-term; dressed in shorts and sandals, while we huddled out of the wind in fleeces and woolly hats.

Near the Dorsetshire Gap, a distinctive break in the hills with, of course, more contours to contend with as well as a flooded section of path, the clouds started to condense into dark grey horseshoes within a lighter grey background. None of us had seen anything like it before. By the time we started picking up signs to Cerne Abbas, our destination for the day, they had coalesced into a solid dark grey mass.

We almost made it. The rain came as we were only about a mile short of our destination, gentle at first as we climbed to the camp-site at Giant's Head overlooking the village and getting heavier as we started down from the ridge to the valley, by way of the Giant's feet. Amazingly we met a couple of wet hikers going up, perhaps they were camping, followed by a wet family climbing to see the giant. The parents must have been desperate to get the kids outdoors.

Cerne Abbas looked like a lovely place with an old abbey and lots of old houses but our focus was on one thing only: 'Abbas', the tea-shop.

"Sit down anywhere," the girl said, as we entered and created lakes on the floor. Were all the other customers wearing Wellington boots? We hoped so. She seemed alarmed when we didn't sit but started to remove clothing, until we told her that we were there for the B&B. Once installed upstairs of course we had to return, dry, to the shop to check-out the cake (with tea) and to hide from the ferocious storm raging outside. I risked the sticky carrot cake again, in-spite of the two flights of stairs to the room. I didn't think we'd be going anywhere for a while. Eventually we did venture out again into the wet, but only for about fifty yards to the pub, where we'd arranged to meet Paul's friends, Richard and Jenny. They too thought we were mad!

Cornwall and Devon had been hit badly and so, reported the BBC, had South Dorset. We'd heard the storm from our attic room overnight and the 'no camping' principle started to make a lot of sense. The morning started bright and clear, and the rain had washed the dust from the atmosphere. The views from the ridge above the village were spectacular. On the way up we'd paid our respects to the chalk-cut giant from the viewpoint by the road and again from a much better place half-way up the opposite hill. We'd been watched by roe deer in the woods and had gone through fields thick with pheasants. In the distance we could see the twenty-six massed masts of the BBC World Service on Rampisham Down a very, very long way away. Paul and Lesley found it hard to believe that we would walk under them later on.

But once up, then down again. This time to the village of Sydling St Nicholas, where the church is reputed to have a fireplace in the porch to keep people warm during parish meetings and where there were some lovely old thatched houses bathed in the early morning sunlight. It was also where we met our only dog-walker of the day.

Up the hill and down the other side to the less lovely Maiden Newton. Perhaps it wasn't all bad but we took against it as the church was closed and so was the churchyard, where we'd been banking on a bench for a short break. Now, why would you close a churchyard?

The next section had nowhere to stop, being alongside a small river on a thin path bounded by overgrown brambles and weeds and deep in sticky, slippery mud. We struggled along for mile or so, until we came to a beautiful cottage and a lovely church with no less than three benches around it. Take note the churchy people of Maiden Newton!

As we sat, a few drops of gentle rain panicked us into battening down the hatches but we felt a bit silly when we set off again in bright sunshine. Three men with spades and a pack of mixed yappy dogs were digging a drainage channel on a puddle-strewn track near a farmhouse.

"Good job you weren't here five minutes ago," one said. "Or you'd have had to swim across."

The rain came again when we stopped once more, this time

under the BBC transmitters, the masts of which seemed to be supporting giant cobwebs and the base of the clouds. They were still transmitting when we were there but all fell silent for the last time just five days later. Next, we were treated to thunder, lightning and even some hail, and decided to take a little short-cut avoiding the highest ridges. 'Cheating!' do I hear you cry? But it was horrible up there and we *were* inventing our own route after all. A lady dressed in a white jumper and blue jeans rushed out of her remote house and ran past us to a parked car. Strangely she didn't stop to chat, but gave us a nice wave and big smile as she tried to run us over.

The thunderstorm had almost stopped and we were walking down a tarmac lane when one of the most worrying episodes of the whole trip occurred. Paul pointed to the rear end of a parked vehicle and said,

"That tractor's got a sexy face don't you think?"

As we approached Lesley agreed. Had we drunk too much beer? Had we been away from people too long? We did expect to meet more folks walking the long-distance trails, and especially in half-term week, but maybe the weather had something to do with it.

We should have gone to Beaminster, but I'd drawn a B&B blank, so instead headed South to Netherbury, a small hamlet with a massive church, straddling the river Brit. The B&B farmhouse was huge. We were met outside by Tina and a sheepdog, and led round to the front to enter via a huge conservatory, a big dining area and an even bigger sitting room which dwarfed the staircase to one side. It led to our large double room and Paul's even larger 'single' one. Given our state it was touch and go whether we'd be able to make it through the building.

Tina was a grandmother. We found this out when she gave us a lift to the pub a mile and a half away in her Land Rover and Paul tried to get into a child seat by mistake. She chatted as she drove and we learnt about the farm (over 20 years there so far and her husband worked it before that), where the Channel 4 'River Cottage' series had been filmed, about Madonna's local house and about Parnam House, recently restored to stately home from nursing home. A lot for a five-minute journey.

The pub was nice. Three small rooms, one occupied by the ex-teenagers of the area, now in their thirties, one by the next generation up with their friendly dogs and the other an eating area. They had a special ale called simply 200. It was to celebrate the 200 years of the brewery but as we'd passed the 200 miles of our walk, we just had to try it. Another, 'Tally Ho', kept in a cask round the back proved to be our favourite. We felt a bit guilty sending the barmaid outside so often and contemplated asking her simply to bring in the cask. The feet didn't seem to be so bad on the way home in the running shoes. A mile and a half in 25 minutes! Tally Ho!

We hadn't even left the farm's driveway in the morning before a torrential shower hit us. It was to be the order of the day: short, sharp wet patches. There was some way to go before we regained the ridge at the site of a Roman fort on Waddon Hill, West of Beaminster. And once again it was across the grain of the countryside.

If you go there make sure to look out for 'assault course path'. It's about a mile further on and entered via a stile that leads to a sunken lane. For the full experience, go just after it's been very wet when the high mud banks on each side are especially slippery. It slopes steeply downhill with fallen trees across it; some to limbo under and others to hurdle over. Part way down, when you've had a bit of experience you can start to enjoy some limbo-hurdle combos, where the underfoot steep, slippery mudslides add speed and interest to the descent. Heavy backpacks are recommended, both to add inertia and also to create additional challenge while limboing. Fortunately, the good people of the nearby pretty village of Stoke Abbot have provided a drinking fountain on a wall complete with chained copper drinking cup, now green with moss. We got most of the mud off.

The start of the next footpath led us to a small lake before it disappeared in front of a set of gates, each leading into a different field. All sloped steeply upwards. We chose the very steepest bit we could find to climb, in the hope that it was the path. Hurrah! We emerged triumphant, right by a hidden stile.

The wyverns led us through lovely old beech woods and then out onto Cockpit Hill, which was perhaps the steepest

68

ascent to any hill-fort so far. It was exhausting but, we read, it had been inhabited at the time of the Roman invasion and they had considerably left behind a ballista for the archaeologists to find, much, much later. We stopped for a rest. Another shower came. Did you think that we'd finished with hill forts? We did, but apparently not. After all this was only number thirteen!

Soon we turned off the Wessex Ridgeway to do a mile or so of the Monarch's Way, at 615 miles the longest inland path in Britain. It follows the escape route of King Charles II after the final battle of the Civil War. Six hikers were coming the other way. They'd started at Lambert's Castle our next destination and were heading for Cockpit Hill where we'd joined the route. The man with the map said that he hadn't told the others about the contours yet.

Down into the valley, across the river Syndeford and up the other side we went. A roe deer and her teenage fawn came running towards us. We stayed still and they didn't spot us and came quite close before heading down the other side of a hedge. Somewhere here we also crossed the county boundary and entered Devon, a county with apparently no walking signs and farmers who delight in eliminating any paths. We had a particularly unexpected battle with a field of tall maize, well above head height, and after bashing through for some time were relieved to come out at a road right next to a stile.

A little later the farmer seemed to have unilaterally rerouted the paths by means of electric fences. We must have missed a turn completely. It was the only time on the entire trip that we seriously ended up wandering around the landscape with map, compass and GPS, crossing fences and hedges and even fording a small stream to try and find the path. In the end we gave up: clearly the path was not where the Ordinance Survey had left it. We set a compass course to intersect where a lane must be and, incredibly came out within 200m from where we should have.

Lambert's Castle (guess what that is!) was a big expanse of turf on a hilltop guarded by a band of beech trees and obviously back in Dorset, judging by the carved finger-posts. Just off the top near the trig point Lesley found a bench overlooking the plain to the East. The shower that had accompanied our 'lost in Devon' experience gave way to almost-sunshine. A second hill-fort lay just to the South, Corey's Castle, and that of course meant a drop and climb again, but it was our fifteenth and last. We all felt a bit sentimental about that. But from here we could clearly see the sea and Lyme Regis, our destination for the day and the start of the South West Coast Path adventure before us.

The pace quickened as we dropped down the contours, first through fields of sheep and then woods and finally cabbages. It was almost dark when we reached the B&B and we'd been in boots all day. The feet were complaining. The knees were complaining. Lesley's shin was complaining. We'd done enough. Fortunately, our rooms were on the first floor. We were greeted with tea and Jaffa cakes!

Later we managed to get down to the seafront, thus completing the Wessex Ridgeway. We stopped in the Pilot Boat for food and were surprised to find it claimed to be the original home of Lassie the Wonder Dog, but not surprised to find the truth very different from the Hollywood version2.

We made the excellent breakfast last as long as we could, abandoned the rucksacks and went for a look round Lyme. The BBC had promised rain all day and here it was in bucket-loads. It was horrible. Not Lyme but the weather. Lesley took to hiding in shop doorways while Paul and I strolled around getting soaked. We debated visiting the museum but didn't have the enthusiasm, and ended up voting to head off and get the short section planned for today out of the way.

Back at the B&B:

"I suppose catching a bus is out of the question?" our hostess asked.

"Yes, that would be cheating."

"What about the air ambulance? I believe that they are very

---

2   Half collie, Lassie was owned by the landlord of the Pilot Boat. On New Year's Day in 1915, the Royal Navy battleship HMS Formidable was hit by a torpedo from a German submarine off Start Point with the loss of more than 500 men. One of the ship's life rafts, containing many bodies, was blown by gales along the coast and was washed ashore in Dorset. The bodies were laid out on the table of the pub. Lassie, began to lick one of the bodies, and someone noticed the man was reacting to it. They managed to revive him.

prompt." After due consideration this suggestion was rejected as well.

"It doesn't often rain <u>all</u> day," was her parting offer, and with that we set off through the town and finally onto the SWCP.

"At last!" I hear you cry. "The South West Coast Path! About time too." Just think of it as a big build-up to increase the drama.

Well, it should have been dramatic, but perhaps not on this day. It started through an old wood on an old landslip with some great trees; their big roots, a slippery trip hazard, stretched across the path. We met a couple out walking their dog.

"Should be better tomorrow," they said.

The rain was unrelenting. The path started practising being a roller-coaster, with little steps where it was steep. No-one felt like stopping. Eventually it headed inland and dropped down to Seaton across a deserted golf course, the bunkers acting like reservoirs. The water was rushing down the river Axe into the sea. The harbour and marina were deserted except for a solitary chap covered in bright red waterproofs tipping water out of an inflatable. We walked along the deserted sea-front feeling miserable, wet and tired, desperately looking for somewhere dry to stop. Eventually we spotted a tea shop.

It was warm and dry in there; at least it was before we arrived. We parked the rucksacks out of the way by the front door and went to a table near the back, where we took off our waterproofs and hung them on the backs of chairs. They soon made embarrassingly large puddles on the floor for which we had to apologise. We came to the conclusion that none of our waterproof jackets were; waterproof that is. Paul claimed to be nurturing a small aquarium in his boots. I do hope that no tea-shop owners are reading this.

We stayed in the tea shop for some time. The windows, clear when we arrived, started to mist up. We ran out of tea and cake and only left when we noticed people outside with furled umbrellas. It wasn't far to Beer and our stop for the night, but it was more or less straight up and down again. For the first time ever I believe, I was awarded brownie points for the location of the B&B. Perhaps it was because it was just about the first building we saw when we started looking. Perhaps it was because it was close to the sea. Perhaps it was because it was right opposite a pub. Most likely it was because it wasn't halfway up a hill!

We knocked on the door and it was opened by Tony, perhaps in his sixties, with a pot belly and holes in his old green polo shirt. The house was absolutely crammed with pictures all along the hall, all along the stairs, all along the landing, and even in the bedrooms. The rucksacks were banished to the shower trays for a while until they stopped trying to irrigate the carpets and the picture hooks formed useful hanging points for wet garments. We were absolutely soaked through. Well done again to Lesley for championing the 'no camping' principle!

Once warm, showered and in dry clothes and with the rain finally stopped, we took a short look around Beer. By now you won't be at all surprised to find out that we soon retreated to do some more work on the beer log in the busy pub opposite the B&B.

Al Bowlly was singing in the kitchen when we emerged for breakfast. We'd never heard of him although guessed the decade of the recordings. Tony gave us the potted life history ending with his death in the blitz in 1941. The dining room was even more crammed with stuff than the rest of the house. It was like a museum. I asked about the history of all the pictures and it turned out that Tony and his wife were auction victims.

"I've told her that if she doesn't stop buying pictures, we'll have to build more walls to put them on," he said.

It was hard to believe that we were in the same country as yesterday. Blue sky, no wind and warm. Absolutely gorgeous for what was predicted to be the toughest walk of the trip; not as long as some but massively hilly; around four or five times as much climbing as on the inland days. It started with a steep climb out of Beer, a stroll along around the cliff-tops of Beer Head and then a long drop back down to sea level at Branscombe with its pebbly shore, little boats and traditional sea-side shop selling buckets, spades and umbrellas. For the first time we encountered both dog-walkers and hikers in reasonable numbers.

Up again onto the cliffs we went, with the white chalk

behind and below us and red sandstone stretching ahead and into the distance. The sea was still and very blue. We dropped all the way down to Weston Mouth and all the way back up again, this time encountering our first 'killer steps'.

Killer Steps? Yes, these are the ones that good people have built into steep hillsides to 'help' with the walking. Often, they are made of vertical wooden retainers filled in with earth behind. The steps themselves are invariably of the wrong height or the wrong spacing; too tall or too short to step up onto comfortably, too close together or one and a half paces apart. Or perhaps just varying enough to make sure that you break your hiking rhythm. They seem to make the steep inclines less slippery but are much more tiring to conquer than a simple slope; knee jarring on the descent and lung busting on the way back up.

Two more such downs and one up later, we arrived in Sidmouth, with its long promenade. We bagged the first available bench, right by the lifeboat station, wondering if we were going to be turfed off for being under-age. Strangely we were quite comfortable, hot even, sitting there in shorts and t-shirts. Everyone else seemed to be wrapped up for winter. Paul thought it was because they'd come on holiday and that's what you wear on holiday on the South Coast in October. On breakfast TV they'd been advertising National Bird Feeding Week, but obviously this didn't extend to Sidmouth. There were notices everywhere saying don't feed the sea-gulls, along with pictures of a gull for those who didn't know what one was.

When we got up and tried to carry on, the legs and feet really didn't want to know. We hobbled off so slowly I thought we were going to get run over by a couple of the motorised Zimmer frame things that seemed to be de-rigour around there, but soon we managed to pick up momentum and started the climb out of town past some young things wearing fleeces and even a sheepskin jacket. Eventually they were all left behind as we tackled the last serious climb of the day, High Peak.

A ghastly caravan site was waiting for us on the other side, although offshore were some impressive red sea-stacks. The cliffs got flatter but we seemed to be going slower and slower, and I started to get concerned about the distance to go and the time to do it. We stopped at the World War Two observation post at the top of Brandy Head and someone must have fed Lesley a Mars Bar. No problem now, she shot off, with Paul and me trailing some way behind all the way along to the end of the cliffs, where they are punctured by the estuary of the Otter river. Here the path turns inland for three quarters of a mile or so to find a bridge, so that it can cross and come back to the sea again on the other side. On the way there were groups of people pointing binoculars at the wading birds, who were happily paddling around on the submerged cricket pitch.

In Budleigh Salterton the 'Don't feed the Seagulls' signs seemed to have been replaced by 'Don't Steal the Beach' ones. Catherine, a tall, broad lady let us into our B&B when we arrived just before dark. Nice bright clean rooms, nice welcome tea and home-made cake on arrival. Coffee and walnut again. Lesley ate half of hers before she remembered that she didn't like it and handed it over. Paul ate all of his. It turned out that Catherine had done a fair bit of long-distance paths in her time, mostly backpacking. Of the Lizard she said her everlasting memory is one of interminable fields of cauliflowers and thick mud. She knew just the sort of pub we needed for food.

Our final day, and there was jazz on the CD for breakfast. I'm informed by Lesley that it got stuck, like a record in a groove repeating the same bit over and over and wasn't supposed to sound like that. Mercifully Catherine seemed to think so too and silenced it.

Back on the coast path we climbed gently up to a high point with views back to Budleigh and views onwards to another enormous caravan park at Straight Point. We had to walk all round three sides of the caravans. It was more like a small village of cheap housing and really quite nasty.

We hit tarmac at Exmouth, just after passing an obelisk celebrating the Jurassic Coast world heritage site award. Well, tarmac that is except for the bits where the sand-dunes had blown across it. Everything was shut. The amusements were closed, the little shops were closed, the kiosks selling fishing trips had signs up saying 'Next Sailing April 2012, and the toilets were closed. Obviously, no-one comes here in the winter, and if they do, they don't need the loo. Or perhaps they close the loos to discourage winter visitors. It wasn't at all welcoming.

We missed the ferry to Starcross by five minutes. It could have been worse. Had we been two days later we'd have missed it by six months! Our first section of The Path had been completed. At this stage of course we were completely unaware of the significance and just headed off down the quiet Devon lanes. First to Kenton with its painted houses and huge (closed) church, and then onto Kennford. Nearing the end, Lesley discovered a pot of gold, or rather a polythene bag containing about four Euros in small coins. We achieved five miles in two hours, an impressively quick ending to the walk. We must have been keen to get there or something.

Paul had made sure that there was some appropriate celebratory beer waiting in the fridge for our arrival: 'Hoppy Hare'. His friend Letty arrived with a bottle of bubbly (we liked her immediately) and we all set off down the lanes to the pub at Kenn to mark the completion of the 263-mile, sixteen-day Hare-Brained Hike. Oh, and the fact that we were still able to walk!

4. The Penzance Practice (St Ives to Penzance March 2012)

So now, at last, we get to the first proper South West Coast Path trip. But it was accidental really, just a rehearsal for something else. And it was not looking good for a long weekend's walking around Land's End. The BBC had been consistently forecasting heavy showers sweeping in from the West. Paul had bought new waterproofs the day before we started, but it hadn't changed their opinion.

However, everything was organised and so Lesley and I left home anyway and drove to Paul's house arriving early for the lunchtime rural bus into Exeter. We switched on the TV and got an updated forecast. Even worse. The showers had joined up into solid rain. The city proved a good place for some emergency shopping. Waterproofs guaranteed for ten hours of deluge, in rather lurid colours, were half-price. Rations for a three-hour train journey were stuffed into the rucksacks.

As soon as it was decently possible to call the Friday work-day complete, Paul once again transformed into the KK in the works disabled loo, ready for a rendezvous in the car-park and a route-march to the railway station for the 16:44 heading West. While it was light it was a lovely trip. The train followed the coast right by the sea, and near Plymouth crossed the wet bits on scenic viaducts. When it got dark, we produced the emergency rations and Paul's eyes lit up: giant pasties and cans of beer. Well, we were heading into Cornwall after all, so what else did you expect? The journey seemed to pass in no time, in spite of the fact that we had three changes to make. Each train was running later than the last so we missed the final connection and didn't arrive in St. Ives until almost nine.

It was very dark away from the platform but:

"This way," Lesley said as she spotted a narrow alleyway leading up the hillside away from the sea.

How did she know? But she was right. Amazingly, we emerged onto a road right opposite the entrance to our hotel. The restaurant was closed.

No problem, we thought, as we set off on a foraging trip into St Ives. It was downhill all the way from the Hotel and, on a Friday night in March, deserted. We tried a pub: 'Food stops at nine'. We tried the sea-front with bunches of teenagers hanging about, the guys in groups looking cool and the girls strutting their stuff. We managed to find a chippie but as we were in arty St. Ives, what we got were French Fries and not the wholesome chunky things served in darkest Bucks. As we stood in a doorway enjoying the teenage antics, the rain started and they melted away. Perhaps we too had been soluble at their age but, as our previous trips had shown, we certainly weren't now.

After a suitably sized, non-arty Full English the next day, we set off to tackle the fifteen and a half miles of Coast Path planned to get us to Pendeen. It was rated 'Severe'. The rain had given up, leaving threatening clouds. The narrow streets of St. Ives were deserted. We walked through the town and around the bay, cutting the corner of St Ives Head from which, we later discovered, people had been watching dolphins swim with the tide. Instead what we saw were the first neoprene clad surfers of the day, tackling the waves.

The path was uneven, narrow and rocky underfoot, and after a while we began to understand the severe rating. A heavy shower came through, but only lasted for twenty minutes or so; not really a good test for the 'ten-hour' waterproofs. A little later we met a wet couple with two very muddy sons. They'd left their waterproofs behind and tried to follow a path marked on the map inland alongside a stream.

"It doesn't exist," they said. "Only bog." And one of the boys had got in to thigh depth.

"I bet it was exciting," we offered.

"Oh yes, great," he said, as his parents looked on disapprovingly.

We had a few more showers, but nothing of more than five minutes or so, and the scenery was lovely with cliffs falling away into a blue sea. We could see a lighthouse in the far distance that never seemed to get any closer. Rather depressingly we concluded that it must be Pendeen Watch, our objective for the day. A few old tin-mining pump-house chimneys were to be seen and at one point we needed to cross a small field.

'Notice to Dogs', it said on the gate. 'Please do not chase the sheep or steal eggs from ground nesting birds. Thank you for your cooperation'. And, on the other side of the gate:

'Notice to sheep. It is illegal to go beyond this point without a movement licence. Failure to comply with this law may result in a fine, imprisonment or both'.

Eventually we did reach the lighthouse, brilliant white under contrasting dark clouds, and turned inland along the road to the village itself. A small shop replenished our chocolate supplies. We'd hit them pretty heavily during the day, as no-one had done much practice for the walk and we were all feeling the 'severe' grading a bit.

The CAMRA Cornwall pub of the year 2003, The North Inn, had lovely purpose-built B&B rooms around the back with views out across the sea. They had beer. They had food. By now you will have realised that it was our sort of place.

Pendeen to Porthcurno was advertised as sixteen and a half miles, but only graded 'Moderate' so we thought we'd be okay. The weather seemed to have improved, and although we got a few showers during the day nothing was too heavy or too prolonged. The waterproof purchase insurance policy seemed to be paying off.

The paths were easier underfoot. You'd have thought that following the coast path would have been easy: just keep the sea to your right. However, there were an awful lot of paths and the ones nearest the sea frequently ended in dead ends at the cliff edge. The Coast Path proper, we discovered, was often less conspicuous and further inland. As we continued West, past disused tin mines with lots of tall chimneys and ruins of pump-houses, we seemed to spend a lot of time trying to rediscover it. At one point we ended up climbing a bit of cliff covered with prickly bushes and were picking splinters out of our hands for days.

We went round Cape Cornwall, admiring the rocks in the sea that Paul called 'President Charles De Gaulle in the bath' and then the path started doing a bit of the 'up every cliff and down to every cove' stuff. Paul spotted a small village far in the distance.

"Sennen Cove," he said. "I wonder if we can get there before the pub closes?"

So, on we marched, past people fishing off the rocks and an apparently lost surfer carrying his board along the cliff path.

The pub was open. In fact, it was heaving with people doing Sunday lunch and we did weaken when we saw plates of proper chunky chips. As a bonus we missed the heaviest shower of the day and weren't tempted by the rather empty café at the Land's End theme park. Last time we were there it was blowing a gale and the weather was smashing doors and windows, but today it was rather pleasant with great views of the lighthouses and rock arches offshore.

The path settled down a bit and the scenery was even more impressive than before, with sea stacks on one side and desolate dwarf gorse and ruined buildings on the other. Just before dark (yes, we'd been pretty slow and taken our time, but it does get dark earlyish in March, you know) we came across the car park to the open-air theatre (not in use in March) and a very steep drop down into Porthcurno. This village is famous for being the place where the first trans-Atlantic cables came ashore and most of the buildings were built by the wireless company. Today there is a museum (shut by the time we arrived) a big car park (empty when we were there), a very welcome B&B and a so-called pub which looked okay from the road but turned out to be the old social club.

It too was empty, except for four people playing cards and a large brown dog with too much energy that bounced all over the furniture. One lady went outside to smoke and when she came back and turned to sit down, the dog, which had been quite happily sleeping on the floor, had just jumped into her chair. It caused yelps and confusion from both of them. The cook, a young girl with nothing much to do except feed us, was rather scary. She kept talking about shooting and generally killing things and how she'd been let off a court appearance. But perhaps because we were nice to the dog, everyone seemed to smile at us, gave us beer and Sunday roast and we managed to make it back to the B&B unmolested.

Only twelve and a half miles for the last day, Porthcurno to Penzance, but ten were graded severe. This time it was owing to the yo-yo nature of the route. It was hot and sunny and we were soon in shorts and t-shirts. Some of the way was through welcome woods of low, twisted trees and one section took us right down to a boulder strewn beach to leap from rock to rock, not easy with backpacks on. We drank all our water as we negotiated the gradients, hampered by the dreaded 'killer steps'.

The scenery was lovely and there were a few people out walking. We met a German sounding lady.

"How far to ze top?" she asked.

This confused us as there wasn't really a single top, just lots of them.

"It's very rocky," she continued. "I fell over back zere."

We watched the white ferry on its way to the Isles of Scilly and went past sandy coves and rocky cliffs, and a lighthouse. Finally, we could see St Michaels Mount in the distance and could drop down onto the tarmac road into Mousehole.

The route took us right along the back of the small harbour and past a pub. The owner of the last B&B had told us that few people pass there without stopping and we were no exception. All the hard work should have been done now and we had plenty of time. Outside was Fitzroy's barometer built into the wall. He's the chap who introduced the weather forecast as we know it. Unfortunately, just beyond the harbour a finger post sent us down to walk on a promenade right by the sea, but the corresponding sign to get us back up to the road again was missing. We ended up running out of promenade at a heap of rocks, beyond which was just, well, sea. It meant a last cliff-climbing event back to the tarmac.

The great fish warehouses of Newlyn had a distinctive smell; we didn't dally. Soon they were behind us and we were entering the outskirts of Penzance. The prom stretched forwards and took us all the way along to the bus and railway station. A seagull came to see if we had any food. What, us?! We'd long since eaten everything. But we had a cunning plan. Lesley had been waiting for this since seeing the original itinerary: a cream tea.

That autumn we went hiking again. The bug had really caught us. But it wasn't the Coast Path; we went North. Even after the successful Penzance Practice and in spite of the fact

80

that we'd managed a decent distance over one of the less easy sections and hadn't even got too wet, we were not irrevocably hooked. We could have walked away (sorry about that!). But obviously we didn't.

5. The Holy Hike: walking on water (The alternative Coast to Coast September 2012)

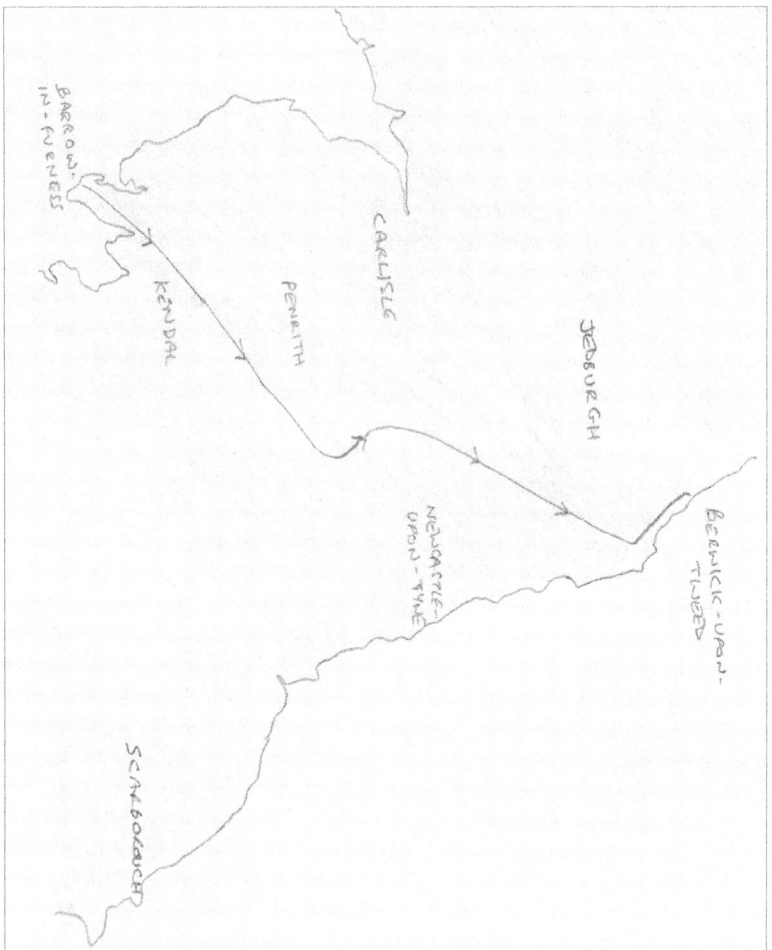

Why, you may well ask, did we set off into what were to be the worst September storms for thirty years to attempt a two-hundred-mile walk based on the contents page of an out of print book and a high-level route drawn on a road atlas.

It had seemed like a good idea six months before. Paul had found reference to the "Alternative Coast to Coast". It had good write ups. It started on one island off the West coast of Cumbria and finished in a symmetrical fashion on another island off the East coast of Northumberland. There was only one small problem: the guide book published in 1999 was out of print and unavailable. No second-hand copies could be found. Detailed information of the route did not appear anywhere on the Internet. The challenge was laid bare.

I managed to find the contents page of the guide. It very helpfully read chapter 1 a to b, chapter 2 b to c and so on which gave a good idea of where the start and end points of the days should be. Then I found a very high-level route map which seemed to have been drawn on a road atlas. Assuming that the paths had more longevity than the guide I was sure that I could work it out.

A couple of weeks later I had it cracked: the route was planned, the B&B's booked, and the train tickets had arrived (25 tickets in total for three people! Paul suggested that we could have half a game of cards if we got bored!) Then reality set in. In April the water companies had banned hose-pipes and issued dire warnings about the levels in the reservoirs. This resulted in almost constant rain throughout the summer. During the wettest drought on record we'd done hardly any hiking and then crammed all our practice into the three weeks before the expedition began.

All too soon the big day came. As our train left Manchester, a very odd modern skyscraper, where the top half looked like it was about to slide down over the bottom half, was visible.

"That's the Manchester Hilton," the middle-aged and slightly portly chap next to us explained.

With some encouragement we then had a very lengthy conversation about beer. We never did find out why, but he knew all the breweries and nice pubs around both Wing and Kennford. Once his expertise had been established, he started telling us about all the local beers and microbreweries we were to find on our route through Cumbria. It proved to be an important lesson, but one that was cut short when he missed his onward connection to the Windermere Brewery and got off at Preston. He didn't seem overly put out.

"There's two good pubs here and an hour before the next train so I'll try a pint in each."

The train carried on around the Cumbrian coast and we admired the salt-marshes, sometimes to the left, sometimes to the right and occasionally on both sides of the train. The hills however, remained invisible, covered by low clouds. Professor Beer had not been complimentary regarding Barrow-in-Furness and we soon found out why. It had lots of low-cost housing, much of it boarded up, around a centre with a mix of low-cost shops and once-grand buildings. Some were now in disrepair and others had evolved into pubs or charity shops.

And then we got lost before the walk had even begun! We'd booked into a hotel in Duke Street and walked up and down failing to find it. Google unerringly led us to an MOT station. However, the walking wardrobe and the Berghaus bags were eventually left to relax inside the warm dry hotel rooms and, pretending that it wasn't trying to rain, we set off for Walney Island, the Beachcomber café and the formal start of the walk.

In the late nineteenth century Barrow had the largest steelworks in the world and in the twentieth it was an important military shipyard. From the 1960's it specialised in building nuclear submarines. Someone had parked a big, wet, grey sub with slimy green streaks near the bridge across the docks.

It was Saturday afternoon and as we walked through the giant-sized BAE industrial units, the streets were deserted. All the doors were tightly closed. A road bridge over the Walney Channel took us to Walney Island and the massed houses of Vickerstown, built to house the workers for the shipyards. The seashore was on the far side. There was no sign of the café, just a boarded-up building that looked like it might have been one once, or maybe just public toilets. Google told us that the nearest Beachcomber café was in California, where it was sunny and hot and wouldn't we like to go there instead?

We walked up and down the coast a bit trying to find any

evidence of tea and cake but without success. Only a few cold dog walkers and masses of offshore wind turbines were there. In the end we simply declared the Holy Hike started and followed the Cumbrian coast path around the golf course, inland past the airport perimeter, and back to the Walney Channel and our first 'walking on water' experience.

The tide was out and there were little boats marooned on the mud flats. The map showed a track across the channel but it looked like we were going to get very wet and muddy if we took it. Just as we were voting to retreat and go back over the road bridge, along came a chap pushing his bike along the shoreline.

"Yes, you can get across on a line of stones," he said. "But it's very muddy on the other side". We went to see.

It was perhaps the strangest 'bridge' we came across. It seemed to be a line of what looked like paving slabs on supports, so that they are just out of water at low tide; in this case very low spring tides. So low, in-fact, that we were able to avoid the mud by walking on the mussel beds and complete our first task: a crossing of the Irish Sea.

Later we went to a pub recommended by Professor Beer. It was packed, even by 7.30. The beer was incredibly cheap, getting on for half of what we pay at home. There were three girls on the next table each demolishing their own bottle of wine and looking like they were just doing the normal Saturday night thing and getting ready to party. We moved on to somewhere quieter, but left around nine to find bouncers outside all the pubs guarding queues to get in. We felt very old. Late at night the streets were full of noisy girls and the town hall clock chimed every quarter, but by the next morning, Sunday, the place was deserted and we set off early through the town to try and beat the rain. The weatherman on breakfast TV had forecast 'the only blue thing you'll see today is my shirt!'

On the outskirts of Barrow, we came across a lake where fishermen, who'd camped out overnight, were just waking up for their first cigarette of the day, but they very quickly retreated back into their tents as the rain came. Persistent and sideways, but mostly from behind us.

Our route cut back over the railway line, along a very

overgrown path of prickly and stingy things from ground level to way above head height, to gain the Cumbrian Coast Path on the edge of the Duddon Channel, which we were to walk along for most of the day. The tide was low, so we had no problem working our way along the salt-marsh towards Lowsy Point where there are two paths marked on the map. One goes all the way around the edge of the sand dunes that bulge out into the channel, while the other simply goes straight on across the neck of the bulge to reach to coast on the other side. In view of the weather we opted for the latter.

What a mistake! Inside the crescent of dunes, the waterlogged land was criss-crossed with water channels, only some of which were visible. We continually went forwards only to be stopped by a deep bit and forced back and around. In the end we more-or-less went around the inside edge of the dunes anyway, while we watched a very wet jogger running around the top, and then back again.

As we emerged on the other side, we came across ponds set aside for the rare Natterjack toads. A couple of women were out with their dogs.

"You can walk from here all the way along the beach to Askam," they told us.

It looked a bit dodgy to us. We could see Askam in the distance, not too far away across the sands, but also a rocky headland between us and the town. The tide had risen and there didn't seem much room between the headland and the water. But local knowledge said we could do it and the alternative, an inland route, looked a long way round, so we delayed our 'promised-to-ourselves' tea stop and gave it a try. The dog-walkers were vindicated. The rocks were slippery and wet and the sea was right up to their base in places, but we did get round. I wouldn't have liked to have tried it fifteen minutes later though.

There was no shelter from the driving rain, so on we continued to wet, windswept Askam pier. No shelter there either. Perhaps there would be a covered bus stop in the town? No. We ended up in the deserted waiting room on the platform of the railway station, drinking tea and coffee. There was no door. It was cold but dry. It did have a fire-place. A short debate followed about using it, but Paul was quick to point out that we had nothing dry enough to ignite and especially damp were his boots and the garments around his crotch region!

Back at the coast there were 'don't even think about entering here' signs on the golf course and the map marked a path between it and the beach. But the sea had other ideas. It was sending waves right up to the grassy bank supporting the golf course fence. A chap in tall wellies with a small dog on a lead came towards us; the dog was getting swamped from time to time as the waves came in and having to swim for all it was worth.

"You'll have no problem getting round," he told us. Aha! That'll be more local knowledge then. We set off.

It proved rather exciting. We rushed from sandy patch to sandy patch when the waves went out, and retreated to grassy bank and unfriendly golf course fence as they came back again. Further on, the path went a little more inland through what appeared to be a swamp. There were sheep here and the water was so high that a small flock had marooned themselves on a cut-off hummock. We laughed as we walked past but ten minutes later, we found that we'd walked along a spit with deep water channels on three sides and we were cut off too. As we went (sheepishly) back, the sheep seemed to be laughing at us, "Baahaha, baahaha".

Finally, we found a way forwards, hugging the railway line, and eventually came to a coast path signpost. 'This footpath may flood at high tide,' it told us (thanks!) and pointed to an alternative route inland across the railway line. We took it. It proved even worse. Mucky swamp mud, augmented by 'cow-slip', above boot height. Lesley's new waterproof socks were working overtime. We struggled and struggled but, in the end, more-or-less just had to wade through it for a mile or so to the safety of tarmac.

Kirkby. Another railway waiting room. Time to empty the boots and wring out the socks. Even Lesley's waterproof ones had failed when submerged to knee depth. We kept to tarmac lanes as far as we could for the next three miles to Foxfield and the next railway station waiting room. But we never made it. Only a few metres to go and we found The Prince of Wales.

Professor Beer had told us that it had its own micro-brewery, and a warm pub easily trumped a cold draughty railway waiting room. From the warm, dry safety of the bar we watched as the rain-gods opened up the tap to full.

With only a couple of miles to go, streaks of weatherman-shirt-blue sky and occasional rays of sunshine started to do battle with the rain-clouds. We even glimpsed some hills in the distance. The path left the coast to give us a taste of the contours to come before dropping into Professor Beer's Mecca, Broughton-in-Furness (four pubs all with good beer). We were booked to stay in one of them. The food was spectacular: pub prices, but restaurant-style fancy stuff. While our belongings were spread out to dry in our rooms, we took full advantage. The chef even apologised to Lesley about the colour of her mushroom upside-down pie. It was a grey, mushroom colour. It seemed alright to us. Anything that wasn't a mud-cow-pat-mix colour would probably have been alright!

As you can tell, we were perhaps not having so much FUN as we'd expected. But we'd had wet at the beginning of walks before and the weather had improved. It very rarely stays this bad for very long, we reasoned. I think you can guess where this is going. What would you have done I wonder?

The next morning, we headed inland through rather boggy cow fields and followed the valley of the rather-larger-than-it-should-have-been River Lickle (poor name in the circumstances!) to the small but pretty village of Broughton Mills. Before long we'd stopped and donned full waterproofs as the first shower of the day hit. We also practised more 'walking-on-water'. We didn't seem very good at it. We kept on sinking.

Broughton Mills, once rich in wool, corn and bobbin mills but now just a number of stone houses surrounded by flowers, marked the sudden and abrupt start of the Cumbrian mountains. A river-like lane out of the village took us up, up, up to a remote farm on Dunnerdale Fell, with views all the way back to the sea and to the flat marshlands of yesterday. Beyond the lane a river, sorry, path, up a valley took us to a saddle and into the mountains proper, and our first bog-of-the-day. We traversed behind the peak of White Pike to come to the remains of an old slate quarry high above Seathwaite. A group of three hikers approached.

"You're the first people we've seen today," we commented.

"Same here," they said. "We expected the Lake District to be crowded."

Soon after, we turned up a well-made dirt path that went steeply up to the summit of Brown Pike and the wind hit, strong and gusty. We could see another band of rain coming, so hunkered down in a stone horseshoe-shaped shelter, donned a few more clothes, ate the odd Mars bar, drank coffee and waited. The fog closed in as the rain got closer and we could hear an odd flapping sound that seemed to be getting louder. What could it be? Vultures perhaps, waiting to see if we'd make it? Eventually a solitary chap appeared out of the gloom and struggled into our lair. It was hard to talk, what with the wind, driving rain and flapping waterproofs, but when it seemed to ease a bit, we all continued the short distance up to the cairn on top to admire the magnificent views back to the coast.

A jagged ridge now stretched along Dow Crag, and in the swirling mist there were a few small groups of miserable-looking people sitting behind rocks eating lunch. So why were they there do you think? After all, we had an excuse, we were on a journey. But for day trippers, surely you'd find a better day and go and look at the pencil museum or something. Perhaps day trippers are made of sterner stuff or perhaps there is a limit to how many consecutive days they can stand the pencil museum.

We had trouble walking along the ridge and paused frequently when the wind got too strong. Just short of the Old Man of Coniston we enjoyed a shower of hail of the sideways, painful type. A party of four were on their way back down:

"You can't see anything from the top," they told us.

A scream from behind made me turn to see Lesley's hat bouncing irregularly like a rugby ball across the short turf at high speed. I chased across to intercept it and, after a complicated manoeuvre that I like to think of as reminiscent of an Olympic hockey goalkeeper, but which others later reported as more like a collapsing wardrobe, I was on top of it. It was just then that the mist lifted to show the edge (and fantastic views) alarmingly close, but probably fifteen metres away. An unexpected number of hikers were looking to see what all the screaming was about.

We carried on North along the short grass and rocks of the ridge, dropping down again after a mile or so and then climbing back up to Swirl How, at 802m (every metre was counting by now) our highest point of the day. It has been described as 'the pivot of the Coniston Fells, the summit to which all ridges lead'. We described it less poetically as 'freezing'. The path went steeply down, over more wet rocks which involved scrambling in places, to a big cairn at the end of a well-marked track that led across the hillside. Did we take that well marked track? Nope, we went for a much tougher zigzag trail heading for one last steep climb.

The wind was so strong that one gust actually blew me over. The way down was terrible. Marked by cairns on the ground and a path on the map, it more closely resembled a precipice. It's not too often that you have to walk backwards down a hill when hiking. Not surprisingly, this section took ages and for some reason we were all tired. I missed a left turn and took us along another ridge as the rain came in again, the heaviest we'd had all day. By the time we'd spotted my mistake, we were still high up and with cliffs on both sides. Did Lesley and Paul make a big deal of my error? No, they were much too tired for that. The way back was too tough to attempt. Our only option was to go on. The rocky ridge turned into steep, wet, slippery grass and Paul had a very spectacular sitting-down slide going a long way before coming to rest at Lesley's feet. He was upset when we realised that the map said we were crossing Birk Fell.

Finally, a ladder stile was spotted in the distance and a steep path beyond led us back to the major track along the valley bottom. It wiggled its way along the river before finally releasing us to a woodland path that ended cruelly with steep steps up a hillside and into fields. It was just starting to get dark but fortunately these were the grounds of the guest house we were booked into for the night.   It had been a fantastic walk, but we were all absolutely beat.

Our hosts were wonderful. Until two weeks ago they'd both been teachers in Liverpool. But when they'd turned fifty-five, they'd wanted to do something else. They were now running the Guest House and, after a hand-over from the previous incumbents, had been managing on their own for a whole week! They had been almost fully booked last week, but we were the only guests tonight. And when they saw the state we were in, they stuffed our boots with newspaper and put them on the AGA to dry, let us have hot showers and then ran us down to the hotel/bar at Skelwith Bridge so we could get an evening meal. They even picked us up and took us home again later on. We must have reached the tourist area. Beer prices were back to normal.

After that day, perhaps we should have given up. But no, if nothing else we are determined! In the morning we set off along the long-distance Cumbrian Way, through the grounds of the guest house and then over fields to Skelwith Bridge. Tarmac lanes went past Loughrigg Tarn and then along the length of Grasmere and into the town itself. The lakes and the hills looked lovely in the morning sunshine and we passed road signs warning of red squirrels. A whole 'collective noun' of hikers were going the other way (according to Google, hikers don't warrant a collective noun, perhaps we should invent one - 'boot' perhaps?). We almost ran out of 'good mornings'.

I didn't like Grasmere. It was all very touristy, with coachloads of people doing Wordsworth things and looking at sheep of all shapes, sizes and functions in the many tat shops. They charged for use of public toilets and I got a little confused about which roads were marked on the map, and so we did an unnecessary up and down past the shops until we escaped into the lanes beyond. Lesley and Paul were not impressed.

Eventually we crossed the main 'A' road, went through a gate and started climbing up the open moorland, along a grassy valley, brown with contours on the map and marked as 'Great Tongue'. It was very steep, but we had a lot of uphill to do. We came across some nice stepping stones at one point, keeping our feet dry for once, and had fantastic views back the way we'd come. A noisy but spectacular military transport plane flew along the valley below us and still we climbed. Lesley and Paul were not impressed.

Finally, and exhausted, we crested a ridge and could see Grisedale Tarn in the dip in front. Everyone coming the other way seemed well wrapped up.

"You won't be dressed like that in half an hour," they said looking at my shorts and t-shirt. "It's very windy and cold on top".

Overlooking the tarn and the steep hillside of Dollywaggon Pike on the other side, two elderly ladies approached. They asked what we were up to and seemed to think that our walk was quite a reasonable thing to do. Were they mad? Apparently not, just locals who did a lot of walking and who'd just popped out for a little stroll.

"It's not a day for the fells," they told us. I wonder what they would have made of the previous two days.

Lesley and Paul spotted the zig-zag path on the steep grassy hillside opposite; our next 'challenge', the Southernmost peak of the Helvellyn spine. They were not impressed.

As we ascended, now wearing far more garments as predicted, fighter jets screamed along in the valley below us. Once on top the views were fantastic, when they appeared in windows through the clouds that is. A broad, grassy ridge stretched North, with a well-defined path along it leading to the summit of Helvellyn a couple of miles distant. Along the way a memorial marked the first landing of an aircraft on an English mountain (in the 1920's), and a mountain 'wind break' in the form of a cross offered some protection to people sitting eating lunch. Just as the sun came out, we arrived at the trig point on the very top. The highest point of our trip. The views were stunning and the ridge of Striding Edge between two adjacent hanging valleys looked suitably sharp and imposing. At last Lesley and Paul <u>were</u> impressed.

It was rather cold and very windy. Too windy, we thought, for a safe descent via Striding Edge and we noticed that, although there were several groups of people on the summit, the edge itself was hiker-free. Swirral Edge offered a similar but easier option and from there we picked up a well-made path that stretched down the hillside and into Patterdale, a long, long way below.

We'd stayed at a farm in Patterdale on the Coast to Coast walk last year and I'd phoned to book again. The lady had recognised my voice and she'd still let me book! Not only that, but at the same price as well. When we arrived, the pack of Australian sheep dogs that we'd met last year greeted us with enthusiasm and put muddy paw-prints on the waterproofs. All the farming talk was of how wet it had been all year, except during May for the lambing. It was so bad at the moment that they'd given up on the hay harvest and would have to do without this winter. Hardly any of the B&B guests had made it up Helvellyn this year; we were the first since May, she said. The weather had just been too bad, too wet and too cloudy.

At breakfast a couple doing the coast to coast joined us. Yesterday they'd taken ten hours to do the allotted section and had ended up at the hotel in Patterdale as it was getting dark, and stopped for dinner. The lady was so tired she couldn't eat it and the B&B hostess had taken pity on them and gone to fetch them later in the evening. It didn't look like they were going for an early start and we knew that their next section was another tough one. I wonder how they fared?

We left them to their bacon and eggs and, after being licked by all the dogs, set off up the road to cross the river and find a track that went the length of Ullswater. After the excessive contours of the last couple of days I'd promised a 'nice flat walk alongside the lake', but Paul had spotted that the mapping program thought it was six hundred metres ascent and descent.

"How can that be flat?" he challenged.

I argued, "It's by the lake and the water must be flat." But, as we went further, the horrible truth emerged. The path did remain close to the water, but went up and down, up and down over any hummocks in the way.

Nevertheless, we were going well. We'd crossed the high Cumbrian mountains. A flock of outward-bound clones, dressed head to toe in identical red waterproofs, brown boots and big blue rucksacks, was looking nervously at a wide river crossing the path. It must have been at least an inch deep. Lesley in shorts, tee-shirt and big boots sloshed noisily across in front of them and Paul and I dutifully followed in similar fashion. Last we saw, lead clone had got about half way across gingerly and slowly, making each step while the others looked on from the safety of the far bank.

A steamer boat went by on its way North to Howtown and,

after a while, a whole stream of people started to come the other way on our path. They were well wrapped in fleeces, waterproofs, woolly hats and, mostly, gloves. One couple stopped to let me past.

"I seem to be wearing less clothes than you," I observed.

"You must be from a different planet," came their swift reply.

The track turned into a quiet road and a pair of joggers appeared from behind. Lesley joined them, Berghaus bag and all, impressively running with them for several hundred yards until she felt she'd shown them how to do it. After a final section by the lake, where sailing boats were moored, we arrived in Pooley bridge emerging right opposite Granny Dowbekin's tea room.

Our friend Jenny had told us about this place.

"It's famous", she said. "And it's got a big garden by the river where you can sit outside."

So we duly put on more clothes (it was rather chilly truth-be-told, in spite of the bravado with the Outward Bounds and the boat people), sat by the river and ordered tea and cake. The cakes were lovely. We thanked Jenny for her 'local knowledge'.

"Oh, I've never been there," she said. "Just read about it in the Caravan magazine."

This point marked the end of the Lake District. The mountains had been dropping behind for some time. Now the scenery changed to rolling, green, sheep-filled fields. Soon we came to the old church at Barton, featuring a lovely wooden barrel-ceiling, memorials to William Wordsworth's grandfather, aunt and cousin, and a strange design with a short square bell tower in the centre. A chap was mowing the grass in the graveyard.

"That must take a long time," I commented.

"Oh, we each have our own bit so it's not too bad, but look, someone has strimmed round *my* headstones. I don't mind that, but they haven't picked up the cuttings."

We walked off in the sunshine, past the impressive Kirkbarrow Hall and through the back of Stockbridge to find an unexpected but welcome 'Footpath to Penrith' sign. Ahead, in the distance, we could see the next set of hills and moors rising above the lower land, but those were for tomorrow. First, we had a railway and motorway to negotiate. The tunnel under the motorway seemed to be being used as an impromptu tractor museum. I'm not sure that they had many visitors. There was plenty of dust.

Amazingly, we reached our next B&B, a substantial terrace house on the way into Penrith, at about four. We even had time to relax before setting out to look at the big, old, red sandstone buildings in the centre of town; not just the banks, but old-fashioned hardware shops and butchers as well; very imposing in a sort of grand empire style. All were shut. In search of food we tried one of the many available pubs, selected on the basis of its odd name, the Board and Elbow. It was quiet inside and looked rather shabby, but Lesley, peering over the bar to look at the labels on the beer pump, got a bit close to an unguarded pint.

"What are you doing?" the challenge came, when the chap returned from the loos, but when she explained, the ice was broken, and the owner very reasonable.

"Oh, you should be drinking this, here have a try." So, she did. The whole episode seemed to amuse the barmaid as well. After what seemed like a respectful time we left and went somewhere less run down!

Overnight there was heavy rain, and the forecast on TV was terrible again. And next we needed to tackle the North Pennines. We worked our way through the backstreets of the town along with the heavy rush-hour traffic and heavy drizzle, and out into a whole succession of quiet lanes. It was a good job that we'd seen the hills in the distance yesterday so we knew that they were there. Today their heads were quite invisible. As we approached, we were gradually able to see their feet, but nothing more.

The land was flat here, well flat by the standards of the last few days, that is. By late morning we'd got to Ousby, where the map showed a track that climbed steeply up onto the Pennines by the side of a river. There was a new fence here, also right by the side of the river. We skirted around for a while and then accepted the inevitable. With so much rain the path and the river had become one and the same. The water wasn't too deep, just several inches above boot height ensuring wet feet for the rest of the day.

After a few hundred yards, a track did emerge from the riverbed and up we went, this time into yucky boggy cow fields. Higher still and the rain eased a bit, most probably because we were inside the clouds now rather than under them. Finally, an old tractor-width lane between two stone walls took us onto the open moor itself, a really impressive bog-of-the-day. We were looking for a junction with the Maiden Way, an old Roman road that leads to Hadrian's Wall. What we came across was an old wooden post sticking out of the bog that looked the same as any other part of the bog. But it was where the GPS thought the junction should be.

There seemed to be no evidence of the Roman road on the ground, and there was a certain amount of mumbling and grumbling that these wretched Romans just didn't build things to last. Look, just 2,000 years and it's not there anymore. The map was consulted, the compass came out and off we set across the bog on a very indistinct sheep trod, in the all-enveloping mist.

Finally, we found a few rocks and sat down for a break on solid ground. The clouds swirled about and momentarily a window through them opened up, showing a fabulous view back the way we had come over the flat ground and back to the Cumbrian mountains. Even better we could see a succession of cairns marching ahead across the bog in a straight line marking the road. But just as we saw them, the clouds swirled back and they were lost once more.

Once beyond the rounded summit of Malmerby Fell, the mist did lift a bit so we could gradually see the views ahead. The path did develop a slightly raised outline, offering a gentle, spongy but slippery surface. Eventually it joined a new-looking gravel track that seemed to be servicing grouse shooting stations and which led us all the way down to another river crossing. No bridge, just a ford to make sure that proper foot hydration was maintained.

An old cobbled track, that we assume must have once been the main road, finally led us to our first, brief encounter with the Pennine Way and the old market town of Alston. We'd arrived soon after five having covered 21.5 miles. An amazing effort.

The tourist board seems to think that Alston is remote; twenty miles from the nearest town. It certainly felt like it! We hadn't seen a single person all day. Its steep cobbled main street, covered marketplace and seventeenth century stone buildings were famous ten years or so ago, due to the apparent lack of women. A nationwide campaign supported by some of the national newspapers (guess which!) found there was a ratio of seventeen men to every woman. In the rain it just seemed empty. Perhaps the women never came, and the men left as well.

We were staying in a B&B just behind the church, in a couple of nice warm rooms in a conservatory near to the main house. Our hostess took in our horrible wet boots for a drying session and had even heard of the Alternative Coast to Coast Walk. What's more she knew where it started and finished and where we would be walking to tomorrow. She seemed keen that we should go to what had obviously once been a pub and was now an Indian restaurant. It was a strange setup. The owner, a Chinese lady, had let the kitchen to a Bangladeshi family who lived in Newcastle. Every day a chef drove from Newcastle to Alston. The food was good, and the chef came to chat after we'd eaten. Well, he gave us a lesson in Bangladeshi history while we listened. Sadly, we all felt more in need of an early night than an education.

Breakfast was unusual. Instructions were: 'eat anything you find in the (well stocked) fridge'. Strawberry cereal with strawberry yoghurt and covered in fresh strawberries seemed to taste of, well, strawberries.   There were chocolate chip brioches, crumpets and lots of other things. A much shorter walk was planned for today, so we didn't rush and we even had time for a stroll around the village before setting off. Apparently there hasn't been a market here for years, but today there was a solitary lady sitting on the wall of the marketplace selling eggs.

Now, you may be thinking that we'd just been unlucky with the weather until now, and everything was going to be fine. Well you'd be wrong. Very wrong. Do read on!

The dry boots lasted less than half a mile. The lane out of town was muddy and attempting to morph into a river. Better tracks led steeply up onto Mohope Moor (misread owing to lack of specs the first time as Nohope Moor) and first official bog-of-the-day. But not just any bog. This one had signs up saying that it was a Site of Special Scientific Interest and important for blanket bog plants.

On the map a path was marked, but in reality, an occasional post showed the way. Black grouse rose up all around, making their laugh-like alarm calls. Walking was a bit like Russian roulette. Mostly the green bits, presumably the all-important blanket bog plants, would take our weight but every now and then one wouldn't and a cold boot-full of muddy sludge was the result. We came to a gate. Perhaps it marked the Cumbria-Northumberland border. It was surrounded by deep, black water. Lesley claimed to have seen a goldfish in it.

Finally, and gratefully, we came to a pebbly track, and stopped for a break and to wring out the socks. But it was horrible; loose pebbles heading steeply downhill and pretending to be a riverbed. It eventually took us to tarmac, and a bridge and little church at Ninebanks. Isaac Holden was baptised here in 1805. We hadn't heard of him either. He was a lead miner who became a travelling tea salesman and also raised funds for the poor. Today there is 37-mile circular walk bearing his name. It's fun. The signposts were mostly teapots or cups and saucers attached to gateposts and stiles. Unfortunately, it led us back uphill and into the land of bogs.

Eventually we came to the minor road at the top of Dryburn Moor (another misnomer if ever there was one!) and rested on top of a large manhole cover that was busy making loo-flushing noises to itself. We could see two tall chimneys a little further on, and from them, two long but distinctly rounded hummocks snaking their way to the valley below. Very odd. On the map they were marked as the lines of old flues but looked to us more like something produced by giant moles. Later Paul did some research and found that they carried fumes from the lead smelting operation in Allendale village up to the chimneys on the moor. This was not, as you might believe, to get the poisonous gasses away from the village, but so that any remaining lead and silver in the vapour could condense on the walls of the tunnels and be chipped off by some unfortunate in due course.

We were due to stay the night at Thornley Gate just outside Allendale. I'd booked it especially for Lesley as on its website it advertised itself as 'a B&B for lovers of fine cats and fine gardens'. It didn't mention the souvenirs from all around the world. We had tea in the living room on arrival talking to the cats, three big toms and one tiny six-week-old kitten that went straight for Lesley's lap. Upstairs there was a female ginger who seemed to think she owned the place and, in the bedroom, we found signs saying 'All guests must be approved of by the cats' and instructions for a children's safari round the gardens.

That night we walked the half mile into town. It was quiet again. They were playing sixties' Summer of Love CDs and Paul and I just had to sing along between courses, while Lesley looked embarrassed.

We woke to a heavy frost, blue skies and a breakfast room even more stuffed with strange things from around the world. The tea-pot was a blue-footed-booby from the Galapagos and coffee was served in an elegant silver and gold pot from Damascus. Hot water came from a silver jug with English hallmarks. We got chatting to our hostess, Elizabeth, and she showed us a set of wall tiles in her kitchen: 'cats of St. Petersburg' and a wall hanging market scene from Cuba. There was a cat statue from Egypt and a Steinway Grand in the music room. Mozart piano concertos had been playing at breakfast. No singing for Paul and me then, but Lesley just couldn't help herself.

We asked about Elizabeth's next trip.

"Oh, a boot-camp in Bulgaria with all the big Bulgarian ladies," she said. "They starve us and make us do exercise and then take us for a 15Km walk, but I left the others behind last time; they were too slow." As we left and walked down the drive she called after us,

"If you've had a nice stay, please put an entry in Trip Advisor so I can get more guests. Then I could afford to get a camel to keep with the donkeys. I do love camels but donkeys cost £1,500 each per year and camels are twice that."

The thought of the lady in her big house with her cats and donkeys kept us amused for several hours as we climbed through the appropriately named village of Catton and up onto the boggy moorland again. We tried to look up her biography but didn't get far. She'd done a degree in Slavonic studies in London in the early sixties and had got married at some point. Perhaps she'd been a cold-war spy!

Up on the moor, Rebel Hill was the highest point and once again the so-called path was marked by a series of posts sticking out of the bog. The way led due East to a patch of woodland, a short stretch of tarmac and a trig point near Lords Lot. For once we had warm sunshine and we lay in the grass by a gate, drinking coffee and soaking it up; the sun, that is, and not the sodden landscape for once.

We had one more stretch of bog-moor to do on the North Pennines before dropping down to Professor Beer's next landmark, the microbrewery in the old drovers watering hole, the Dipton Mill Inn. It was so nice we sat out in the garden and talked to a pair of black labradors and their owners. The dogs thought we were lovely. We hoped that the attraction was the crisps that we were eating and not the state of our clothing!

I'd had trouble getting anywhere to stay in Hexham. There seemed to be some sort of festival going on and it was Saturday, but eventually I'd found a big place, big enough to be shown on the map and with a half mile private drive leading to the edge of town. Its website claimed 'it dates from 1780, is comfortably furnished, with many antiques adding to its essential 18th century character.' We would need to walk through its grounds on our way to Hexham and it was only lunchtime, so I called to see if we could drop off our rucksacks on the way past. The lady who answered the phone had a very posh voice, and I joked with Lesley that the accent was like hers and the Queen's.

When we arrived, an elderly lady with a friendly white dog let us into a very large, grand house, more like a stately home, really. Our room was enormous, with antique furniture, posh wallpaper with birds painted on it and old-fashioned round pin electrical sockets. There was a chandelier in the bathroom. It was that sort of place. We found her watching horse racing on TV when we went to ask for bath towels.

This was our official rest half-day. So, what did we do? Well, we walked the mile or so into Hexham for a look-see. Stalls filled the market square and the park behind the abbey, but they didn't offer much for us: mostly kiddy things. We visited the abbey and went shopping (more walking). Paul was in search of waterproof socks and, much to our surprise, found some. We walked the mile back from the Abbey to get showered, and then back to Hexham again to meet up with Lesley's friend Anna who lives there. She'd left her husband babysitting and came out to the pub with us instead. It was a late night; ten thirty!

A girl in her late twenties with short-spiky hair served us breakfast. She turned out to be a portrait painter who'd recently taken on a part time job at the B&B as it came with a tied cottage. I managed to serve marmalade with a knife rather than a spoon and Paul managed to put his tea cup down without a saucer before she told us that the lady we'd met yesterday was a cousin of the Queen Mother. We felt out of place again.

Hexham was our gateway to the Northumberland National Park. It was pretty empty early on a Sunday morning as we walked past the Abbey and down to the river, although we did find a few dog-walkers out here in the early morning mist. We headed North, and even a bit of West, over more moors and through misty woods. It was the wrong way for our Coast to Coast route really, but Paul had never seen Hadrian's Wall so we needed to walk on some of it. By the time we reached Black Carts, the fog had burnt off and we were all impressed. It even looked like a wall. There was a German couple walking along it for a week. They were well wrapped up.

"Aren't you cold in your t-shirts?" they asked, but we were acclimatised by now and were only cold when we stopped.

After a couple of kilometres heading West along the wall, we came across a car park at the Roman Fort of Brocolitia. A cheery chap in shorts and a big jacket was hiding in a small 50cc three-wheeler advertising 'Fresh Coffee' on its sides. Soon he was out in the cold making us hot drinks, telling us about the history of the wall and correcting our pronunciation of our next destination, Bellingham (Bel-in-jem for the record). He pointed out a radio mast on the horizon a very long way away.

"It's in the valley behind that," he told us.

We left the wall for the moor proper, heading through bog-of-the-day in a straight line for miles. Coffee man had told us it was the old trading route between the river fording points, but now it seemed to be mainly being used by sheep and a large flock of outward-bound types, looking lost and peering at maps. The bog plants seemed to have changed a bit; less green flat stuff and more ankle-breaking tussocky things, mixed up with heather. As you can tell we were getting pretty expert with bogs by now.

Right on the boundary of the Northumberland National Park, we joined the Pennine Way. Famous for going straight through bogs, it didn't disappoint. At least we were heading North again and in the sunshine the views were magnificent. We followed it all the way to a road just short of Bellingham, reducing speed all the time as Lesley's feet were very sore. Eventually we turned off and walked, very slowly, down the gated one-mile long track to Bridgeford Farm where we planned to stay. It was in the middle of nowhere, but the rooms were spacious, warm, dry and comfortable and well suited for what had become the nightly wash-the-other-set-of-clothes routine, hoping that they'd be dry by morning.

The map showed a river crossing right by the farm that would take us to the town tonight, and onwards North again in the morning. But was it a bridge or was it a ford? Just outside the farm was a 'no river crossing' notice. We checked with our host.

"Neither! That's right, no crossing. There hasn't been one here for years, not since they built the reservoir. It's marked on the map right enough, and we often get people walking down here and they suddenly find out there's no way over. They seem to think it's all my fault. It's about four miles if you go round."

You can imagine how we felt! This was very bad news. Very bad indeed. We felt a bit better after showers, but with sore feet stiff limbs we certainly didn't fancy the two mile walk to town to get fed, two miles back again and then an extra four miles tomorrow, simply to get to the other side of the river. He took pity on us.

"I'll run you down to the village," he said and, as we got out of the car, "what time would you like to be picked up?" What a hero!

Our bodies seemed to have recovered by morning, but there had been yet more heavy rain and strong winds. The TV news reported that someone had been killed by a falling branch in Kew gardens. As we dallied over breakfast, postponing the inevitable for as long as we could, a woodpecker and nuthatch were on the bird table in the rain, outside the dining-room window.

I planned a new route that didn't involve the extra four miles.

Overnight the track to the farm had transformed into a river. We splashed up it (wet feet yet again!) to re-join the road, the Pennine Way and our new detour to the village. There was a strange clock tower in the High Street with pointy turrets, and a gun brought back from China in 1900. A little further on was a tourist centre with an old railway carriage acting as a café. The lady asked what we were up to. "Walking to Otterburn, but as the weather is so bad, we'll take the minor roads rather than following the Pennine way up and over the tops of the moors. Those peat bogs will be pretty horrible today."

"The thing about bogs," she replied, "is that they're boggy. It doesn't matter about the rain, they'll still be boggy anyway." Good point, and well made, but we decided to stick with the tarmac as far as we could.

We passed a couple of farmers attempting to move hay bales out of the rain and instead of the normal "good morning" we got a cheery "nasty day!"

By the time we got to West Woodburn and the end of the lanes, we were ready for a break and to escape the rain for a while but there didn't seem anywhere to stop, not that is, until we reached the A road and found a pub. It was open and advertising coffee and tea. But we were soaked and they had a carpet in there. Fortunately, they also had a side entrance that led to a passage with a flagstone floor and hooks to hang soaked garments on. By the time we'd all undressed and made our way into the carpeted bar, all our good intentions to have hot drinks had evaporated and we ordered the usual: beer.

103

There were a small group of people inside and they asked what we were up to.

"Well I just hope that you've got good waterproofs," one said, when she found out.

At that point Paul, who was at the bar, turned around with his usual damp patch in an embarrassing place on his trousers. Although predictable the response was almost instant.

"Oh, you must have been so excited to get inside," the girl said, while an older man patted him gently on the shoulder and said,

"Don't worry, it's an age thing you know."

We stayed as long as we could but the weather wasn't getting any better. I re-planned the route again to avoid both the A road and riverside paths that I'd been planning to use. Before long we were heading cross country, high above a deep river valley and enjoying that bog-of-the-day experience again. Mostly there were no signs or visible paths on the ground and the heavy sideways rain obscured the view, making the route finding rather challenging. Lesley and Paul went into 'smug mode' after I owned up to having saturated feet. 'Money well spent' was the general verdict on the waterproof socks, so much so that Paul did a little rain dance in an unsuspecting patch of bog.

We arrived at a remote little church, all alone on the hillside and surrounded by old graves. Inside was a wooden cross sitting beside a pile of rocks and a sign saying 'You are invited to place a stone at the foot of the cross to represent your prayer". Is that a Christian thing do you think, or a bit pagan? Then we had more invisible path through bog, this time with five-foot-high bog reeds to add variety, before we finally reached the road into Otterburn.

It turned out that years ago our Guest House had been the old Co-op shop. We sat in our warm, dry room watching the news on TV. It was all about the weather. It had been bad in the South. Tonight and tomorrow it was expected to be worse where we were. Paul had to confess that the waterproof socks had proved only 50% effective. He'd ended up with only one dry foot.

A couple of buildings down the street was the Percy Arms Hotel which served food on a Monday night. Unfortunately, a coach party of forty pensions had arrived just before us, and so we just had to sit at the bar and drink the half-price ale that the hotel was trying to finish off. Eventually the pensioners started filtering off to an upstairs room and we could get some food. Later, of course they started coming back again, the advance party being two elderly ladies who started giving us lots of light-hearted grief about our trip. Well, they did until they let on that they were due to visit Alnwick Castle tomorrow. We knew that it was the location of Harry Potter's Hogwarts and we turned the conversation to broomsticks, black pointy hats and the relationship of these things to the two elderly ladies in front of us. Then the hotel ran out of beer. How could that possibly have happened?

It rained heavily all night AGAIN! The news reported that parts of the M6, M1 and A1 had all been closed yesterday, due to excessive surface water. Some places had received a month's worth of rain in one day and there was plenty more to come. Breakfast TV was full of footage of people being rescued from floods from all over the country.

I looked again at the maps and re-planned the walk: No river Valleys, too flooded. No crossing rivers or streams, too deep. No woods; the trees had been throwing things at passers-by, too dangerous. It didn't leave many alternatives but I had spotted a network of tracks over the moor that might serve as an almost bee-line to our next overnight stop. There were a few slight drawbacks. First, we had to reach them, second, they weren't all marked as public rights of way and finally, big red script in block capitals all over that bit of the map saying 'DANGER AREA'. At breakfast we asked for some local knowledge and as usual were told,

"You'll be fine. It's all tarmac roads round the army firing range!"

We couldn't avoid the bog just North on Otterburn on Fawdon Hill, and the map did show one small brook to cross. But for once there was a discernible, albeit faint, path through the ankle-breaking, knee-wrenching tussocky reeds, as well as the usual post markers. Normally, I guess you'd just step over the brook, but not today. It was about two metres wide. It was deep. It was the colour of last night's beer. It was flowing strongly. We started diverting upstream to where the channel might be narrower, but up there the bog got even more waterlogged. Soon we had all been in to mid-shin height and no amount of waterproof socks or boots could protect from that.

Just about now my phone went. It was the publican from the pub we'd booked for tonight.

"Are you still coming?"

"Yes, we're on our way, but we're not sure when we'll arrive because of the weather".

"Be careful" he advised, "The rivers are all over here. If you get stuck give me a call and I'll pick you up." A kind thought, but one that we obviously took as a challenge to see if we could get there without any help!

Eventually we did find a place where, rucksacks off, we could demonstrate our Olympic long-jumping capabilities with a leap, or was that a lunge, over the torrent. But by now we were well away from the path and had to contour up the hillside yet further to meet a track in a small wood, where, for what it was worth, we indulged in the wringing out of socks ceremony yet again. There was an enormous forestry digger up here and inside, a chap drinking tea. He opened the door to chat as we passed by and we told him that we were headed for Alwinton.

"Be careful," he said, "It's very flooded over there". He didn't offer us any tea!

The noise of machine gun fire greeted us as we left the wood and set off along a tarmac road, and now and then there was the deep thump of a bigger explosion. We seemed to be right on the edge of the range. From time to time, army Land Rovers went past us and, at one place, there were big trucks shedding camouflaged soldiers, who were setting off single file down a wooded gully and looking very wet. None of them stopped or spoke to us. They too carried big packs, but we didn't think they had mistaken us as foe. Whereas they had foliage in their hats and carried guns, we carried flasks of coffee and ate chocolate. We guessed that we were probably okay doing what we were doing.

Eventually a not-too-boggy and not-too-long footpath took us away from the range, down a hill and into a forest. The wind had dropped and I'd re-planned the route again, betting that tracks through woods would be better than paths not far from rivers. It seemed to work; the tracks were plenty wide enough and took us without fuss to a minor road near Harbottle. Briefly the phones woke up with messages of concern from various friends and relatives, but then the signal was gone again and we couldn't respond. As we carried on towards Alwinton, we could see that the fields down near the river, where our original footpath was, were entirely flooded. Not only that but as we got closer, we could see that it wasn't the usual static water, but more closely resembled rapids. Even our little road was flooded in places but the feet couldn't get any wetter, so we waded through.

We arrived at the pub soon after two, completely drenched in the footwear department but the publican let us in, and lit a big log fire in the guest sitting room just for us, where we relaxed, dried out and drank tea for the rest of the afternoon. We watched the rain get heavier and heavier through the afternoon, and the river water gradually creeping up the fields getting closer and closer to the pub.

In the evening the pub was quiet. After a while, one couple came in, obviously well known. Their drinks were poured even before they'd placed an order.

"We couldn't get out of the village." they said. "You are doing food, aren't you? We've only got some salad and two chops in the house. We seemed to have eaten everything else." Exhausted Lesley went to bed and another couple came in.

"The water on the road just beyond Harbottle is above the bonnet of my Freelander," he said. I'd almost decided to come that way instead of through the wood. Paul and I tried a little whisky to celebrate that we'd made it through. After all, we were within ten miles of the Scottish border.

In the morning the news was full of the worst September storms for thirty years, and the worst hit part of the country seemed to be exactly where we were. I'd looked at the map but there wasn't a good alternative to the planned route today. We needed to cross the Cheviot hills. It wasn't actually raining when we set off, and when we had come into Alwinton yesterday we could see a steep hillside rising behind the pub. After a big breakfast, the track took us straight up it.

We even got some views of the surrounding countryside as we went, and all agreed it was very much like parts of Scotland. We swung up past the edge of the huge area of Kirkland Forest, bits of which seemed to have burnt down at some point, and as we continued the showers came and went, but with increasing frequency and ferocity as the morning wore on. North of the forest a rough track took us to a really remote farm at Uswayford, where the publican had told us there was a new bridge. Just as well, as the torrent beneath it would not have been passable. A farmer was busy doing things in his farmyard but, unusually, he didn't acknowledge us.

We stopped for coffee in the next wood, in what turned out to be the last dry(ish) spell of the day and then climbed up to the open moorland beyond which we met the Pennine Way again. Someone had been very busy laying huge stone slabs to make a pathway across the black peat bog. Once again, the feet could get no wetter, so even where the slabs were underwater, we just splashed through. At least they were a firm footing. Sometimes the slabs had sunk so much that peat as well as water had covered them, and in one place Paul, attempting to use the edge where the water might be shallower, put his foot completely off the block. Down he sank, one leg on the stone and the other thigh-deep in the peat without his foot touching the bottom. The suction was such that he couldn't free himself and we had to Paul him out (as Lesley put it). Sorry!

By now the mist was down, it was raining hard and blowing a gale. It was cold and absolutely disgusting. Visibility was probably less than ten metres, just enough to follow the stones. My 'escape route' in case of bad weather was of no use, as it went down the hill to follow a river in the valley at the bottom and crossed many tributaries on the way. We had to stick with it.

We stopped to put more clothes on where the stones and the map indicated a path heading South. The GPS gave a reference saying we were at the summit. It was freezing. Only when we set off again did we find the real summit, marked by a trig point on top of a tall plinth, only a few metres further on. The stones led us on again through the murk and wet.

We had to do another couple of miles of this before we were able to take a turn and set off down an invisible spur along a path through yet more bog. But this one was different. High on springiness, but low on sinkiness. Lesley led the way down, travelling fast and mostly getting away with it, and earning a new nickname: The Queen of the Bogs.

Much, much later we came down below cloud level, the rain stopped and we were able to rest on a more solid patch of ground, looking down on a small-river-turned-large, forging its way down in the valley below. Fortunately, the road near to it still looked intact. When we got there, it was clear that yesterday the road had been submerged, and in one place a whole section of riverbank had washed away, leaving unsupported tarmac and BT ducts swirling around in the torrent.

But we did finally get through to the stone-built market town of Wooler. It seemed to have a lot of pubs and shops, but we were in no presentable state to investigate. A note on the door of our B&B was addressed to us:

"I'm sorry I'm not in, you are in rooms 1 and 3, Rachel".

Perfect. Radiators were turned to max, wet clothes, boots and laundry hung all over the place. It made a terrible smell, and only later, when it was too late, did we find that the windows were all painted shut.

After a while Rachel's partner turned up, a mid-thirties, athletic-looking chap in shorts ("I always wear shorts"), and we asked where was good to eat. His suggestion was to go into a few pubs, order a beer and keep going until we found one we liked. Fortunately, we managed to like the second one we tried. As we sat by the fire, two big chaps turned up and sat at the bar. We could hear them talking about walking over Cheviot today and how terrible it was. It turned out that they were two firemen from near the border, doing St. Cuthbert's Way to raise money for a defibrillator for their small town. Apparently, it would take an ambulance so long to get there in an emergency, it would be too late. Now there's a coincidence. Our plan was to follow St.

Cuthbert's Way all the way to Lindisfarne and the official end of the route tomorrow.

In the morning we found that Rachel did really exist, bouncy, plumpish and sort of horsey, which explained the rosettes and pictures of show jumping on the dining room walls. We seemed to have 'accidentally' left the door of our room open before and during breakfast so it didn't smell too badly (or so we thought) by the time we left. Although the storms seemed to have ended, much of the land was very flooded, but fortunately for us, St. Cuthbert must have had similar issues and his holy footsteps kept to the high ground wherever it existed. Perhaps he was about as good at walking on water as we had turned out to be.

Once out of the outskirts of Wooler, we went uphill through tall wet bracken onto a heather topped hill. Some of the heather was still flowering and the views of the floods were impressive. In the valley below the map showed three large rivers, but all we could see was a succession of lakes. An elderly couple with a half-grown, very friendly sheepdog puppy stopped us. They'd just moved up from "busy Berkshire" and told us how lovely it all was up here and how friendly everyone was. Somehow, we felt, they must have missed out on that regular 'bog of the day' experience.

The path was well signposted, except where it needed to be. Coming off the hill, we followed a path on our map that seemed to be a very overgrown trail on the ground and we ended up dropping very steeply indeed, down a hillside beside a wood, through more tall, wet bracken towards a bridge ahead. Just beyond the bridge, the road was flooded. A car approached and backed off.

"You'll be okay," they told us, through their windows. "The road dips here but there are good verges."

Indeed, the verges looked like green banks of grass between the flooded tarmac and the flooded fields on either side. More local knowledge then. When will we learn? It turned out that it was long grass with the tips floating on the flood and, in reality, the water was about knee height. Of course, we only found this out part way over, by which time it was too late to take the boots and socks off. Finally, safe on the other side there was a long pause while we wrung out the socks and drained the boots. Paul found he could actually wring out his boots as well!

Roads and good, dry tracks took us through the rolling agricultural landscape. Behind we could see yesterday's mountains with their heads still in the clouds, but for once we had sun and blue skies. We stopped for coffee and to change into dry socks, and the firemen from last night caught up with us. They'd missed the path off the hill and had gone straight on and miles around by roads. But it did mean that they'd also missed the flooded bridge. Bizarrely, they seemed disappointed; something to do with wanting to follow St. Cuthbert's footsteps exactly. But still clad in fleeces and waterproofs and sweating profusely, in contrast to our shorts and t-shirts, they continued.

"We should see the sea over the next hill. We'll stop then"

Several hills and several miles later we found them taking a rest in St. Cuthbert's cave, a good-sized overhang under a rocky outcrop surrounded by pine trees.

"We were going to carry on until we could see the sea," they said, "but it never happened." We climbed up behind the cave and there, in the distance, was the sea and our first sight of Holy Island and Lindisfarne Castle. It looked a very long way away.

Next was quite a bit of walking through boggy woodland. A whole different type of bog we expertly surmised. So much so that it provoked an outburst of community singing. Paul had learnt all three verses of the 'Hippopotamus Mud' song, for just such an occasion.

We stopped again on a bench just short of Fenwick, and the firemen came past once more. The shorter, bald one looked like he'd had enough, and complained that the taller one had a much longer stride and kept on going too fast, but it was an easy two miles cross-country to the start of the causeway connecting the island to the mainland, and we didn't need to get there until around five to give the tide chance to go down enough to expose the road.

We did arrive a bit early, to find the firemen sitting on a concrete block, waiting for the tide. As we drew near the parked ice cream van, it started up and moved further down, towards the queue of cars. Naturally we followed it. By the time we'd got to where the queue was, the vehicles had started crossing, the ice cream van among them. How inconsiderate! What sort of customer service is that?

The map only shows one way over: to follow the tarmac in a big arc across the sands and alongside dunes to the village on the island. But we'd been told (you know where this is going don't you: more local knowledge, more walking on water!) that there was a direct route: a pedestrian way over the sands marked by a series of posts. Well, the road was quite busy and the sand looked fairly dry and the posts were easy to spot. There was a whole line of them, about three meters high and with 'tree houses' from time to time in case you got the tides wrong. And the Alternative Coast to Coast description had said that we should cross the North Sea.

All was well to begin with. The sands were firm and wet, with a thin layer of water but as we progressed, they became rather slippery with green stuff and black ooze, and a bit sinky. But the posts were there to keep you out of the real quicksand, so we'd been told. Further on it became wetter. The tide hadn't gone out far enough, but we managed to hop around and over channels for a bit until we met a really deep one and stopped. We were, perhaps, two miles from the start of the causeway and only had a short distance to go to the village but the water looked deep. We waited. The firemen caught us up and had a debate. They decided that the lure of a pint in the pub was greater than the threat of wet feet, and went on. We watched with interest as they splashed through. At its deepest the water seemed to be about crotch level. We waited.

In the end we got bored and started to get cold, so followed their example and got the boots flooded for the second time in the day, but at least the water level had dropped to about shin level. Apparently, it doesn't go a whole lot lower than that.

As we entered the stone houses of the obviously very touristy village, past the large car park, we enjoyed a restaurant sign: "Food to Go And Sit In".

We didn't try that but instead shared a beer with the firemen in the Crown and Anchor, our B&B for the night, while they waited to be rescued by a wife. Their walk was over, but we had one more day to do.

112

In the morning the boots were still completely sodden, so we had wet feet from the outset. The plan was to potter around the village, take a look at the ruined Abbey and then walk up to the castle. It was all rather pretty, with little boats pulled up on the beach as foreground, and the castle standing proudly on an outcrop of volcanic rock. Unfortunately, it was National Trust and therefore closed until just about the time when we needed to head back across the causeway so as not to miss the tide. Instead we went for a walk round the island, along the coast and through the sand dunes, and started back to the mainland. After our experience of yesterday we took the long way via the road.

On the mainland the causeway met the Coast Path and turned North. Quite unlike the Cumbrian 'get your feet wet' one this seemed almost ashamed of the sea. It took a nice safe option along the edge of solid ground with sand dunes and miles of wet sand flats, full of flocks of wading birds, between us and an invisible sea. At one point we lost the path and ended up even more inland than we should have done, but it didn't seem to matter much. Just a few more miles!

We started passing a long, thin golf course that stretched between the railway line and the coast. It seemed to go on for ages, but finally we came to the club house and, especially after our previous golf course experience, an amazing sign: 'Walkers Welcome'. Given that they'd made the gesture it would have been rude not to stop for a rest in their bar, especially as we could see what turned out to be the only rain shower of the day approaching fast. Inside a party of large Dutchmen were asking the young barmaid,

"What is gammon?"

After a pause she said

"Pig", then "thick bacon, very nice". They asked for beer and the older barmaid hissed quietly to her

"Give them lager".

In spite of being made welcome, we did feel very scruffy and out of place.

A bit further on and the coast got itself sorted out and started looking like one, with small cliffs, sandy beaches and a car park full of dog-walking transports and an ice cream van. Our pace quickened and this time the van didn't escape. At last it started feeling like a holiday.

The last couple of miles went through Spittal, which seemed to be a built-up suburb of Berwick, along long straight roads and through the old dockland area. Ahead we could see three arched bridges across the Tweed, each rising higher than the last, such that they looked like a three-tiered Roman aqueduct. Our final approach to the city was across the most seaward and lowest, the 'old bridge'. It was like something out of Pratchett. Tall old houses dominated by a tall clock spire, hiding behind tall, thick city walls on the edge of the river, and with just the bridge creating a gap in them. Inside, cobbled streets and tall old buildings jammed close together reinforced the effect.

Our B&B was one such building, and a small plumpish lady opened the door. Just inside was a bowl of sweets. Lesley took a few. By the stairs there were toffees. Lesley took a few. Up in the room there was a bowl of fruit, biscuits, and chocolates on the pillows. Lesley was in trouble! Then the introductory lecture started. She told us about the fridge in the corridor with milk, and complimentary beer and wine, where the best pubs were (for real ale 'The Barrels' at the bottom of the street), and the best places to eat; again, lots of choice and none very far away. Later we tried The Barrels, an old-fashioned pub, dark and stuffed full of artefacts, and no sign of food. We went to the Indian just down the road and then back to the pub.

"Did you enjoy your curry?" asked the cheeky barman.

"Yes, how can you tell?".

"Oh, the smell," came the reply. Still, it must have disguised the smell of the dirty clothes, or maybe he was just being polite.

In the morning it turned out that it was the husband, Rocky who was cooking breakfast. Now, we only know one Rocky and that's the troll from Terry Pratchett who's counting skills go one, two, many, lots. We were a bit worried. As we started on cereals, fresh fruit and yoghurt, the lady said,

"I've got croissants today; would you like one while you look at the menu?" We did that and Lesley ordered bacon, while Paul and I fell for the house special. It came. It was enormous! Lesley had five giant rashers, while Paul and I got everything imaginable, including both black and white pudding, gammon steak, sausage, bacon, eggs, mushrooms, tomatoes, beans and even haggis. It seemed like the counting mechanism was in action. Two of everything. "Would you like toast?" asked the lady. Aargh no! We did our best but couldn't finish and had to go for a walk round the town walls for a bit, while waiting for the time to go to the station and catch our trains.

When we came back to the B&B to pick up our bags, Rocky himself opened the door. He didn't look like a troll at all: small and round.

"Fantastic breakfast," we told him, "so sorry that we couldn't finish it".

"Don't worry," he said, "few people do. There was a chap who came here once with a friend who'd been before. He came down first, before the friend, and told me that they had a £100 bet that he couldn't finish the house special. Well, I had some liver and kidneys in that day, so I did them as well. But full marks to him, he stuck with it for an hour and did finish".

"Was he a big bloke?" we asked.

"Oh yes, thirty stone at least." We felt a bit better!

Some months after completing the walk we did manage to get hold of a second-hand copy of the Alternative Coast to Coast guide book. I was not to live it down! My route had gone a to b and b to c, over all the highest and most spectacular bits of landscape I could find. The 'official' route stayed low; river valleys wherever possible, and much less strenuous. Would Lesley and Paul ever trust me again?

Normal life took over. We imagined Paul back at work now, respectably dressed, but with a secret damp, soggy grow-bag under his desk into which he stuck his feet at regular intervals to maintain some of that holiday feeling, while Lesley had a major birthday to get through. I got stuck into Open University Exam revision, all about storms, weather and seawater. Amazingly just days after the exam was taken an email arrived from Paul:

"I've been getting beer withdrawal symptoms, not to mention itchy feet (they're obviously too dry), and have been giving a little idle thought and research to the next venture. How would you and the Ageing Assistant (many happy wossnames by the way) feel about continuing the Penzance Practice in an Easterly direction sometime?"

The seed had been sowed, and now it had germinated! Despite all the awful weather we'd had, we were actually contemplating 'doing' the South West Coast Path. Perhaps it was that investment Paul had made in waterproof socks that was driving him on.

The mpg calculation.

Taking 220 miles as the on-route total we get: Paul 42 mpg, Tim 48 mpg and Lesley 135 mpg.

However, if we include scrumpy, lager and stuff not fit to be called ale, a slightly different picture emerges: Paul 38, Tim 38, Lesley 122,

6. To Looes – La Trek (Penzance to Looe March 2013)

It was going to be March tomorrow, and after the hibernation that comes with winter, we were ready (in mind at least) for another walk. For the sake of continuity, we wanted to start at Penzance and continue East. But how far to go? We decided to aim for Looe, for no better reason than it had a railway station that we could get back from and because it offered some great, but perhaps predictable, project names: The dash to Looe anyone? In the end we settled on a reference to a French Impressionist painter who liked to drink.

We decided to do it, even though it involved shopping. For Paul, waterproof over trousers with full length vents to avoid overheating, whilst also avoiding the embarrassing wet patch in the crotch area. For me, waterproof socks for the inevitable 'is this a stream, river, lake or path?' days and to bring me in-line with the others in terms of gear, and for Lesley, Mars bars and other chocolates!

We decided to do it even though this part of Cornwall has estuaries and the ferries don't run out of season. A state of mind that says that a thirteen-mile detour should be nothing to be worried about was going to be important.

We decided to do it even though it had been raining heavily for weeks and the long-range weather forecast for March was terrible, including heavy snowfalls for our first week. Landslips and missing sections of path had also been reported.

After the traditional curry last supper, we held a ceremonial weighing of the packed rucksacks (for the record, Lesley: 9kg mostly Mars bars and home-made bikkies, Paul: 10Kg mostly sensible stuff, Me: 13.5Kg mostly sandwiches and nardicot oranges), and set off through the grey skies and light drizzle to walk the five and a half miles from Paul's house to Exeter train station.

The rucksacks seemed heavy, but I managed to persuade the others that sandwiches and nardicots needed to be eaten on a bench outside the station while we waited for the train, and so mine was better after that. So much so that we managed the additional 50 yards to The Great Western Hotel, that local-knowledge-Paul assured us had a reputation for real ales. The customary beer log was opened.

Having admired the fields of daffodils in bloom as we travelled through Cornwall, we arrived in Penzance just before dark and headed up the High Street to the distant edge of town, where all the B&B's huddle together safely out of the way of anything harmful, and soon found the big Victorian house that was ours. Victoria, a sixtyish, roundish lady with a strong Cornish accent ushered us in and bustled around us.

"Oh, you look single," she said to Paul, as she pushed him into the nearest bedroom.

"Thank you so much" he managed.

"No, the other two look together," she replied. Good recovery!

Later, we went in search of food. The steep road took us to the promenade, but just as we got there, a board outside the Alexandra Inn advertised a special price on Betty Stoggs: £2.50 a pint.

"That's good beer," Paul said. "We must try some".

Inside it wasn't busy and we ordered a couple of pints, and a half of something stronger for Lesley, and the barmaid was soon asking us for money; £8.50. Something seemed wrong. We gently suggested that she'd overcharged us. Suddenly, everyone else seemed to find some urgent reason to be elsewhere and the place emptied. She looked at the till, she looked at us, we looked at her, we suggested that two times £2.50 might be £5. She went to talk to what seemed to be the owner. We drank the beer. She came back and all was okay. Bar brawl averted. The manager had forgotten to set up the special offer on the till. We paid and people started drifting back in. Strangely, we didn't stay there for food, but it *was* good beer!

Instead we took a stroll down to the harbour area and the rather touristy Dolphin Inn, with air smoky with the steam from their speciality sizzling dishes, but somehow, after eating, we found ourselves in the not-so-touristy Dock Inn next door. Victoria had suggested that we go there, or maybe it was just Paul that she'd invited. It was their quiz night and she was in a team. Fortunately, the quiz had started by the time we arrived, so we didn't have to enter but sat quietly in a corner trying to get the answers anyway. Well, it would have been rude to compete and beat the landlady wouldn't it. As it was, she came over at half time:

"Did you know the answers to that last round?" she asked. We couldn't get them at all. We gave her our guesses:

"They'd better be right, otherwise it's burnt sausages for breakfast!"

They turned out to be wrong!

The next day started badly. To save weight my phone had been told to act as an alarm clock. It seemed pleased with its new responsibilities and went off loudly, enthusiastically and persistently, to the increasingly aggressive cries of "switch it off, switch it off" from under the bedclothes to my side as I, blind without contact lenses, poked and stabbed at various parts of the screen to no avail. Eventually I managed to turn off the entire phone but it had worked well; we were both now wide awake and looking forward to burnt sausages. Later, when things had calmed down a bit, we switched it on again and both poked at it, without result.

Victoria had relented, as her team had won the quiz, and breakfast was good. Good that is until someone pointed out that we had managed five pubs so far, and not even started the walk proper. We set off through Penzance, down to the promenade, past the Alexandra Inn and headed East to the harbour, with its gold post-box commemorating Helen Glovers gold medal at the 2012 Olympics. We then continued out of town on a raised bank separating the railway line from the sea. Dominating the scenery was St Michaels Mount, the castle silhouetted grey on its grey island in the grey sea under a grey sky.

As we progressed, the beach seemed to be swarming with people out walking their dogs, and as we approached Marazion the sun came out and the path took us up through the village, with its closed tourist shops and narrow streets. We stopped and watched as the first people managed to cross to the island, over the causeway that had been revealed by the falling tide. The official path grading changed from 'easy' to 'moderate', and we followed it along the low cliffs to a big bar overlooking the

119

long, empty beach of Perran Sands. We sat inside in the warmth, ordered tea and coffee and admired the view through the picture windows still dominated by the castle on the island. Outside the wind was bitter. It was woolly hat weather. The grading changed again, this time to 'strenuous', and the path started making some hefty climbs and descents as the cliffs got higher. The National Trust had installed groups of small Shetland ponies at various points up here. They seemed a long way from home, presumably on their winter holidays. We found some spectacular black and white zebra striped cliffs, and a whole class of geologists, easily recognised by their yellow hard hats, inspecting them. Rounding a corner, we surprised a red setter and two collie dogs coming the other way. They seemed to have taken themselves off for a walk, but seeing us they turned around and loped easily off uphill. We could see them happily trotting off for miles in the distance.

As we neared Porthleven, there were the chimneys of old mine engine-houses sticking proudly out of the landscape, and then we dropped down to the pretty harbour itself, full of little boats and with a breakwater guarded by cannons. It had seemed a long time in coming. By the time we'd found the small family run hotel we'd booked into, we'd done 15.9 miles of the planned 14.5. How had that happened? The official South West Coast Path had Penzance to Porthleven as fourteen miles. We'd done a bit extra at each end to find accommodation as usual, but not that much, surely.

In the hotel they told us about the beer festival in the pub about three doors away. It seemed too good an opportunity to miss. We were just going to pop in for a look, you understand, and then find somewhere else to eat, but they were very kind to us and found us a table in a cubby hole by a window, so we didn't get trampled on in the busy bar, and kept supplying us with food and drink. Between us we sampled another eleven ales, making twenty so far for this trip. With twenty-one miles walked that seemed a fine ratio and well in the spirit of our guardian French Impressionist!

The phone alarm clock was less resilient the next day. We managed to get it to shut up in under what seemed like a decade, and even managed to make it sound like a clock and not a cockerel with an American accent, but not before we were both wide awake again.

It turned out to be another cold, cloudy but dry day. The hotelier told us that the coastal path had been almost impassable with mud just two weeks ago, but we had found it dry, firm and good. Then he asked about the beer festival; he was intending to go that night and perhaps he was worried that we'd drunk everything.

Our plan was to do 14.5 miles, graded moderate, to the Lizard. We were to find that it was a mile longer than that and some sections were much more moderate than others! But to begin with, it was fairly easy, crossing Loe Bar, a spit of shingle that separated the sea from Loe Pool the biggest lake in Cornwall. It was Saturday. We started to come across people out with their dogs but we seemed to be the only non-locals.

"What entertainment have you lined up for tonight?" asked Lesley. How was I going to follow the quiz night and beer festival?

"Karaoke," I said, knowing that both she and Paul would hate it. After an appropriate show of wounded feelings and resistance, I allowed myself to be persuaded to pretend to cancel tonight's fun.

The path generally kept to the cliff-tops as it headed South down the side of the Lizard peninsular, but dived down to the sand at Church Cove near Gunwalloe. The church dedicated to St Winwalloe was shut, which was a shame as it is supposed to have some typically Cornish images of the apostles in it (whatever that means!). St Winwalloe is some sort of saint of fertility and the legend says that his wife was known as 'Gwen the triple breasted'. None the wiser, we stopped for a coffee on the foreshore and watched coastal erosion in action, albeit on a small scale, as a little stream cut itself a winding river-bed through the sand. Lesley and Paul had to suffer a geology lesson.

There were packs of golfers on the hillside opposite, braving the bitter wind, and after a while a surfer appeared in the sea, got washed up on the beach, picked himself up, and set off running up the track past the church. How strange. Then the path started to show its true coastal nature; up to the top of the cliffs, down to each cove and back up again. Nothing too steep, just lots of it. We were reintroduced to our old friends from the last trip, the 'killer steps', somewhere near the monument to Marconi and the early days of radio. A couple of bays later we found ourselves in Mullion Cove, the venue for many a holiday in the past, but now, out of season, just shut.

It was a steep pull out of there, but once on top we more or less stayed there passing lots of long, empty sandy beaches below. We met a couple of elderly ladies who'd walked from the Lizard to Mullion and were now going back again, checking out a walk they were due to lead for a local hiking group in a few weeks' time. They pointed out a village visible in the distance.

"It looks close," they said, "but it's a long walk to get there from here."

They were right! As we ventured further South, the rocks went a bit weird (technical geological term you understand): reds, blacks and knobbly all over, sticking up in spectacular lumps among the grey laminated schists. A bit sort of tortoiseshell, really. We stopped in a small valley for coffee and sat on them. I took a small sample and fended off questions like "What is it?", "Call yourself a geologist?" and "Can you get your money back from that OU geology course you've been studying for years?". The further South we went the more there seemed to be of this stuff.

Eventually we rounded Lizard Point and came across England's most Southerly gift shop, most Southerly disused lifeboat station, most Southerly house, most Southerly eggs (for sale on a doorstep), you get the picture, and what claimed to be the largest lighthouse complex in the world. Although there were only a few other people about in the cold wind, we decided that perhaps, at some times in the year, this place might just be a tad touristy.

Rounding the corner, a kestrel was hovering in the wind absolutely still, but moved off as soon as the cameras came out. We had to snap a pair of unsuspecting choughs that were probing the grass on the other side of the path instead. And then we picked up a footpath that headed inland to the village of Lizard itself and our B&B for the night. I was rather worried. I'd booked by a series of text messages as the chap had no phone or Internet connection and his mobile only worked when he was outside the house.

It turned out to be a tall old building, painted bright blue and joined onto a pub. We knocked on the door and after a while it was answered by Adrian, complete with long pony-tail, earplugs and always talking, (were the earplugs so that he couldn't hear himself speak?). He even seemed to be expecting us, although we had to pick our way around the doors to his kitchen cabinets, that were laid on the floors between big antique furniture, to get to our rooms.

Apparently, the house had been built in 1830 as an extension to the hotel, and when guests booked in, they were allocated rooms in "The Top House", which is now the pub, or "The Bottom House", which is now our B&B. Clearly after a couple of days walking, we were bottom house type people, but at least we only had to go next door to get food that night.

In the pub they had several model lighthouses made of the weird rock. We asked the young barman what it was.

"I think it's serpentine," he said uncertainly.

But when he went away, we had a debate based around the fact that we all thought that serpentine was green, drank our beer and ate our food.

I had two good pieces of news to report at breakfast.

Late night research (Adrian's Internet connection had been restored) had revealed that serpentine is produced from mantle rock when it reacts with seawater and can come in many colours. Importantly one of those turned out to be green, so we could all feel smug. There are three distinct types, one of which is called 'lizardite' and the reference site for that is Kennack Sands, which we were to walk through that day and so perhaps could solve the mystery of the knobbly rocks.

Secondly, and of more immediate relevance, was that we'd come to an arrangement with the phone/alarm clock. If we agreed not to stab or poke at it, but just stroke it gently in a diagonal direction it would allow us to oversleep. Or maybe by now it was just as tired as we were.

Breakfast was a lengthy but extremely pleasant affair, with Adrian doing everything. After a while his wife and demanding baby daughter wandered through, so we understood why.

Strangely the most memorable items were the tomatoes. They were exceptional. A recipe from an Italian guest apparently.

All too soon we set off again under more cold grey skies. There was no rain, but the wind had picked up and it was bitter as we followed a track back to Bas Point, a large white castellated building and the coast path.

Soon we came across the new lifeboat station with a visitors' centre and lookout on the top of the cliffs. A cliff railway ran down to the boat shed and a steep slip-way stretched from there to the sea below. As we admired the white-caps on the sea we wondered why there were no "The most Southerly active lifeboat station" signs. Maybe the tourist board people hadn't made it this far.

The map marks the 'Devil's Frying Pan', just South of Cadgwith. The sea had cut a hole through the cliffs, leaving a rock bridge from one side to the other but it was difficult to see any resemblance to any type of kitchen utensil. Perhaps it looks different in the summer, when people actually come here (allegedly!). Then the path went down through somebody's steeply sloping garden, all the way to the little village of thatched cottages, lobster pots piled high by the roadsides and even a fishing boat parked on a blind bend in the road.

The route so far today had been rated moderate, with a few strenuous sections. We came to the conclusion that it must be a 'how rocky is it underfoot' rating rather than a 'how many more times do we have to go up and down these huge cliffs' rating. It was exhausting, and especially tiring where those lovely tourist board people had 'upgraded' the path to killer steps.

The wind got stronger and our resident expert, Paul, classed it as least force 6: i.e. Rough.

Kennack Sands turned out to be a windswept crescent of sand with rocks at each end. We headed for the far side to be sheltered from the wind, and sat down on what turned out to be more of those tortoiseshell knobbly rocks for coffee and the last of the home-made bikkies. There didn't seem to be any other special types of rock here, and definitely nothing green so we decided that the chap in the pub must have been right all along. Lizardite. Lesley's rucksack was getting distinctly light now, what with her wearing all her clothes and being in need of a restock on the provisions front. However, for some reason she didn't seem keen on me filling it with some of the exciting rock samples lying around.

As we approached Coverack village, down a steep path through woodland, an old gent with a stick asked if we had come from the Lizard and how far we were going. For some reason Lesley seemed to have got food on her mind, and so the response the poor chap got was:

"To the village pub. Where is it and do they serve chips?"

Now, Lesley, who it must be said, had been lagging a bit, put on a spurt of speed, pounding away to the repeated chanting of a new mantra: 'chips, crisps, beer and chips.' Paul and I struggled to keep up!

The pub was in the cove, by the sea, and provided a warm haven, big plates of chips and of course, beer. Soon we all felt much better. Much better, that is, until about an hour later when we stuck our noses outside the door again and the wind seemed stronger and colder than ever. Lesley appeared to be inclined to hide in the porch, but was extracted eventually and off we set along the road around the bay and back up onto the cliffs on the far side.

As we walked through some big quarry workings that looked like they were still in use, a seal watched us from just offshore and then the Coast Path headed inland to the hamlet of Rosenithion. We left it there and took the road for half a mile or so to our B&B in the centre of the village of St. Keverne. It was also almost next to the big village pub.

Except for a small fire in one small side-room occupied by babies and young children, the pub was unheated and freezing. Eventually the babies left and we had a choice. Stay where we were and enjoy tonight's entertainment, Bingo, or go and sit by the fire. You can guess which we did. Not really the choice of an adventurer and it would make me feel better if I thought that you would do the same.

The walk had been fifteen and a half miles, a mile and a half longer than planned. What was going wrong? Lesley and Paul were starting to lose confidence in my planning. Can't blame them really, especially as soon we had to tackle the first half of the massive detour around the no-ferries-in-winter Helford

River.

The plan was to head back down the road again to re-join the coast path where we left it yesterday but Mary, the roundish, sixtyish, grandmotherish B&B lady, had other ideas.

"There's a lovely footpath that goes from the back of the church all the way down to Porthoustock," she said. "I'll point you in the right direction, I'm just taking Boris out into those fields anyway." Boris was a very friendly working springer spaniel. He'd head-butted Paul on arrival as a way to say hello.

We've had trouble with B&B-lady routes before, so I gave the map a good long inspection. There was the path, marked as Mary said, all the way back to the coast, cutting out the road and re-joining the Coast Path where it returned to the sea. It seemed like a good choice. So off we all went through the churchyard and into the fields beyond, with Boris bouncing around excitedly in front and Mary telling Lesley how she'd broken her toe so hadn't been walking him as far as usual lately, and how he's ever-so faithful and won't go far. She pointed out our way through the fields, described the onward route and we said our goodbyes.

After the fields, the path dropped down through woodland to a lane which we were supposed to cross, but the way was barred with orange netting and 'path closed due to landslip' signs. Boris was still with us and we thought he looked a little confused as we turned left up the lane to attempt to meet up with the Coast Path a little further on. Soon we found the acorn signs of the long-distance route and followed them to the sandy cove of Porthallow and the signpost marking the halfway point of the Coast Path.

Boris had seemed to know the way up until now, but he looked confused again as we climbed the cliff on the far side of the cove. Up on top, we went through fields and Boris shot ahead having a lovely time, bouncing all over the place, chasing his tail and chasing seagulls when he saw them, but soon there was another 'path closed' sign and we were diverted away from the cliff edge and onto a narrow tarmac lane. It ended with a gate into fields and the map showed a footpath crossing them. The second field had sheep with lambs and a sign on the gate: 'Dogs on leads.' Now what were we to do? Deep in the bowels of my rucksack was a strap for my camera bag. That would have to do and Boris seemed quite happy with the idea.

But halfway across there was a shout from the house in front of us and we could see someone waving. On the breeze a distant shout of "No footpath here" wafted over. But where then? We shouted back but couldn't make out the reply. Instead the figure headed out towards us and joined us in the middle of the field.

"It's down the other side of the hedge," she said.

"Okay, we can do that, but the map shows it going straight across and heading straight for your house."

"I'm in the long-distance walking association and so know all about footpaths and maps."

I showed her the map.

"Oh!" she said. "When the people moved in over there, they had the path diverted around the houses but it's not like that on the map is it."

Then we had a long chat about where we'd been, where we were going, the diversion and how lovely the next bit of the route was, and we left her and her sheep and went around the other side of the hedge, and eventually found our way back to the cliff-tops and the Coast Path.

Once off the 'lead' Boris bounced around like a puppy again on the short turf near the lookout at Nare Point and showed no sign of leaving us. We started to think we should phone Mary in case she was missing him, but of course we had no signal. Round the point we had to head almost due West through lovely woodland, following the coast to get around a small estuary and somewhere round there we got just enough to make that call. No answer. We left a message saying that Boris was alive and well and would she like to collect him. We dropped down into the sandy coves of Gillan Harbour and, as we sat drinking coffee, the phone burst into life. It was Mary.

"I've been going frantic," she said. "I've had the whole village out looking for Boris."

He was currently busy playing in the sea, but twenty minutes and several cups of coffee later a car drew up. He recognised it immediately and raced towards it, tail working at maximum velocity.

Mary said, "He's never done that before", but thanked us for walking him (just the five miles) while her friend, Bob, dried him off with a towel.

On we went, somewhat behind schedule now, and wondering how much trouble Boris would be in. We rounded the small estuary and then there was a lovely section along the edge of the Helford River, through woodland, passing lots of deserted sandy coves, and all the way to Helford itself. We'd made a special effort to get there without a stop, encouraged by the PH marking on the map near where the summer Ferry stops. It turned out to be the Shipwright Arms, very closed and full of builders building! We had to be content with a bench by the crossing and looking sadly at the sea, willing a boat to appear.

It didn't of course. And that meant a thirteen-mile detour. Instructions for the route are in the official book, so I put away the maps and started following them. After about an hour and a nice circular walk in National Trust woodland with early flowering bulbs, I threw away the book and got the maps out again. Frenchman's Creek (named after Daphne Du Maurier's book rather than vice versa) was very atmospheric. Even at low tide with exposed mud flats it was attractive in a muddy sort of way, but perhaps a bit more atmospheric than we'd bargained for, if you get my drift.

After the creek we crossed farmland to pick up lanes. We went much more quickly now, worried about our arrival time at the B&B in Gweek. Would we still be let in after dark? But amazingly it was only five when we knocked on the door. The walk had been seventeen and a half miles, a whole two miles longer than expected. This was getting worse!

Later, in the pub, the doggy theme continued. The beer was called Hamish and had a bust of a dog's head on the pump. There were lots of real dogs, including one that was almost a bearded collie. Paul instantly fell in love and accidentally seemed to open negotiations on a purchase price. Fortunately, we managed not to take it with us when we walked home!

We were late starting in the morning. Our hosts had been very chatty at breakfast. Wherever it could, the route around the rest of the Helford River used footpaths, some through fields of daffodils in full bloom, but mostly it was tarmac. Still, we're pretty fast on tarmac. As we tackled one of the many hills, a lady standing on her doorstep called out:

"You're very brave, there are some big hills round here".

We didn't feel brave at all, just ready for beer and crisps when we finally got back to the ferry crossing and the Coastal Path proper. It was 11.30 when we arrived and the pub was just opening. We sat outside looking out at the water and again spotted no ferries, just a few sailing boats going up and down.

Beyond was fairly easy going on short turf along the cliff-tops until we rounded the corner at the end of the estuary, where the wind hit us. But we carried on to Maenporth without stopping. It turned out to be a sandy cove with a café at the far end. In winter of course the café is closed, but the picnic tables are still there so we made full use of those before taking to the cliffs again and tackling the few miles to the outskirts of Falmouth and our hotel.

We'd been delayed getting there due to a narrow bit of path and, for the first time, lots of people out wandering along the cliffs in the sun. We'd covered almost fourteen miles and bits of body were starting to ache a bit. The receptionist turned out to be charming and pretty. The plan was to drop off the bags and walk through the town to the ferry terminal to check out the departure times for tomorrow, and then walk back round the long pointy-out bit of land and around Pendennis Castle on the coastal path, so we could legitimately say that we'd done that bit. Paul gave serious thought to staying at the hotel with the receptionist for the rest of the day, but in the end the adventure called to him. How could he miss a section? It might mean that he'd have to come back and do it all again? Or worse, we may never let him live it down? Three set forth once more.

The High Street was a bit like any other high street really. Lots of chain shops, many shut for business, but further on as we started to navigate round the point, a strange wooden boat was sitting on the mud. Unfortunately, its significance was lost on us until we saw it again on TV a day later. It turned out to be a replica bronze-age effort that they were trying to paddle round the harbour to see if it floated. Further on, in the dry docks, a very modern warship was having its bottom wiped clean.

It seemed an awfully long way round the Point and back to

the hotel, and Lesley's feet seemed to give up so I pretended to cancel the dance arranged for this evening and instead we headed for the closest pub. It looked grotty from the outside but had been given the thumbs up by the pretty receptionist and had big squashy sofas and candlelight and food inside. All very welcome after eighteen and a half miles.

Three large estuaries join at Falmouth and our first challenge of the day was to find a way across all of them. Although it arrived late, the boat that went over to St Mawes was running and that took care of the first two wet bits. It dropped us off at a rather deserted quay on the other side where, during the summer, a second ferry crosses the Percul river to Place (yes, that's the name of the, err, place).

Now we had some options. We're not very good at options as it means we have to make decisions and once in expedition mode that ability seems to leave all of us. We could walk round the river, a nine-mile detour, and pick up the coast path, follow it round St Anthony Head and then carry on North East to Veryan. This would make a very long day, over twenty miles, and we weren't sure if our aching feet and tired legs were up to it. Alternatively, we could do a detour and cut across inland, missing out the point and part of the official path, making it much shorter. We'd just about decided to do this, but on the off-chance I tried a call to the local taxi company. It normally only operates down here during the summer. As luck would have it, he was just driving someone close to where we were and was happy to perform a rescue and take us to the ferry terminal on the other side. We sat in a café drinking tea until he arrived. It felt very much like cheating! Lesley and Paul tried to convince me that it wasn't.

It was worth it. The walk around the head was nice. It had a lighthouse with a warning of loud noises and a picture of someone pulling the same face that Lesley does when a police car goes past, sirens wailing. It had an old gun battery. It had a 'wreck post' designed to help practice rescuing people at sea. It had some scenic Scots pines on the cliff-tops and the path was easy, flat(ish) walking all the way to Portscatho where the pub was open in spite of building work. They seemed to be repairing the chimney. Inside, a half brick came bouncing down and into the bar where we were sitting. We moved further in. The talk was of the announcement of the closure of the Axminster factory and the loss of hundreds of jobs.

The going was easy further on, the sun came out and we all felt great. Even a copper-coloured slow worm was out on the path, basking in the sunshine. Maybe it was the numbing effect of the lunchtime beer on the feet, but by the time we got as far as Carne Beach, about three miles on, it was only mid-afternoon. We decided to change the plan. Instead of cutting inland to Veryan we stuck to the coast path to go round Nare Head, adding on three or four miles, but meaning that we didn't have to do them tomorrow. The cliffs were higher here and we found it much more strenuous, but it was a lovely place.

Eventually we left the cliff path and climbed steeply to join a road to Veryan, famous for five thatched houses built for five daughters. The houses are round, so that there are no corners for the devil to hide in, and topped by crosses.

Our B&B had changed hands since I'd booked, and we were the first guests for the new owners. They gave us a lovely welcome but they seemed a little uncertain. After a while, they owned up to having read a book on how to do it, and kept forgetting bits.

No special events in the pub tonight. Just a dog eating mint-imperials. Well, what do you expect in a devil free village?

In the morning we were greeted with a cheery,

"Did you sleep well...? Oh no, I'm not supposed to say that, in case you didn't."

But we had, so it was okay. It was raining hard for the first time on the trip, and misty too. We lingered over breakfast but in the end accepted the inevitable.

First stop was the graveyard to inspect the 'long grave', where nineteen bodies from a German boat that ran aground in 1914 had been laid end to end. They were identified by name and job title: Captain, First Mate, Sail-maker and even Ship's Boy.

Then we headed back to the Coast Path at Portloe and a climb back onto the clifftops. The next section was very tough; frequently up and down all the way from sea level to the top of the high cliffs. We were all still tired from yesterday, but

131

eventually made it round to East Portholland where the sea was trying to invade the land. The rain had eased and turned into heavy Scotch mist, and it was a good pull back onto the cliffs, followed soon after by a long descent into Porthluney Cove. There was a spectacular castle just inland, but unfortunately there were also a number of 'Coast Path closed due to landslip' signs, including an enormous one that looked like it had been stolen from wherever they make road signs. We took the hint and diverted steeply up fields onto the flatter ground well away from the cliffs and onto narrow lanes. Eventually they dropped back down to the coast, sea level, and yet another climb up the cliffs.

At this point I think I need to put in a reminder that we do this for 'fun'. Sometimes, for some reason, it may not seem like it!

Our next challenge was Dodman Point, with a bronze-age settlement across the end. Unfortunately, the cloud base was lower than the cliff-tops, so we could see almost nothing. Up here the rain and the cows had made the paths noticeably muddy and slippery, and so the going was slow. Eventually a tall granite cross, at the point dedicated (in advance presumably) to 'The Second Coming of The Lord Jesus Christ', loomed up out of the mist.

As we dropped down into Gorran Haven we stopped to chat to a chap who looked local. After a while we asked "Where's the pub?" and got a very strange look.

"It's not very good," he said, and recommended that we carried on to the next bay. A little further on a couple unloading their shopping also gave the pub a thumbs down.

"They're trying to be a smart hotel," they said, "and they've lost all the local trade," before adding: "The path to the next bay's a bit wet: very character building."

By the time we'd built up our characters and dropped down to Portmellon on the outskirts of Mevagissey, the mist had lifted, the sun had come out and the pub was shut. However, we had a chance to clean off a bit and even remove some layers and expose t-shirts, so we arrived at the B&B looking almost respectable. Good job too, as it turned out to be a Grade Two listed building boasting some impressive rooms. Paul's was spectacular: huge and with a fancy ceiling and chandeliers, while we had a more modern 'add on' with a picture window looking out over the town and its harbour.

We woke to warm sunshine rather than the never-ending rain that had been forecast. We didn't quite break into shorts; it was only the beginning of March, but the thought was there. We climbed out of the winding streets and crammed-in cottages of Mevagissey, and back onto the coast path. It followed the cliffs above the harbour and then set off determinedly North.

The next three hours were very tough going, the hardest yet: steep ascents and descents with hardly any respite between, and killer steps by the dozen. And we'd started with tired limbs and aching feet anyway. We were exhausted, and then horrified when the GPS told us that we'd only done three miles. Across the bay we could see the outline of Gribbin Head and we knew that Fowey our destination was round the other side.

"How can we possibly get that far today!" Lesley exclaimed.

She had a point. But what could we do? We carried on.

At a summit just after some particularly nasty killer steps, we met a couple walking the other way. In a broad twangy accent, they told us of a nice pub at Polkerris, while we stood there gasping for breath. Then they mentioned that the Coast Path beyond was closed due to a landslip.

We stopped at Portpean, a little South of St Austell, because we found some picnic benches and were in need of coffee, and because the police were providing some sort of show. They seemed to have roped off the road and were searching for something. Whatever it was they didn't seem to be finding it and, after a while, and lots of speculation about buried bodies, we lost interest and remembered that we still had an awfully long way to go.

One more big climb up and down and then the path became gentler. With the china clay slag-heaps of St Austell gleaming in the sunshine, we started to pick up some speed and before long we were in Charlestown dock, admiring the lovely looking village and tall ships; all masts and stringy bits and looking like they needed to be out exploring an ocean somewhere instead of sleeping here.

A long, thin and very busy golf course took us past St Austell and as we approached a big factory, we met a chap coming the other way. He'd walked from Fowey and said that the path was a bit strenuous in places but not too slippery. He also mentioned the landslip, as well as the nice pub at Polkerris and said that Fowey was only a couple of hours from it. Maybe we would make it after all.

Spurred on, a limping Lesley declined the suggestion of an emergency bus or taxi and changed into her 'evening' footwear, a pair of old trainers. She seemed a bit better after that, as the path diverted round the factory by the docks and wriggled inland on roads before emerging back at the coast on the dunes behind Par Sands. It was still easy going and at last we seemed to be making up time.

A helpful lady at the far end of the beach, with more 'local knowledge' (when will we ever learn!) directed us back to the Coast Path on the cliffs via a short-cut. This meant that we missed the 'path closed' signs and had to go back when we met a couple coming the other way who spilled the beans. The diversion was up a steep footpath, along the Saints' Way, through fields. As we approached a junction with the main road, we spotted a bus. Lesley declined. And then another bus, followed by a third. Still no takers. Well done team! No cheating!

The diversion came back down to the sea at Polkerris, a very small bay with about two houses and a beachside pub with a patio overlooking the sea. It was even open, and Lesley seemed a bit better and even more determined to make it after a reviving prescription of beer and crisps. When it was time, she shot off, up and along the cliffs on the other side, way ahead of Paul and me. We didn't seem to take long to get to the red and white navigation tower at the end of Gribbin Head. Then, at last the coast turned North again, heading for Fowey.

We couldn't see the town in the distance. Tucked away at the top of an estuary, it kept its secrets right until the last moment, but what a relief when we finally came around the corner and spotted it. Unfortunately, our hotel was well up above the old part of town, but it did, to be fair, have a great view over the river. We arrived just before six, as it was starting to get dark, having completed a very exhausting nineteen miles. The B&B lady made us tea and told us about the closest place to eat, while we all firmly sat still in her drawing room not wanting to get up and use those feet again.

But eventually we did, and went down the hill to the town. We went into the back door of the first pub, and then straight through and out of the front door. It was packed in there. Paul asked if we could stay, he'd spotted the pretty barmaid.

The next pub was bigger and we found a table. A band was setting up. Paul asked to leave, even though the pub seemed to be inhabited mostly by women. There was a rather large scary one with an American accent on the next table. We stayed put. The band started. It was a long way off and we couldn't see properly but the musicians seemed excellent although the singer wasn't great. We all helped him along a bit. When we left, we realised that the band *was* the singer, with a CD machine for all the backing music.

After our final cooked breakfast, the day started with a walk down to the ferry terminal next to last night's pub, and a small red boat that took us across to Polruan on the other side of the river. There were lots of Coast Path signs - all to Polperro, five-and-three-quarter miles. However far we walked they seemed to crop up, and before you ask, no, we weren't walking round in circles.

The path led us to the top of the cliffs and headed East, with yet another dose of the yo-yo hiking experience. Eventually we stopped for a break on a bench and, as we got up to leave, a couple walking the other way took our places. They told us that they'd walked from Polperro and the lady, who was most obviously not English, told Paul that the path was easy, not steep at all. Soon after we came to the conclusion that she must have come from the Himalayas! Not-steep it was not!

Polperro was a lovely looking harbour village and the path went right by the door of the Blue Peter pub. Expecting sticky-backed plastic and food of the 'here's one I made earlier' kind, we went in and found it full of strangely-dressed people. There was a lady in a black bodice, tartan skirt and high heeled boots, and the barman had a tartan cap. Others also seemed to have a slightly Scottish theme. Aha! The rugby would be on, then.

A chap was pulled down the steep staircase by a large dog on a lead. As he swept by us, he cried

135

"I didn't want to come down you know." and the dog swept him outside.

People started telling us about the landslip after the next bay, and how far and how steep the detour was, but when we got there, there were 'Path Re-opened' signs. Hooray! There were even some people coming the other way.

"Ooh! It's steep," they said.

After a bit we decided that they must have come from Norfolk! Steep it was not.

Finally, we rounded a corner and came to the outskirts of Looe itself. We still had a good mile to go before the bridge over the estuary, but the tarmac and therefore the houses had stretched out this far. We passed, and paid our respects to, the statue of Nelson; no, not the man with one arm, but the scarred Grey Seal that had made Looe his home for over twenty-five years. The shops were shutting as we approached town and everyone seemed to be standing around in the sunshine eating chips, but it seemed too early for us and we had a train, or two, to catch.

The first headed inland to Liskeard. It had to zig-zag up the steeper bits and took half an hour or so to do the nine miles, which seemed pretty quick to us. We had an hour to wait before the train from there back to Exeter, and headed for the 'Old Stag' at the top of the road, in search of food. No such luck: the kitchens had been flooded, but the barmaid, who had the strongest Cornish accent yet and who called everyone 'Me Lovely', kept us amused, told us that Scotland had lost at Rugby, and fed us crisps and beer until it was time to go.

On the train, the beer started talking. It had a discussion about the feasibility of doing the next section of path: the bit from Looe to Plymouth and beyond. Much, much later, back at Paul's house, we had to resort to wine and an impromptu 'what's in the freezer' meal. That stopped it! But the slippery slope had been started.

A few days later, a report from the official team A.R.S.E. (Ale Recording and Sampling Executive, Paul) arrived. He reminded us that, on the Holy Hike, our beer related miles per gallon came in at 38 for the boys and 122 for Lesley. Clearly our French painter had an impact. We were now down to 33 mpg and 96 mpg respectively.

7.   BANCSI – Bude Along North Coast to St Ives (April 2014)

So now we seemed committed to a full-scale assault on The Path. To do it properly, as it were. We decided to do the previous section of the South West Coast Path. Yes, that's right, the previous section so that we ended up at St Ives which is where the 'Penzance Practice' had started.

In the past rigorous(ish) training and careful lightweight packing had preceded such expeditions, but not this time. The wettest winter on record gave us a good excuse not to get fit. To be fair Lesley had attempted a couple of jogging sessions per week that had given her a strange perspective of time ("three miles: that's half an hour isn't it?") and Paul had dragged out his trusty treadmill and installed it in his spare bedroom opposite a TV. After a session while watching 'Heartbeat' followed by nightmares about having to run on a treadmill at 'police speed' while being shot at by 1960's villains, the normal activity of the treadmill was resumed (i.e. collecting dust and acting as a clothes horse, and sometimes a guest towel rail). Meanwhile, in order to make sure that I was able to contribute fully towards the creation of the beer log, I trained hard in an appropriate way.

But we weren't concerned. Our planned mileage was about five miles per day less than normal because of where I had been able to find B&Bs. So, we thought, we should be fine, and even have time to potter around all those picturesque villages on the way, rather than walk straight through.

Hmm...

Paul took us the scenic route for our 'shake down' session from his house in Kennford to Exeter: through an industrial estate, then the park (beware women with push-chairs!), along the river and then via some narrow, steep residential roads to the Exeter bus station. The rucksacks felt heavy in the warm sunshine. As we walked past cyclists old and young, joggers and people just out strolling around, talk was of when we should stop and change into shorts. But we held out and were soon installed on the back seat of the coach and heading for Bude, with knees suitably covered.

The chap in the seat in front of us had a local paper and showed us a couple of pages with recent photographs of Bude. It looked great. We'd only chosen it as our starting point because that's where we could get to by bus from Exeter. We chatted and he seemed to produce bus timetables from every conceivable pocket. We spoke of next year and the section of The Path from Minehead to Bude, notorious for its difficulty.

"You won't be able to get a bus to Minehead," he exclaimed in a broad *Devon* accent. "It's in Somerset!"

By 14:30 we were in Bude and in shorts at last, passing their millennium statue (a sort of multicoloured rocket nose cone coming out of the earth) and heading for the beach. Dogs were playing on the sand and I got into trouble for not properly researching the spectacular geology. Something had been seriously bending those rocks! The path climbed quickly out of the bay, over short turf to the lookout of Compass Point Tower and then settled down to ambling gently along the coast. It seemed easy, although the internet rated it 'strenuous'. In the hot sun we felt good and confident.

We passed a bookshop, well, a wheelbarrow of books for sale that someone had positioned next to the path, but we decided that books were heavy and continued without. Soon we came to the village marker for Widemouth Bay and Lesley obliged with the obvious face for the camera. Later, the people who lived there tried to explain to us that it is pronounced *Wid-eh-mouth*. A likely story!

Almost the first building we came to was the Bay View Inn, our stop for the night. It was packed with people on the terrace admiring the view of the dunes, the sea and the surfers. It was Mother's Day. As Lesley had mentioned beer about four times on the path since Bude, we took the hint, ordered some, started the log and sat with the mothers on the terrace. It started to feel like a holiday.

As you might imagine, we enjoyed the Bay View Inn; good food, lovely views from our balcony (we'd had a room upgrade), helpful staff and a big late breakfast, but now it was time to tackle the fifteen-mile section of the path to Boscastle, graded strenuous.

It started along the sand dunes that backed the beach, never easy to walk on, and then climbed the cliffs at the far end of the bay. But it wasn't too bad underfoot and, after a mile or so, Lesley was prompted to ask whether the person who'd graded it had been in a wheel-chair or if they were wearing high heels. Soon she was to regret this as the path yo-yoed between clifftops and the sea, a good 100m rise and fall each time. Before long we were all exhausted and wishing that we'd done more training and eaten less breakfast.

Below the cliffs, the rocks had been messed about with again: black ridges bent into dramatic swirls and zigzags that stretched across the fore-shore and continued up into the cliffs. About lunchtime we dropped into Crackington Haven, the first real settlement we'd come to since leaving Widemouth Bay. The sun was out, we were in shorts and t-shirts again in spite of the pessimistic BBC weather forecast and it marked the half-way point of today's section. We celebrated with a pint and a rest outside the pub.

But the path continued to be 'strenuous' with many sections of the dreaded 'killer steps'. At one point we could see before us the customary descent and, on the rise that followed, two paths etched into the turf. One went straight up and the other zigzagged across it. It was clear that a number of people had started on the former and then been forced to adopt the latter. Lesley and Paul tried the vertical, so in the spirit of scientific enquiry I went for the other. They beat me to the top by a good margin and felt that maybe they weren't as unfit as they thought.

We could see Boscastle long before we arrived but we had been much slower than expected. Lesley phoned the Hotel to say we were still coming and got a sympathetic ear. She was asked whether she was enjoying herself and was unsure of how to reply! It turned out that the receptionist, barmaid, waitress (all one person) used this section of the Coast Path as training for trekking in the Himalayas.

The Hotel, an old coaching inn, was a fabulous building. For a start from the outside it looked a bit like a castle, and inside it had grand rooms with lovely furnishings. It advertised 'The

Long Bar' and Paul was rather worried in case they needed us to walk from one end to the other. We seemed to have done enough walking for one day!

Based on yesterday's experience, we started with an earlier breakfast and could hear the waitress coming down the long corridor to the dining room saying "hot, hot, hot!" to herself as she bore our laden plates. The plan was to walk only fourteen miles to Port Isaac today, and although it was graded 'severe' we should have plenty of time, shouldn't we?

Almost immediately we found ourselves back on the top of the cliffs, with the lovely scenery looking its best in the spring sunshine, and heading for the first major milestone at about five miles, King Arthur's ruined castle of Tintagel. Just before we got there, a woman dressed all in pink was walking slowly up a steep bit. She was only going as far as the ruin but when she heard that we were aiming for Port Isaac she started to say,

"The book says that the stretch from Trebarwith Strand to Port Isaac is... but I shouldn't be telling you this should I...?"

"Go on," we encouraged.

"Well, it's rated severe and is known as the seven gullies."

"Oh dear!".

Did King Arthur really exist do you think? Or is the whole story just a nice legend? The visitors' centre seemed real enough, as did the bridge to the island where the ruins are. So did the 'Don't eat your own food here' signs. However, just a little further on, up the cliff, there is a convenient bench for a coffee stop where you can see lots of believers struggling with the steep paths to the ruins.

Another couple of miles and a steep drop took us to Trebarwith Strand, where we overtook Mr and Mrs Stripy, elderly hikers wearing garish tops. We asked where they were going.

"There!" was the answer they gave, pointing to the pub below. We went 'There' too.

The next section, immediately above (yes, I use the word 'above' rather than 'beyond' deliberately) the pub was the hardest yet: a climb of almost 100m so steep that it needed 'killer steps' all the way. Thus started the ordeal of 'The Seven Gullies'. As we reached the top, we met a chap going the opposite way. It turned out that he was going 'There' as well. No wonder 'There' was busy.

The Seven Gullies lived up to their reputation. We even counted them to make sure that we didn't miss any, and felt that perhaps we shouldn't have been so disparaging about all those people struggling to visit King Arthur's place. We knocked on the door of our B&B in Port Isaac, after fourteen distinctly 'severe' miles, at five-thirty. Nellie immediately produced tea and biscuits. We liked her!

Anita and Rosie were at breakfast. It turned out that they were also walking the Coast Path and told us that, after a few strenuous miles, the path settled down a bit and became more reasonable. I got the impression that everyone else had done more research than I and prepared an argument along the lines of 'it's more exciting this way, not knowing what the next bit will be like', but Lesley and Paul seemed to be more interested in the full English and the dire weather forecast than in teasing me. Or perhaps they were just being kind, even when it transpired that Anita and Rosie were getting their luggage transported between B&Bs so that they didn't have to carry anything, and that they were catching a bus to bypass the first few miles (which they claimed to have done last year).

Nellie told us all that Port Isaac was okay now, but terribly busy when Doc Martin was being filmed, and in the summer, with American visitors coming to pay homage to the TV series. Anita and Rosie seemed impressed, but Lesley and I had never heard of Doc Martin. Paul had, but had never seen it so we were rather at a loss. However, when we walked through the admittedly rather attractive village in the drizzle, Doc Martin's Cottage was unmistakable. It had a big sign pointing to it.

After a stiff climb, we were back on the clifftops and tackling steep gullies again, now made all the more difficult by slippery tracks, the need to wear full waterproofs and tired legs from yesterday. We had to put in a fairly good time today in order to cross the Camel estuary; the last ferry was scheduled to depart at four-thirty.

In spite of the rain, the scenery was still lovely, but not many other people were out on the path. Three or four gullies and a tea stop by a stream on the edge of a little beach later, and the ladies were proven right; the route became flatter as we walked round Port Quin Bay. The rain eased and by lunchtime it stopped altogether, and we'd reached Pentire Point and could see down the Camel estuary, which seemed to stretch a long way. We'd done only seven miles and so, at that rate, would miss the ferry. No lunch stop today.

The surfers were out in force off Polzeath, although the tide was low and they had a very long walk to the water from the road. Rather than walk all round the edge of the houses and cafés, we cut across the sand, thus discovering that my new and rather expensive boots were not as waterproof as I might have wanted. The rocks were dramatically arranged in mauve and turquoise stripes. I hadn't researched these either.

Beyond Trebetherick Point, we entered the mouth of the estuary and continued walking quickly inland on the sands. Wads of people came towards us periodically, like cars released from traffic lights, which we took to be a sign that the ferry was still running. Eventually we saw it: a small yellow landing craft shuttling from the sand on one side to the sand on the other, as the water was too low for it to reach anywhere sensible to moor on either side. It was just after four.

A stocky chap with a huge rucksack boarded with us. He'd walked from Bristol and was going to Land's End, having done John O'Groats to Bristol last year and then rested during the winter rains. He told us that he'd come down to the Coast Path from Exmoor and it had been a bit of a shock; much tougher than anything on the rest of the route. A big notice on the Ferry told us that the timetable had changed on 1st April, two days ago, and it was now running until five-thirty, so we needn't have rushed.

Winnie, a rather fierce B&B lady, told us that all the pubs in the village were okay for an evening meal but we managed to find one that wasn't. Packed with rather drunk people, talking about how to kill each other with martial arts, and a large landlady with more piercings than a pincushion, we retreated to the one next door. But then Winnie was encouraging us to patronise one of the many, rather posh, designer restaurants rather than a pub. Her rooms were equipped with corkscrews and wine glasses rather than the more usual coffee mugs.

Perhaps Padstow is not for us!

The onward route took us North, back up the estuary and onto cliffs at Steppe Point, with a tall round tower at the point where we turned South West again. It was easy underfoot and a group coming the other way told us that they were local and had never known it so still up there. There was scarcely a breath of wind. They also told us about the legend of the Pentire Steps, where the giant, Bedruthan, had used sea stacks as stepping stones to cross the bay, but that was for tomorrow, and another piece of research I hadn't done.

The walk was easy on the turf of the clifftops and the scenery magnificent. Gulls were nesting on the cliffs and a kestrel hunted nearby. After a while we caught up with Anita and Rosie. They were sitting on a bench and looking at their guide book so we asked them about the stripy rocks. It didn't mention them. Instead they told us about an historic church that they'd visited in Polzeath yesterday, which we'd missed.

We left them behind and carried on to the beach village of Harlyn, where we found a pub next to a church and sat in hot sun in the beer garden round the back making a contribution to the beer log. When Anita and Rosie walked past, they didn't see us. We found them again, on another bench, on the next section looking at the map. Paul helpfully pointed forwards and said,

"It's that way" while Lesley accused them of conducting an extensive survey of benches (a "benchmark" we later decided, sorry!). We tried to convince them that they must have overtaken us while we were visiting the church in Harlyn, but I don't think it worked.

The easy cliff walking continued, past the pretty Mother Ivey's Bay, with a new-looking lifeboat station, and on to Booby's Bay. A World War One wreck had been uncovered by the recent big storms and was there for all to see. This is what the chap hanging out of the window of the house next door had told us as we'd donned our boots this morning outside the B&B. Well, it wasn't obvious to us, so Paul and I went down to the sand to investigate and soon found some lumps of iron cunningly camouflaged as rocks. It seems like the recent non-storms had been busy covering it up again. This wasn't in Anita and Rosie's guide book either.

Eventually, after another spectacular bit of coastline that looked on the map like fingers pointing out sea and which therefore took a while to walk around, we dropped into Porthcothan. There is only one B&B in the village and I'd booked it, so I wasn't very popular with Anita and Rosie when they found out. We left them waiting at a bus stop to get a lift a couple of miles up the road to Old MacDonald's Farm. Yes really!

On the hill above the village there is a pub and both our respective B&B hosts gave us lifts there to get food. Anita and Rosie had found out about my Geology course and asked me about those stripy rocks we'd seen at Polzeath. Fortunately, I'd had a secret session with the internet, while Lesley and Paul had been relaxing with 'Pointless', and was able to deliver an authoritative lecture on the Polzeath Slates (yes, that's their official name), which are formally described as 'Striped' and 'Purple and Green'. Maybe this geology stuff isn't as hard as the Open University would have you believe!

Tom, the B&B owner, ran a professional photography business and over breakfast told us it was well worth taking the steps down the cliffs to the beach at Pentire to see Bedruthan Steps and so, when we got there, we did. Well I did and Paul partly did. It was very steep and at the bottom the tide was high and lapping around the bottom step with no beach to get onto. Fortunately, in the nearby National Trust loos there was a sketch of what we should have seen (as well as men with paintbrushes sprucing them up for the new season).

We carried on along the clifftops in increasing sunshine and could see Anita and Rosie ahead in the distance. As we dropped into the bay of Trenance, an old-looking lady was coming the other way. In her eighties (we think), she told us that she walked some of the path each year and so knew it well, but could only manage about four miles each day now. Good for her!

Anita and Rosie were ending their walk there and we found them one last time. No bench this time, but table and chairs in a little café by a bus stop. We asked if this was an example of one of those historical churches that they favoured.

Further on and the sea was speckled with black blobs:

surfers, we decided, and when we emerged from a hedged section of path that led us down to the main seafront at Watergate, the place was heaving with people wandering around in wetsuits, carrying surfboards or just sitting in cafés behind large trendy sunglasses. Sadly, we still had quite a way to go and so didn't join in.

Then we had to tackle the metropolis of Newquay. All the public toilets were closed for refurbishment and, to really make the point, the council had erected great fences around each of them. Each had a sign saying that it would reopen at Easter, two weeks away, which seemed a rather long time to wait. Each had directions to the next one, which was likewise closed. There didn't seem to be an official route through all the buildings and shops of the town, but we tried to follow what was marked on the map which took us straight down the busy High Street: rather a shock after the empty clifftops.

Near Pentire Point we picked up a Coast Path sign post that didn't match the map at all and seemed to point the wrong way, so after a while we retraced our steps and resorted to the route on the map, right around the point itself. The problem seemed to be the need to cross the River Gannel. On reflection, the map must expect people to only want to do this in the summer when the ferry is running. The signpost, on the other hand, must rely on low tide when there is a little causeway that can be used. Perhaps some more pre-trip research would have been useful after all.

We stayed in the village of Crantock, where our room looked out onto a hedgerow full of birds and a field full of rabbits beyond. There are two pubs in the village, right opposite each other and clearly very competitive. As soon as we poked our noses through the door of one, we were set upon with drinks and menus and given somewhere to sit. We didn't put up much resistance!

The weather wasn't good the next morning; grey with drizzle and occasional rain showers, although it hadn't put off the surfers. We found pairs of fulmars cuddling together on ledges in the cliff below the path and saw seals in the water. Near Ligger Point, where the cliffs are high, the coastguards were practising winching each other up from sea level to clifftop, but

145

soon we were tackling the sand dunes that run for a couple of miles behind the long, sandy Perran beach. They were very hard work with steep uppy and downy and twisty and turny bits, all in soft sinky sand. We gave up on the 'official' route and took to the beach.

Eventually the sand dunes gave way to rocky cliffs near Cotty's Point. Did we have to climb that cliff yet again, or could we squeeze around between the cliff and the sea? Yes, you've guessed it the 'give it a go' vote was unanimous. It looked like we could make it. But at the last point, only visible on arrival and with only about three meters of rock left before the next bay, the waves were still breaking against the cliff. So, did we turn back and climb that hill – no! Did we take off shoes and socks and wade around – no! Just for once, we settled on the appropriate course of action. We stopped for a cup of tea! Ten minutes later a black Labrador appeared from around the other side of the rock. The water was low enough for us to get through and head across the sand to Perranporth.

The next set of cliffs seemed to be riddled with old mine workings and open-cast heaps. They were an interesting mix of colours, some pale grey, some yellows and some deep ochre red. There were chimneys and old ruined buildings here as well. We really could have done with a geologist on the team! The weather improved so much so that by the time we reached Trevaunance Cove, we decided to push on round St Agnes Head so we didn't have to do it the next day. It was lovely easy walking, on high clifftops with great views.

Beyond the head itself we turned inland, heading for our B&B in the nearby village. We gained height and entered low cloud. A girl, out jogging with her dog, ran past and we could see her heading off up St Agnes Beacon. It looked easy enough so we decided to follow her instead of taking the road as planned. Mistake! Perhaps she was one of those apparitions that appear and lure sailors to their deaths, although obviously a land based one rather than marine. It was blowing hard up there, with almost no visibility, and thoroughly nasty. We came down quickly but couldn't spot any paths heading in the right direction. The girl and dog were long gone. It seemed a very long walk into the village and to our B&B.

We had planned to stroll back down to the sea to eat in the real ale pub that night, but the B&B landlady suggested the Queen Agnes Hotel, just down the street. With sore feet it seemed a better (i.e. closer) option. It was packed in the bar and we were ushered into the adjacent restaurant. For some strange reason they seemed to be alternating 1940's tracks with early 70's rock music, and eventually the 1940's stuff seemed to win the battle and take over completely, settling down on Andrews sisters' songs. It finally dawned on us that there was a live group in the bar; three girls in uniforms, 1940's style make-up and hairstyles: The Three Belles. We wandered through to watch. They were excellent, but as usual we didn't last long. We were exhausted!

The wet was travelling fast and sideways across the landscape as we started in the morning. By the time we got back to St Agnes Head (via the road!) it was blowing very hard and we were soaked. After a couple of miles, we dropped off the cliffs to the small cove at Chapel Porth and its small National Trust car park. As we climbed the cliffs on the other side, we could see the attendant emerge from his hut and make his first catch of the day, a small car full of miserable looking kids. Back up on top it was wetter and windier than ever and absolutely horrible, so we didn't loiter.

Soon after midday, we'd covered over eight miles and had retreated to a beach-side pub at Portreath. Looking out over bowls of chips and pints of beer, we could see the rain sweeping across from land to sea. It was hard to find the enthusiasm to leave and tackle the next few gullies.

Visibility and map reading were difficult so we marked our progress by counting car parks as we went. Now is that an official car park as recognised by the Ordnance Survey, or just an overgrown lay-by? It wasn't the most reliable system. Near Godrevy Point, perhaps fifty seals were lying about on the beach. Amazingly six tourists had come to see them, but not so amazingly none stayed for long. The lighthouse marked on the map was almost invisible in the mist. It was white. Now then, what colour would you paint your lighthouse, eh? I assume that one of the objectives would be to make it stand out and be easily visible wouldn't it? How about orange, or maybe that bright yellow they use in the roads? But white?

I'd had trouble finding a B&B here. There are some, but not near places to eat and I didn't think I'd get away with offering a choice between food or sleep. So, in the end, I'd gone for a farm, about a mile down a lane inland from Gwithian. The 'lane' turned out to be a farm track, complete with pot holes, mud, puddles and nasty evidence of cows. It seemed long. Lesley doubted the parentage of those who'd declared it to be only a mile. The cows in the field beside us thought that we were exciting and stampeded around fences and obstructions to keep up with us as we went, so that they could watch what we were up to. We came to a sign: 'B&B this way', and then a gate across the lane but also signed: "B&B keep going". Later (Lesley thought *much* later), there were more: "B&B - it's worth it" and then "B&B - nearly there".

And when we did arrive, we were ushered in, wet, mud and all, into a huge farmhouse kitchen where we stripped off. Our discarded clothing was hung decoratively above a nice warm Aga. Not only that but our hostess fed us tea and saffron buns, booked a table for us at the pub and even gave us a lift there. When it was time to leave, the barmaid phoned and we were collected. What a star! Our friends Vic and Ann from the Citroen Club came and spent the evening with us so we were able to have near normal conversations, well perhaps not, maybe just a different type of weird!

It was still pretty nasty outside when we started our walk after breakfast, but our clothes were dry (at least to begin with). We formally measured the length of the lane with GPS and it was exactly one mile to the tarmac road, although we all agreed with Lesley that it must have shrunk in the wet overnight.

More sand dunes stretched along the coast path, but this time they were a bit flatter and the path was marked with periodic standing-stones of slate. We entered Hayle and had to walk around the estuary and wet bits, and there, just where we had been told it would be, was the Philips Bakery, home of the saffron bun. We had some more on a bench outside, being entertained by a crow whose party piece was to catch any flying morsel mid-air.

Out of Hayle and we could see St Ives in the distance. The

sun came out and we were able to finish the walk in the style we'd started in, shorts. We were, of course, somewhat more exhausted and more weather-beaten and the shorts weren't the cleanest. It was mid-afternoon when we arrived in town. What to do with an hour or so before catching the train home. Any guesses? Did we look around St Ives? Nope, we went to celebrate with a pint and a rest instead.

Paul announced the results of the beer log a few days later. Despite occasional lapses into wine territory the boys had identical fuel economy at 35.1 mpg, whilst Lesley seemed to be in a hybrid hop and grape mode at 119.8 mpg. In nine days, we'd visited 16 pubs and consumed 15 different ales. And we'd been telling people that walking holidays are healthy! We also noticed that the more of The Path we do, the worse our fuel consumption becomes!

8. M to B (Minehead to Bude October 2015)

With a significant proportion of the 630-mile South West Coast Path under our belts, err boots, so to speak, it seemed time to tackle the first section: Minehead to Bude. At last! The start!

The walking wardrobe and its friends, the Berghaus bags, were dug out of hibernation. A plan was hatched. The B&Bs were booked and we were as ready as we would ever be. Paul's kit seemed to have suffered rather and he went shopping again. Once more he seemed to choose his complete outfit from a single manufacturer. The Karrimor Kid became the Berghaus Boy.

During the early morning five-mile walk to Exeter railway station, we were able to reflect on the number of bottles of wine dispatched the previous night at Paul's house. Too many perhaps? But then again, maybe it was just good training for what was to follow. And soon we were all wishing that we'd awoken the slumbering rucksacks earlier and done more (i.e. some) walks with ballast before setting off. The sleepy walking wardrobe and Berghaus bags were seriously slowing us down.

First thing on a Saturday morning and everyone in Exeter seemed to be out doing healthy things. The place was full of hot and cold running people: some were involved in organised events and some were freelance. Cyclists were out in force, the river was full of skiffs and kayaks, and there was some sort of long-distance run happening. C'mon, this is a student city! I don't ever remember student Saturday mornings being like this (Grumpy Old Man alert!),

But we did get to the station on time for the half-hour train journey to Taunton, and we did manage to catch the number 68 bus from a stop that wasn't where the internet said it would be. It took us to the village of Bishop's Lydeard, the terminus of the West Somerset Railway. And that meant that we did arrive at the start of the walk in style: by steam train. The train looked the part, smelt right, made all the right chuff-chuff and clickety-click noises and we all even managed to stay awake during the one-hour journey to Minehead but only just. It felt like we were all on our way to Hogwarts, but no-one tried to sell us live chocolate frogs.

Grey skies and grey seas greeted us in Minehead, as did pink hen-parties and loud stag groups. The main street was full of tacky seaside shops and discount stores, although we did rather enjoy an eye-flashing, skull-wobbling, horror-film-laughing, skeletal Pratchett DEATH in one of the Halloween shops. The official start of The Coast Path was nearby, marked by a sculpture of a pair of hands holding a partly folded map. We wandered along to look at the harbour, very nice too, but soon the attraction of the heating and the tea and biscuits in the big comfortable Victorian house we called 'B&B' became too much.

Our hostess directed us to an Indian for our evening meal, as a curry had somehow become traditional for the eve before one of our walks, and she told us that the hens and stags would give us no problems. She said that they all come out from the local Butlins in daylight, but wear ASBO type wristbands so that they can go back and get locked up at night.

After three pints and comfortably full of curry we returned to the B&B and the normally sport-averse Paul was observed to be watching the last twenty minutes of a World Cup Rugby match with interest. It saw England knocked out of the competition.

Now, this was a difficult expedition to plan because much of the walk goes through quite deserted stretches of coastline with little choice of places to stay or to eat. So, in the end, we'd opted for some shorter than normal days at the start, followed by longer than ideal days on the flat bit in the middle of the trip, when The Path is forced inland by estuaries. Thus, the first day from Minehead to Porlock was only ten miles and, as it turned out, a good thing too.

A lot of faffing seemed to be needed to get us ready, but eventually it was done and we set off under grey skies with mist obscuring the views. But at least it was reasonably warm and not raining. Almost as soon as we passed the map sculpture and the harbour there was trouble. A signpost proclaimed 'Coast Path to Porlock 7 miles'.

151

"That's not enough," Lesley and Paul complained (would you believe it!).

Soon we were zig-zagging steeply up a wooded hillside that eventually emerged onto the open cliff-top. The views were hazy in the grey light, but the path clear and easy. The book advised that the 'rugged clifftop path' was much better than the official inland route and so, especially in view of the 'complaint', we took the former. It kept near the sea and had a couple of deep, steep descents and ascents, crossing streams, to remind us what the Coast Path is all about.

Soon after re-joining the official route at the top of Bossington Hill, we found a sudden steep descent of about 200 feet being tackled by a family of four, with the two kids making rather a meal of it. We tried to demonstrate how it should be done, although Paul's knees thought otherwise. Part way down a finger post showed a contouring path, but the Coast Path was marked as continuing down. At the bottom was another Coast Path sign pointing back up, the way we had just come. What was going on? Back we went, before looking at the map and deciding that the proper way was down to the bottom after all. The mum and kids were coming down.

"Have you seen my husband?" she asked. "Oh, but you don't know who my husband is, do you."

Inside the gents in the car park in Bossington, I caught up with him. A kamikaze fly had dive-bombed into my eye and I was in need of a mirror. Dad told me that his daughter was sure she had broken both ankles and was complaining of a thorn in her bottom. Sounded reasonable to me. The mirror revealed that the fly was still alive, just, but sadly it didn't survive the extraction process.

The loos were also a relief to Lesley (in more sense than one). She'd fiercely uprooted the lower signpost and rotated it through ninety degrees, on the understanding that, had we not found the car park and loos, then she'd have to go the mile or so back and turn it some more.

I'm told that Bossington was very pretty with some lovely cottages featuring tall round chimneys, although due to the fly experience I mostly saw fuzzy mist. Next was Porlock. After walking along green lanes through fields and then a rather confusing maze of residential roads, we reached the old part of the village. The 'rugged clifftop path' had extended the distance to ten miles, but it was now only 1.30 which seemed too early for the B&B. What to do? Follow a stranger down a narrow alley of course, and end up at the back door of the Royal Oak. It was advertising itself as the only pub in Porlock and was busy with Sunday lunches. We managed to find three empty stools by the bar and drink some eye-healing and knee-reviving liquid lunch.

The centre of the village turned out to be charming. Quite empty on a Sunday afternoon, except for the occasional classic car taking part in a local road-run, and full of attractive buildings. It also seemed to have two more pubs. When we went to find food in the evening Lesley suggested that in the interest of research and the beer log, we pop into the Top Ship for a quick pint, before going to eat at the Royal Oak.

Inside, among the dogs looking hopefully at their owners eating and drinking, there were two fireplaces, one at each end of the bar. The two barmaids were having a 'who could make the biggest fire' competition. On the bar was a tap for a dark strong beer called Exmoor Beast.

"Just a moment," the barmaid said. "I'll have to go down to the cellar for that one. We keep it locked up". It was lovely. Needless to say, we never did make it back to the Royal Oak.

The final pub, the Castle, was directly between the Top Ship and our B&B, and from the outside it looked like it had a library inside, so we nipped in to see. Unfortunately, the reality was somewhat different. It turned out to have had an attack of interior designers at some point, and the rows of books were just wallpaper.

We woke to a beautiful sunny day, but we were to spend most of it in the woods. The walk started well enough, cutting down from Porlock towards the sea through Porlock Marsh. It was quite striking with bleached, dead trees above low, flat red and green vegetation. Then over the stones of the foreshore and into the impossibly pretty Porlock Weir we went with boats drawn up around thatched cottages. There was an old Jaguar replica left over from the road-run parked outside the hotel, and a couple having an argument near a convertible Beetle that kept

153

sounding its alarm.

"Stop fiddling with your keys," the lady by the car announced to the chap standing some distance away.

"I'm not," he replied. "Look, my hands are here". He held them up for inspection.

"Well you must be," she said, rooting through her handbag resting on the boot. The alarm stopped.

"Don't do it again". The fiddling in the handbag continued. The alarm went off. She glared at him.

"See, it's all your fault," we told him.

"Always!" he said.

We complimented her on the Beetle and asked about the Jag. The alarm went silent and with both of them talking to us and with no more handbag digging it stayed that way.

We moved on, entering deciduous woods with last years' old, dry leaves underfoot and climbed up and down the hillside. It went on for a while and was quite steep in places. We'd promised ourselves a tea break in Culbone, the home of the smallest parish church in England, but it seemed a long time in coming. As we approached yet another climb, Lesley was heard to mutter (with venom)

"Why do they always put **stupid** churches on the top of **stupid** hills?"

Do you ever feel like that? No? Well, I guess that you might if you do a lot of walking. Our other pet theory, while we are on the subject, is that more often than not, the village pub is right by the village church. It used to work well: head for the church tower and you'll find the pub. But now it's often just someone's house with thirsty hikers outside.

The church, when it did appear, in a small clearing, was indeed small and still contained the original wooden pews and boxes and, for some reason, a number of not original gas lamps. Importantly though it did have a bench outside, very suitable for a tea stop. Then we re-entered the woods that once housed French prisoners of war and later were used for the charcoal industry. The trees and roots were covered in thick green moss and there were plenty of streams to cross as the path went up and down, the trees obscuring all the views.

We found Sisters' Fountain, also covered in green moss, at

the point where Joseph of Arimathea had struck the ground with his staff. (As you'll know, he was the chap who donated his own tomb for the burial of Jesus Christ, but why he should have been walking the South West Coast Path is a bit of a mystery. You'd have thought that he'd have had better things to do, wouldn't you?). The water gushed out of an artificial cave built in the nineteenth century, with a cross on top.

Eventually, we did emerge from the trees and out onto heather-clad open hillside with splendid views along the coast. After over twelve miles, near Devon's most Northern extremity (Foreland Point) a signpost told us that Porlock was eleven miles behind us, A good example of the flexible, variable and quaint approach to distances that we were to encounter (and increasingly, ignore) on many occasions throughout the week.

Finally, a small path that squeezed between the A road and the sea cliff, where kestrels were hunting, took us all the way down to the foreshore of Lynmouth. Unfortunately, I hadn't managed to find anywhere to stay near the sea, and the best I could find was another big Victorian pile all the way back up the cliff in the 'sister' town of Lynton. A 125-year-old cliff railway runs up and down the cliff and it was even running. But I made Paul and Lesley walk. No cheating here, just muttering!

The path crosses the cliff railway near the top terminus, so we didn't have to walk all the way down again the next morning and I was almost, but not quite, forgiven for the climb the previous day when everyone was tired. A tarmac path that the locally famous goats seemed to have been using as a toilet took us to the end of the Valley of Rocks. It was all very squishy. We pretended to be sorry for the group of Eastern European visitors that were wearing expensive designer trainers, but didn't carry it off very well.

'Day three blues', that exhaustion that strikes worst on day three of a long walk, when the initial energy has all been used up, and the body is not yet accustomed to all that exercise, big cooked breakfasts, pub meals and copious amounts of beer, seemed to have struck. To be fair, we had all been training with the eating and drinking bit before we came. It was just the walking part that we'd forgotten about. So, when the book encouraged us to avoid a whole section of road by following a path closer to the sea, it seemed like a good idea. It was even signposted as a 'Coast Path alternative route'. It went through woods and fields for a while and then came to a signpost announcing a landslip and diversion. The diversion went very steeply back up hill and ended up on the road not far from where we'd started. Bah!

Woody Bay had an interesting, but not altogether helpful signpost. It showed the directions to America, Russia, Iceland and New Zealand! Ignoring all of these lovely places, we set off in the sunshine up a rather steep hill with great views. Just before the top, we passed three separate elderly couples out walking and then felt bad because we'd bagged what turned out to be the only bench for miles around for our tea break. Pair by pair they overtook, looking exhausted. Then, of course we overtook them again on the next section. Some had found some small rocks to try and rest on.

A long gentle descent took us to Heddon's Mouth and a half-mile detour inland, alongside a river, saw us at the Hunter's Inn. We had to go there, honest. I told the others it was because I needed to see what it was like. It's one of the few places to stay on this section and although local knowledge (the B&B people) had told me it was a walkers' pub, it thinks it's a wedding venue on the internet.

It turned out to be lovely. Good, remote location, nice grounds among woodland and *six* real ales. We sat on the patio in the sun and, one after another, the elderly couples came in. This time, when the outside seating ran out, we surrendered our table to the last pair, returned to the coast path and a really steep climb before a short collapse on top of the cliff!

A broad, flattish track helped improve the average speed for the day, and one more big climb took us to the cairn on top of Great Hangman, the highest point of the entire South West Coast Path. We had another collapse here. You have to be careful with that up there though. The local legend says that a sheep stealer was walking over the hill carrying a ewe slung over his shoulder. He stopped to rest on a rock and the struggling sheep caused the cord tied around its legs to tighten and slip round the man's neck, strangling him! But we were okay. The walking wardrobe was too tired to struggle!

Combe Martin, a long thin town stretching along a river valley to a sandy beach and a harbour, was only a couple of miles beyond. There were people surfing in the sea there. Yes, in the sea in October. We didn't join them! We went to the inn by the harbour that night to eat. It was rather empty. So, on the way back to the B&B, we tried the other pub nearby. The remains of a wake, celebrating the life of a local lady who died aged 105, had been there since early afternoon. About twenty were playing traditional pub skittles, and perhaps a dozen or so were near the bar, taking it in turns to play pool. One (rather squarish) couple did a very passable impression of a Māori haka when they took on their opponents, and again when the beat them. Jade, in her mid-twenties, was torn between playing pool, rolling a cigarette and the need for a toilet. Her eventual self-proclaimed and rather noisy "wee dance" from one side of the pub to the other settled the conflict. It was very entertaining to us all!

The climb out of Combe Martin was steep and zig-zaggy but soon we were up on the clifftops again in glorious sunshine and, before long, approaching Ilfracombe. We promised ourselves a tea stop there. A sign said three miles. It looked a lot closer than that, but then the path headed off sideways and climbed up and around Hillsborough Hill with an iron age fort on top. Words were said. "Stupid!" for example!

So, our tea stop in Ilfracombe harbour, sitting on a bench in the sun, was rather later than planned. And the harbour wasn't quite how it used to be (another Grumpy Old Man warning!). Since our last visit, perhaps twenty years ago, Verity seems to have turned up. The twenty-metre-high stainless steel and bronze statue by David Hurst depicts a pregnant woman holding aloft a sword while carrying the scales of justice and standing on a pile of law books. On one side she is naked and on the other her skin has been removed to show her innards. Now why would that be a good representation of truth and justice? Perhaps our unwanted apple cores would be a good symbol of something: the hunger of the long-distance walker perhaps. But instead they were consigned to a bin and we moved on.

The path followed a fairly easy track on top of the cliffs and

157

was lovely, before it dropped down along a lane into the village of Lee. Okay, it was a short diversion (half a mile) to the Grampus pub, but Lesley's Great Uncle used to live there, no, not in the pub, although we suspect that his son more or less did, but in the big house over the road. The house was hidden by scaffolding. The pub was open so we felt that some more work on that beer log, with stuff brewed on the premises, was required. See how dedicated we are!

We worried about the next section. Both the book and the B&B people had issued hilliness warnings. It lived up to expectations. Steep out of Lee and then many steep ups and downs. A solitary walker stopped us and asked how far it was to Woolacombe. He was contemplating whether 'tis nobler in the feet to suffer the route back to Ilfracombe, whence he'd come, or to take arms, and the rest of his body, on to the sea at Woolacombe.

To be honest it seemed about 50/50 to us, but somehow, we seem to attract things to our expeditions. Dogs mostly, oh, and bitey insects. Not to mention the leeches. Strangely, the solitary walker was called Boris, the same as the dog who had walked with us for a whole morning last year. He was visually impaired and so had trouble reading a map. But he behaved in a similar way to Boris the dog, although perhaps with less tendency to chase rabbits and seagulls. He followed us closely, sometimes in front and sometimes behind and sometimes alongside, but always chatting away.

The scenery was lovely again, and there were seals in the water at the base of the cliffs. At Morte Point the tide was low enough for the visually endowed to admire the 'spectacular jagged slate ridge like a dinosaur's back emerging from the sea'. However, it turned out that our new companion wasn't as faithful as some of the others, and left us to chase a bus when we stopped for tea on a bench at Woolacombe.

An enormous beach, dotted with surfers, stretched ahead and on the hard sand we made good time. At the far end Paul almost took up a sporting activity. As we climbed up through a car park, an all-female surfing school were getting ready to get wet. The rather attractive instructor (it's okay, Lesley did allow me to say this) stopped to chat when she saw us look at the map to see where the path went. Perhaps it's fortunate that Paul's sports chip had used up its monthly allowance on the rugby on the first evening.

The coast path turns right at this point and goes round Baggy Point, but that was too far for us today so we left it and cut inland a mile-and-a-half through lanes to the village of Croyde and our B&B. Unusually this was being run by a man, although I think he had had chef training as well as a part time job in the local Wickes. Then, an amazing thing happened. He asked if we wanted any laundry done.

Now, as you know by now, we carry all our belongings with us on these trips and so weight is an issue. The rule of thumb for clothing is three of each item (except socks of course when you're allowed six!): one to wear, one to be washed and one to be clean. Normally we'd arrive in a B&B, try and finish drying what we washed last night, wash what we wore today in a basin or shower, and wear the last remaining specimen. So, the offer of laundry and clean, dry, sweet-smelling and above all bendy clothes was AMAZING! Three people rapidly stripped off and the basket provided was filled. Lesley may have gone too far. She had to borrow some things to go out to the pub later!

But it was worth it. If anyone from the Thatch Inn is reading this, some feedback: Bigger tables please for those fajitas that Lesley ordered. Great, but massive!

Finally came the day when we actually arrived at our accommodation in under the planned distance! It was also the day that Paul kept everyone's spirits up by being especially entertaining. It started soon after we'd left the B&B and were heading off through the lanes to re-join the Coast Path to go back and tackle Baggy Point. Lesley asked if Paul had filled his water bottle (as he'd forgotten yesterday).

"Oh yes," he said. "In the middle of the night. I woke up and needed to go to the loo and filled the bottle."

There was a short silence while Lesley and I contemplated a horrible thought but then Paul said

"No, I went to the bathroom and filled the bottle from the tap." Aha!

We were back on the path and tackling Baggy Point by nine. The landscape had changed. Gone were the big drops and climbs of the last few days, and instead we had flat walking on grassy paths, on top of low cliffs. In another hour or so, we'd turned the corner and were heading South rather than West, heading towards Croyde Bay and starting to think about sun cream.

We crossed the sand of the bay and continued along the cliffs, eventually picking up a path above and alongside a road. Where it ended, the Coast Path signposted us down through a gate, across the road and through a car park with the huge length of Saunton Sands stretched out before us. Paul spotted a sign pointing the other way that the book described as 'a better route avoiding facilities'. He seemed keen. After we'd zig-zagged up a very steep hill with killer steps for rather a long time, we came to a stile with a 'Beware of the bull with cows and calves' notice. A great big brute silhouetted on the skyline in the next field was very much in evidence. As we puffed and waited by the stile to recover, we asked, "In what way is this path better?"

We dropped down to the extensive sand dunes behind the beach, The Braunton Burrows Nature Reserve, which Wikipedia thinks is famous as being one of only two sites in the UK where the Amber Sandbowl snail lives. Strangely, when we were there, the snail was not its most obvious feature. A golf course and army training area would be higher up the list for us. As we emerged from the path through the dunes and onto a track, a squad of soldiers were coming down it. We stepped aside to let them pass (and so they could admire the size of the walking wardrobe), and they broke into a jog, which slowed to a walk again further on when they thought we weren't looking. Embarrassingly (for them) we seemed to be catching them up as we continued, but fortunately, we came to our turn-off just before that happened.

With the snails not in evidence and three or four miles of 'track behind the dunes' to do, it has to be said that this wasn't the most interesting section of the Path. Soon we were into route march mode, hot and tiring, but 'getting us there'. Eventually we emerged, turning the corner again to head inland up the big Taw estuary. The problem with this section of the coast is the need to go a long way inland to get around the wet bit. It was to take us a day and a half. The tide was out, it looked very muddy, and boats were being scrubbed underneath. We headed to Braunton and the Tarka trail.

The Tarka trail is a collection of footpaths and cycle paths in North Devon that allegedly follow the route taken by the fictional Tarka the Otter. At Braunton, it starts by following a disused railway line, is tarmacked and is part of the National Cycle Network. Even before we got onto it, we had to give way to four middle-aged and not very proficient cyclists. One overweight lady, who seemed to be testing the 'you never forget how to ride a bike' theory, did apologise to us saying "I haven't done this for a very long time" and her husband was heard to be telling her to change down the gears when she came to a hill, although I'm not sure where he expected to find a hill on an old railway track!

We managed a mile or so on the trail before taking a little (half-mile) detour to a thatched pub and then, feet refreshed and rested, we simply shot along. To be blunt it was dull. A tarmac strip edged by nettles and behind them trees. Often, we were sunk into cuttings and even when we weren't, the trees obscured the views. Boring! And with the ever-present threat of being run over by cyclists.

We tried I spy: something beginning with A - Acorn, something beginning with T – Trees, Something beginning with D.P. – immediate response and in chorus because there was so much of it: Dog Poo. Thanks, Paul!

Eventually there was a soft green verge alongside the tarmac and the line ran so close to the estuary that trees couldn't grow between us and the river, so we could see out. As we approached Barnstaple a new bridge spanned the gap. Well, Paul said it had been there for some time but it didn't appear on my map. It led almost to our guest house, so in spite of walking a long way today we even ended up arriving early and in time for a Pointless Party. (Pointless: a TV quiz show where the objective is to gain as few points as possible. On air from about 5.15 most weekday evenings and okay if you know lots about pop music, football, films and TV. Otherwise good for sleeping through with your eyes open so you don't get caught!)

The pub around the corner, which I'd almost booked as

somewhere to stay, had no real ale, was almost empty and looked awful. Instead we took the recommendation of the B&B lady and went a little further to the chip shop, which had just been refurbished and had a restaurant attached. It was heaving, modern and very nice.

16th October. It was Lesley's birthday again. Yes, I know that seems to happen rather a lot in this book, but she does insist on having one each year, you know! Cards at the breakfast table and box of chocolates rather gave the game away. All the other guests, workmen to the last, wished her a good one. Then it was back for more of that dull, hard tarmac on the old railway line. But at least on this morning, with the tide in covering the mud and with the boats actually floating, the estuary did look a bit more attractive.

After some time, we had the option to leave the track to walk over dunes and around the back of a disused power station. A big ship had turned up on the tide and had just finished unloading what looked like huge piles of earth. As we walked on, it left the quay and headed back towards the open sea.

Now the River Torridge joined the party and we had to find a way to cross that as well. Another excursion inland. We stopped for a tea on a bench on the prom at Instow, and watched the dogs and their owners on the beach. We could see the old shipyard on the opposite side of the river and, rotting away in the mud some quite big old wooden boats. One seemed to be inhabited mainly by daleks.

An old bridge at Bideford allowed us to cross. Hurrah, no disused railway line cum cycle path on the other side, but a welcome return to gentle ups and downs, through woodland and open spaces. We debated stopping for a rest near the bridge, but pushed on to the rather nice town of Appledore. It had narrow streets and houses painted in pastel colours and offered a rest, a beer and a bowl of chips in a nice warm pub. When we set off again, we all seemed a bit stiff. There was still about four miles or so to go, all round the end of the promontory (which mostly seemed to be a golf course) and into the typical holiday town of Westward Ho!

In the morning there were about five groups of people eating breakfast in the pub where we were staying. Two ladies, Isabelle and Tania were speaking to each other in French and looking at a Coast Path guide book. We said hello and wished them a good day's walking and went on our way. We were to meet them again. And again! It transpired that they were Swiss, and complained about the steepness of the path. But surely, they have hills in Switzerland?

"Ah yes, but when you walk there, you either go up or go down. Not this constant changing."

Surprisingly, we did start with a short section of old railway line today but soon the path was back to its old tricks: never a flat moment. There were pheasants everywhere, a tree full of long-tailed tits, a flock of partridges and even a tawny owl. Then the fields and scrub gave way to woodland. The sun disappeared, the wind became stronger and it started to become chilly.

At Bucks Mills the path came out of the woods onto a road and looked at a few houses, but the café was shut and the only bench was taken, so we pushed on again, back into the woods and up the hill to find a rope swing to play on. Eventually we came to a wide, well-made track through the woods, Hobby Drive. It was built by the obviously very wealthy Hamlyn family between 1811 and 1825, but much more interesting is the story of John Gregg, his wife, children and grandchildren in about 1750. Living in a cave near here they were known as the Clovelly Cannibals and are supposed to have slaughtered, pickled and eaten 1,000 victims. We made it intact to the end of the drive and the start of the road down to the village of Clovelly.

Actually 'road' might be a bit of a grand term for the steep cobbled pedestrian track that twists and turns between the whitewashed slate-roofed houses and down to the harbour at the bottom of the cliff. All very pretty and apparently the subject of much literary and artistic time and effort over the years. Because it is so very steep and there is no vehicular access, deliveries and the removal of waste are traditionally by means of sledges. Some were parked outside the houses, presumably for the tourists to admire but as our B&B was one of the listed houses half way down the main street, we were there in the evening after everything had shut up for the day and the tourists kicked out. Firewood and coal were being delivered. On sledges! One chap pulled from the front, another by the side of the sledge seemed to be trying to steer, and a woman at the back was hanging onto a rope for grim death with one hand and a labrador with the other.

Breakfast was served in the front room with the window looking out over the main street. It was nice and warm inside but looked freezing outside. Suddenly Lesley leapt up.

"Did you see that?" she asked. We thought that maybe she'd spotted a donkey pulling a sledge up to the road at the top. But no, it was a woman in bathing costume and pink towel going down to the sea! No risk of losing Paul to the wet women this time. He selected another piece of toast.

The next people to pass were Isabelle and Tania. They peered in and pointed at us and then carried on downhill. We were so surprised we even forgot to do chimpanzee tea-party impressions!

The climb up out of Clovelly took us onto the cliffs again, for a few post breakfast ups and downs, but after a bit the path calmed down and went through fields of sheep, cows and grass. Somewhere we missed a turn and ended up too far inland, our only navigational mistake of the trip. But it didn't matter much and soon we'd found the trig point fenced into its own little mini field. After that we found the white dome on a stalk that is an air traffic control radar. It dominated the view for a while, until we reached Hartland Point and its lighthouse marking the official end of the Bristol Channel (for our Roman readers, this would be the Promontory of Hercules). The remains of the 1982 wreck of Johanna lie on the rocks nearby but there's not much to see now.

Then we had a prelude for tomorrow's yo-yo path, high cliffs and steep valleys. Out towards the sea great ridges of rock stuck up vertically in spectacular fashion. Fortunately, it wasn't so far to the old customs house at Hartland Quay where we were staying. It's been converted to a museum, a little shop and a pub and hotel. The harbour, built in Henry VIII's time no longer exists. It was washed away in a storm in 1887.

As usual Lesley's digital feeding behaviour had struck. She

164

seems to flip instantaneously between 'staaarving' and 'stuuufed', so a late lunchtime beer and chips seemed called for. Isabelle and Tania arrived. They had got to Minehead on Sunday and started walking but elected to miss out all the flat bit round the estuary and had caught a bus instead. "It looked like it would be boring," they said. Too right! They were carrying sleeping bags and tents so they didn't have to pay for accommodation each night but very quickly they'd booked a room at the hotel.

Later, Isabelle joined us for pre-feeding drinks in the bar and it seemed that there was friction within the Swiss team.

"I always have to wait for her," she said. "And she has a problem with her leg so she can't go so far."

We were worried about the next day, from Hartland Quay to Bude. It was fifteen miles, and everyone we had spoken to had said that it was a tough and long stretch, with nowhere to stop off on the way unless you go a fair distance inland. The book didn't help. It told us the section was rated severe, the highest classification. It went on about great jagged ridges of rock stretching out to sea, ten steep and deep river valleys to cross and how arduous it was all going to be.

To make things more 'interesting', Paul's knees were complaining about the unaccustomed amount of beer, or was it the walking? Lesley's weren't sure and my back, which I'd managed to damage somehow on the nice easy flat section approaching Porlock Weir wasn't completely cured.

The hotel breakfast didn't start until 8.15, so we were down early to try and beat the rest. So were the Swiss. Among the food choices the menu told us that it would take eight hours to walk to Bude. Surely that couldn't be right? I'd planned on ten. The book said eight-and-a-half. The tactic worked; we were out and walking by nine. The tide was in and the sea had covered most of the geology so there was less distraction there. The team set off, determined, but rather crippled.

Lesley, currently stuuufed after breakfast but soon to be staaarving, was worried that we hadn't got enough food for the day and after about three-quarters of a mile asked Paul if he'd remembered to 'collect' the packets of biscuits from the room. Expletive. He hadn't and then, another and even louder

165

expletive as he realised that he still had the room key in his pocket.

Only one thing to do. Walking wardrobe removed, I jogged back to the hotel with the key. Good job what little training we had done involved cross-the-cowfields jogging. Isabelle accused me of going the wrong way when I ran past her. On the return trip the wardrobe and team members were not where I'd left them. Another expletive! This was turning into a long-distance run! I jogged on and over the next hill found the Swiss, who helpfully pointed ahead to where Paul and Lesley were tackling the one beyond. Briefly I thought about returning to walking mode and defecting to the opposition. After all they probably had chocolate in their packs, but no, it would look far more heroic to jog past trying not to gasp for breath too much and anyway, if they turned round, Lesley and Paul would see that I'd wimped out and stopped, and that would never do.

When I did catch up (they waited for me half way up the hill so I had the enjoyment of taking the walking wardrobe to the top), it transpired that when I'd left them, Lesley had strapped the wardrobe to her front so it counterbalanced her Berghaus bag and set off. The only problem was that she couldn't see where she was putting her feet down, so on the downhill bits she took one end and Paul the other, and on they went.

By now we'd had some fairly serious ups and downs as well as a nice waterfall that I'd somehow not fully appreciated while running. We thought that we were doing quite well, but after about four miles we came across the first of the river valleys mentioned in the book. It was very obvious. Very steep and very deep. And then four or five more followed immediately, with almost no flat between them, either at the top or the bottom. Lesley and Paul were both using walking poles to help the knees by now. We weren't fast but did keep going. We hadn't seen the Swiss team for some time. As we approached one summit, a sign told us of a pub along a footpath about a mile inland. For once our commitment to the beer log was just not strong enough and we ignored it.

Lunch was declared when we found a bench on top of a cliff. It comprised some Mars bars we'd found in the hotel shop. The next deep and steep followed immediately, and I struggled up the other side, stopped and turned expecting a nice rest while waiting for the others, but Lesley was almost upon me and Paul not far behind.

Eventually, after the prescribed course of ten, and after we'd had the opportunity to admire the GCHQ listening dishes from close range, the path settled down to its more normal yo-yo style and we even found a 'seasonal' café still open that sold Mrs Staaarving her favourite: lemon cake. A few more miles and we could see Bude in the distance with its beach, colourful beach huts, golf course and Sainsbury's supermarket. We'd made it, and in a lot less time that the menu had predicted.

The next morning, we pottered around Bude in the sunshine. Unbelievably, we'd managed nine whole days on the Coast Path, starting in Somerset, traversing the whole of the North Devon coast and ending up in Cornwall without a single drop of rain. But no-one complained about having carried all those waterproofs unnecessarily.

We arrived at the bus stop late in the morning to catch the bus back to Exeter, and who should be there but Isabelle and Tania. It turned out that they'd been lured in by the pub sign yesterday. After that there was no going back to The Path, just a nearby bus stop. They had spent the night in the camp site just outside Bude and a truce had been negotiated. Their new plan was that they would use local buses to do some of the distance and walk shorter sections. Their aim was still to get to Falmouth in another two weeks.

Our bus dropped us only three miles from Paul's house and we made it back by early afternoon. That evening we walked to the pub in the next village; old habits die hard. We realised that we'd done an exceptional job on the beer log so we toasted that. And then it started raining. It was still raining the next day.

9. Lesley, Tim and Suffering (Looe to Starcross October 2017)

Thoughts turned to finishing the entire walk, but perhaps rather prematurely as we still had two biggish sections to go: from Looe in Cornwall round the South Devon coast as far as Starcross on the Exe estuary, and all of the Dorset section from Lyme Regis to the official end of The Path at Poole. We decided that we really ought to leave the end until, well, the end and so 2017 was going to be the year of the South Devon section. Whilst we'd walked almost all of this (or so we thought) over the years what with holidays at various times and with Paul living there, day-trips don't give the same sense of 'journey'. We needed to do it again; and properly.

But there was a very good reason for not tackling this section before: logistics. Out of season many of the ferries across the estuaries don't run and in season the B&B's and pubs are reluctant to take one-night stays. What would you do? Or, in case you are finding this narrative super inspiring, what are you planning to do? Well, I suggested 'in season with tents'. I like camping and the sense of freedom it gives. So long as it isn't wet and there is somewhere warm and indoors to go for food, that is. Lesley and Paul both provided rapid, blunt, focussed and non-negotiable feedback, as you might expect by now. And so it was that, by April, an 'out of season' October expedition had been properly planned and booked. Three long estuary detours had been included, increasing the distance by some 25 miles.

Paul immediately started training. He set off by train for a beer festival, together with The Blind Date (TBD) whom he'd met some years ago, but even after all this time of acquaintance with Paul she still claimed to have no beer drinking experience! The official de-brief went:

'Yesterday's training exercise for my official role as SWCP beer logger was highly successful and I now have a comprehensive guide to over 100 South West breweries and 275 ales. There'll be no excuses for drinking the same ones twice! The education of TBD also went well, despite a slight

communication glitch that left us travelling in opposite ends of a train with no interconnection! She managed to survive without adulterating the ales with lemonade at all and even enjoyed one or two. Between us we drank seven 'new' beers and sampled several others…. if only we could remember what they were"

Then things went quiet for a bit, well, months actually. Paul became the proud owner of a VERY large golden retriever puppy and we went to visit him for his 60th birthday in August. Sciatica had struck! He wasn't walking well at all, or even sitting comfortably for that matter. Puppy walking was punctuated by stops every quarter of a mile and he was now on first name terms with everyone in the chemist's shop. But with two months still to go, everything should be okay; shouldn't it?

In mid-September it was my turn to start training. I went for a run. My legs felt really heavy and the circuit took fifty minutes rather than the usual forty-five. Paul's news was not good either: not enough improvement since August. He had taken to visiting Katie, a physio. Although she had stuck needles in him and found some bits that really hurt when poked, she seemed rather perplexed as to why the right leg shouldn't function and why his reflexes were so bad that if anything caused a small lack of balance he tended to fall over. Not good for cliff walking.

The expedition was looking increasingly 'interesting'. Lesley seemed to be the only fit one amongst us, but perhaps that's because she is so much (almost 3 years) younger!

Lesley and I went to our house in Hungary for a month and were besieged by welcome and well-meaning elderly relatives, which somewhat limited our training. The report read:

'Food and alcohol training going superbly well (you know what those Hungarian meals are like). We have been wearing hiking boots today but not actually doing much hiking, unless getting on and off the open top tourist buses of Budapest counts. We have also gained some ferry experience: a boat cruise on the Danube'.

Paul was not happy:

'On the positive side I'm definitely improving, but it's very slowly in a three steps forward, two steps back kind of way. I

169

can now lie flat, or sit in relative comfort and have greatly reduced my drug habit. Unfortunately, although the comms link seems to have been restored, the right leg is still refusing to come back on-line and even just standing up, to cook a meal for example, is very painful. I've been given the go ahead to try some hill training with pointy stick (aka walking pole) and rucksack .... (but).... I reckon unless I can get up Haldon Hill and back in a reasonable time and comfort, there's no point in even attempting anything on the coast path.'

Well, as chief instigator of the expedition I wasn't going to have that! So, we called from Hungary and started talking contingency plans, which had the desired effect of making Paul determined not to drop out (yet). A week later:

'Emergency panic training has commenced and I did a couple of miles with about 5kg in the ruckie yesterday and another one this morning before physio. This was the penultimate appointment and I took my pointy stick along too, for advice on the best way to deploy it. She squished my back and stuck pins in me again and we had a good chat about epic expeditions. She's doing the Inca trail next week. Opinion on our hike was that I'm now in a fit state to try it and see how it goes, as I'm unlikely to do myself any serious damage or get irrevocably stuck. However, I should:

a) bail out ASAP if it gets seriously painful

b) cheat wherever possible

c) try to acquire bags of ice from the B&Bs on arrival, for insertion into pants.'

And with a week to go:

'Yesterday afternoon I achieved my objective and did a five-mile ascent of Haldon and back with pointy stick and an 8kg pack. I was hoping to report that it was relatively easy and comfortable, but actually it was pretty tough and felt more like a 20+ miler. Nevertheless, I did it, and in a little over two hours, which has given me some confidence for the first day. Although it's further I can hopefully take more time over it and of course I'll have you two to bully me along. This morning I was suffering a bit, but have had a final session with Katie, who gave me lots of homework and was quite positive about my prospects. Still I'm going to be quite slow and won't be up to

twenty-mile days, so I'll need to review strategy if I'm to venture beyond Plymouth. Anyway, we can talk about that later.'

But just two days before:

'First the bad news: I'm really struggling. After a mere 3.5 mile walk with pack yesterday, without much in the way of hills (for Devon) I was back in Marvin3 mode. After a worried night I'd pretty much decided that I was going to take only two day's supplies and bail out after Plymouth, though even that far now looks like a challenge. However, this morning I decided to rest up and look at it all again and realized that the A379 follows the route pretty closely, albeit inland. And there's a bus that goes that way, right from Plymouth to Dartmouth. So, with a combination of shortish walks and/or local bus connections back to the A379, I've found I can follow you round the South Hams without worrying about the estuaries. The only problem will be Sunday, when the local buses don't run.'

And so, it was that on the appointed day all three, Lesley, Tim and Paul (Now Suffering), set forth fuelled by the traditional pre-walk curry from the night before. Long ago we had decided to catch a taxi from Suffering's house to Exeter railway station rather than walk. It meant that we could get to Looe by mid-morning and avoid a really stupid o'clock get up time. You don't think that's cheating do you? After all we had done that walk many times before and given Suffering's condition it seemed like a good thing.

The early morning light over the sea was lovely as we left Exeter. As the train crossed the Tamar at Plymouth, the boats were all lined up in neat rows on the water. Arriving in Looe we strolled down through the town, only stopping to buy lunchtime pasties before being reunited with the acorn markers and the start of the traditional Coast Path roller-coaster. It was lovely walking weather, still, dry and hot in the sunshine, and we were soon in shorts and t-shirts and feeling in holiday mood. The cliff walking was great and at Seaton we dropped to the beach

---

3   Marvin: The paranoid android in The Hitch Hikers Guide to the Galaxy who is always complaining about the pain in the diodes in his leg

and Lesley and Paul marched on at great speed and with great chat, while I was somewhat distracted by the dramatically coloured purple and green rocks.

He felt it later, Paul, that is. All that rushing had tired his back so he walked the next section more slowly and Lesley and I pulled ahead. We met three women on the path walking the other way and stopped to talk to them. Later, when Paul rejoined us, he had a strange tale to tell of being accosted by three unknown females who knew his name and encouraged him with tales of a pub en-route not far away. How could that possibly have happened?

All too soon we arrived at the Finnygook Inn at Crafthole, our stop for the night, to be greeted warmly by a charming barmaid and beer (or was it charming beer and a barmaid, I can't really remember). Paul's back had survived the first test, although the pub did not. A couple of months later, a roof fire destroyed our warm, comfortable rooms upstairs.

The next day, low cloud obscured the view through the large windows in the breakfast area. But we started as we meant to continue with a big full English and then took a sneaky (but legitimate) footpath across a golf course to regain the coast path on the cliffs above Portwrinkle. Paul was determined to walk the next section, as it was one of the few he thought he'd not done before.

We lost some height, enough to now be below the cloud base, and, perhaps rather unkindly, Lesley and I then left Paul to carry on more slowly and stop where he needed to. Our excuse was that our planned distance today was over twenty miles so we'd better get on with it. His plan for today was to do some walking and then deploy 'cheat' mode.

We admired how far the targets were from the shooting positions in the Tregantle firing ranges. Soldiers inside the big solid bulk of the Victorian fort on the far side seemed reluctant to come out. We took some pictures to encourage them, but nothing happened and we went on our way.

The guide book then talks about a road walk followed by a section that 'undulates quite steeply and unexpectedly among chalets and gardens'. It did too, although the 'chalets' seemed more like garden sheds sheltering among undergrowth and bracken on the hillside, golden at this time of year. The going was a bit more 'moderate' than we may have wished for, but eventually we came round Rame Head, the wind dropped, the cloud lifted and the sun came out. We chatted for a while to two women and three dogs, and set them up to accost Paul when he came along. Sadly, they did not meet. The path, now on the top of the cliffs, rounded the next point and Plymouth Sound came into view.

But first we needed to negotiate Cawsand. Emerging from the woods we came to the old village square with a small beach to one side. Sue and Liz, two middle-aged women, were drying themselves. They'd been swimming (!!!) but their current most pressing need was to get a cup of tea. The urgency of the beverage was discussed with relation to the relative importance of clothing, and the likelihood of being served in the square without any. In the end they settled on just socks and the towelling sacks they referred to as 'changing tents' and off they went.

Deeper into the village we lost the route and ended up on the beach. I blamed Paul. Partly of course because he wasn't there, but mostly because he had the instructions (although we did have the map). It didn't matter much in the end, as the correct path was obvious further on, hugging the coast on a grassy track and entering Mount Edgcumbe Country Park. Through woods, steep in places, and then through landscaped gardens with Greek-style temples looking out to the sea, and finally the path skirted right past the house itself. There were people inside, in a tea room. We were tempted but managed to resist, knowing how far we still had to go. Just beyond the entrance gate was the ferry point and as we approached, we could see the little boat just leaving. So, we waited. But the sun was out and we had jam tarts, rather squashed from being in the rucksack since Exeter station. Luxury!

The crossing of the Tamar marked our arrival into Devon, and specifically Plymouth. The Coast Path goes all the way round the city's waterfront and therefore we did the same. There were historical bits, modern bits, nice bits, rather dodgy bits and even a 'Welcome to Plymouth' floral message on a grassy bank in front of a hotel. The acorns marking the long-distance path seemed to have given way to red diamonds and some huge markers, made from what looked like old torpedoes. We were getting very tired by now and so the discovery of a 'Footpath Closed' sign and barriers across the entrance to Sutton Harbour, meaning an extra mile detour, was not welcome. There was even some 'language' used!

Then we got a call from Paul. He'd made it! Walking as far as the ferry, he'd then caught a bus around Plymouth to a second ferry that took him to Mount Batten and our hotel right by the ferry point. We eventually joined him just after six, after twenty-two miles. Lesley refused to leave the bar where we'd checked in to see our room, until we'd all had a (strong) beer.

We ate in the busy hotel bar and Suffering's friend Sue joined us. Strangely she didn't feel compelled to accompany us the next day, but went safely home again.

So, we had reached the section where three big rivers needed to be crossed, without the summer advantage of ferries. We had planned three days for this, each with an eight-or-nine-mile detour. Paul decided on the 'bail out completely' bus option on the first day. Sue, the waitress in the hotel gave him an extra sausage at breakfast upon hearing this just in case the bus had steps he had to climb. Or maybe it was because he hadn't asked her to put ice down his pants.

It was very windy and wet and rocky and slippery underfoot, and so Lesley and I struggled to keep up a decent speed. Offshore, two little warships were practising shooting at each other while we passed some old forts and lots of large hairy chestnut and black caterpillars. Eventually Wembury with its very prominent church came into view and we walked along the beach for a while. A mile or so later we were on the lookout for Rocket House, where the guide told us that the start of the detour round the river Yealm was. We found what we thought might be it, but a lack of house name or footpath signs made us continue. Continue, that is, steeply downhill through woodland, to emerge at the ferry point by the water. There was a sign here. Two, in fact. One said that the ferry wasn't running in October and the other pointed us to a path for Rocket House. It climbed back up the steep hill in a big loop and ended up back at no-name cottage! Would you believe it!

The detour didn't even have the decency to hug the riverside. It went cross-country through fields and woods, rather than the narrow Devon lanes, and would have been lovely except for the severe hilliness, the on-off drizzle that finally grew up into rain, the hilliness, the distance (nine miles) and did I mention the hills? The guidebook let us down again when we encountered an allotment that had obviously been there for decades but which it didn't seem to know about. At the furthest inland extent, a small humpy bridge next to a wide piece of tarmac road took us over the water. All that fuss and in the end just a small bridge. We felt cheated!

As we approached Newton Ferrers, the guidebook yet again disappointed. There was no road sign where it thought there should have been. As we stood at the junction in the rain consulting the map, a car stopped to help and the driver pointed us the right way. The same thing happened in Noss Mayo: road junction, map out, rain, car stopped and driver directed us to the Ship Inn, where Paul and beer were waiting. Lesley drank hers so fast that she had to have another!

Paul had already been to the B&B, a mile-and-a-quarter further on through National Trust woodland. The owner, Sue (again!) was out but had left us a note. We were expected! And when we turned up all wet this time, she gave us tea and chocolate biscuits in a bay window looking out to the sea. It was fabulous! She also said that she was going to a talk on birds this evening, and could give us a lift to the pub and back if we wanted. Yes please, after nineteen-and-a-half miles what an offer! Then she gave us the Terms and Conditions: leave at 6.30 and stay in the pub until 10.00. Tough job, but we thought we could do it!

For some strange reason, the feet were tired the next morning and we had another estuary to cross. Lesley was suffering huge blisters on her heel, little toe and side of the foot. But the rain had stopped, the sun was out and it was t-shirts and shorts weather, and not like October at all. The path followed the route of an old carriage drive, where the local rich landowner used to take his guests. It was a flat, level wide grassy track on top of tall cliffs. Paul was back with us and we took it easy and stopped and admired the view a lot.

We saw Buzzards. We saw kestrels, sometimes hovering motionless above the cliffs. We saw small white dogs. Lots of them. Why almost all of the dogs on this section were small and white we will never know. We saw more large hairy caterpillars.

After Beacon Hill the path changed character back to the familiar ups and downs, and quite severe ones at that. We were quite tired (take that comment as a typical British understatement and translate as knackered!). By the time we got to the Erme estuary, we faced a choice. Either an eight-mile detour or a knee-high wade across the river Erme, which our ever-so reliable guidebook said was possible an hour or so either side of low tide, provided that there hadn't been any recent heavy rain or high seas. Paul's back and Lesley's blisters had no hesitation in making the decision. If it had been a choice of a walk over a bed of nails, or burning coals versus an eight-mile detour, I think the detour would still have come second!

But low tide was at about six and so theoretically crossing would be possible from about five. Then we had a couple of steep uphill miles still to do to the Dolphin Inn at Kingston, our stop for the night. We sat on the beach and drank tea. It was about three-thirty. After a while, I got talking to a couple of dogs and their owner. I told her what we were waiting for and she looked over at the river and said,

"Oh, I think it should be OK now - not more than knee-deep."

We walked across the wide sands to the remaining sliver of river, perhaps twenty metres wide, and peered at it. It was deep chestnut-brown and keeping any hints of its depth to itself. Lesley and Paul courageously sent me in first, to see if I got washed away by the current, sucked in by quicksand or just drowned in the deep water with the heavy walking wardrobe on my back. Actually, it wasn't bad. Knee-deep as promised, hardly any current and not even particularly cold. I made it! The others then followed, but looking at the photos, the expressions on their faces say that they weren't having a great time.

We shot up the hill to the pub, in relief. Too fast for Paul's back as it turned out. On entry, the first thing that greeted us was the traditional village pub atmosphere, and the second was a table with our name on it, reserved for a meal tonight. The third was, of course, beer!

As we sat in the pub the next morning, full English before us, Paul, whose back was not good (but, as we reminded him, the ice in the pants treatment had not been tried) mentioned to the landlord that there was something in one of the brochures in his room about a local bus.

"A local bus?" he responded with incredulity, "On a Friday?" and then a thoughtful pause followed by, "Well, yes, the once-a-week bus does go on a Friday. I'll phone Sue (yes, really, another Sue!) and see what time."

Again, we abandoned Paul, but didn't feel so bad about it this time, as he was in a pub drinking tea and chatting to the landlady. It turned out later that the bus arrived a bit late. But arrive it did and then two further buses took him within two miles of Hope Cove, our destination for the night.

Meanwhile, Lesley and I set off down a very muddy path back to the coast. It was windy and misty, and as soon as we arrived at the sea we found a steep climb up the cliff, followed by some more serious climbs and descents before arriving at the Avon estuary at Bigbury-on-Sea. The tractor ferrying people to Burgh Island just offshore seemed to be running, but, of course, the ferry we needed was not. Time for the third estuary detour.

It started well enough, through fields and woods, and not excessively steep, although in one place the signs directed us to the wrong side of a barbed-wire fence that had to be climbed over in due course. After about four miles we reached a single-track road, which marked the inland crossing point. It was lunchtime: high tide. Looking at the map, the name of the road was 'Tidal Road'. I think you can guess what's coming next!

We could see the tarmac stretching into the river and then emerging a bit further along, but we had no idea how deep it was. But tarmac would be easy underfoot and the edges were marked by a series of poles sticking out of the water, and a detour on the detour would add another couple of miles to the day. It seemed worth giving it a try. So, the boots came off, the shorts were rolled up and everything that mattered was packed into waterproof bags inside the rucksacks.

177

It wasn't too cold, and not too deep either; only about the same as yesterday, and on the far side was a convenient bench on which to sit and dry off, unpack and put the boots back on. But just as we were gloating about our success, around the next corner the tarmac submerged once again, and this time we couldn't see where it came out. But there was no going back now. Boots off, shorts rolled up, stuff packed away and in we went. We went quite a long way this time, around several bends, before dry land was sighted once again. This time though I wandered on a bit, around yet another corner, before kitting up again. Just as well too, as on the next bit there were ducks swimming over the road! More wading and where the tarmac emerged yet again, a chap in a big 4X4 with a trailer was loading up a boat.

"Only one more section," he promised. But this was a bit deeper, just above the knees, and there were people on the other side taking pictures of us crossing!

Boots back on and off we went again, but horror of horrors! Another flooded bit further on. Fortunately, it turned out to be much shallower, just below boot height. Then, of course, we had the four miles back to the coast before continuing on our way alongside the sea in the murky mist.

A good track started at Thurleston golf course and it took us nearly all the way to Hope Cove, although we noticed that the tarmac at Thurleston Sands was lying broken on the beach after the winter storms. A digger was busy making a new road to the hotel. We met Paul just starting to climb the cliffs out of Hope to see what had become of us.

Christine, who ran our B&B, told us later that the section of the cliff path leading into the village had collapsed as well some years back and, at great trouble and expense, had been made up again with lots of concrete. We quizzed her about the 'Hope and Anchor'. Last time we were in the village it had wooden floors, open fireplaces, was quite dark and with fishing memorabilia everywhere. Now it was all stainless-steel London bistro style.

"Ruined it!" she said. We had to agree.

And it was here, at last, that the ice in the pants event occurred! Paul thought that he'd paid enough for the B&B to justify it. Indeed, he thought there should be some scotch in it too. Christine didn't bat an eyelid!

The next section, from Hope to Salcombe we knew well, and it's not too far, only eight and a half miles. We treated ourselves to a leisurely breakfast and a relatively late start. Then we all set off, in the dry but murky morning, through the houses of the village to the thatched cottages of Inner Hope square and up a steep hill back on the Coast Path to Bolt Tail. The views were very hazy but it was still a lovely section with plenty of day trippers, dog walkers and big mushrooms around on this Saturday morning.

We took it slowly and gently, with plenty of stops, and even the steep drop into Soar Mill Cove and climb out again didn't seem as bad as we'd remembered from previous encounters. Soon we rounded Bolt Head and crested a dramatic pass through the jagged rocks of Sharp Tor. The town of Salcombe and the estuary lay before us. It was full of little boats enjoying an end of season race. The sun started to come out.

We stopped at South Sands to watch people being loaded onto a ferry via a tractor thing on stilts, but even so arrived at the B&B in town much too early. The owners were out. Paul sat and waited on a bench in the sun outside their house, while Lesley and I braved the crowds, all speaking with terribly posh Home County accents, for ice creams and emergency Compeed blister plasters and chocolatey supplies. It was all very pretty.

But later on, both pubs recommended by the B&B lady were serving drinks at London prices, and full of the posh people. They didn't want to feed three scruffy bumpkins walking The Path. We ended up elsewhere, also crowded and also expensive, but with food. We clinked glasses over our first drink and wished Lesley Happy Birthday in anticipation of the great event in two days' time. At the end of the meal the barman surprised us by presenting her with an ice-cream with a candle in it. Aaaah!

The next morning, we were so busy chatting to the owner of the B&B about her worldwide scuba-diving exploits that we missed the nine o'clock ferry across the estuary. However, the sun was out and Paul was with us, owing to a rescue service offered by Mary, the hostess of our next B&B. Sadly anywhere remotely sensible to stay was asking astronomical prices, but I'd found somewhere just outside Stokenham, a couple of miles inland. She'd even emailed twice, with strict instructions to call if it all got too much and if we didn't want to walk the whole way.

We sent Lesley (wearing shorts!) out onto the slipway by the Ferry Hotel, looking hopeful. There was no-one else around, but after only a few minutes the ferry came and Paul and I hurried out of our hiding place. The tarmac path, through woods on the other side, soon led to a good cliff-top path through gorse and bracken and eventually to the coast-watch lookout at Prawle Point. The two people inside must have had good sightings of a couple of sailing boats and plenty of walkers with dogs. The cliffs then gave way to nice easy walking on a broad gravelly track on a raised beach.

There was a climb up a sharp ridge near the lighthouse at Start Point and, as soon as we could see over it, a fantastic view, clearly showing where we needed to get to today. The route took us to the lost village of Hallsands, with its viewpoint and information board. The ruined houses below looked very sad and the information told us about the offshore dredging that had reduced the level of the beach protecting the village, leading to its almost total destruction during winter storms in 1917. Further on Beesands was protected by a big concrete sea wall and was still very much there. On a hot Sunday afternoon, it was busy, the Cricket Inn especially so. Famous for being the place of Mick Jagger's first public performance, and perhaps less so for the most expensive pint we found on the whole route, it was also the site of the telephone call for our rescue service.

Mary arrived with perfect timing, just as we were finishing our drinks and before we'd had time to consider the eye-watering wallet-straining pros of a second. She took us to her house deep in the woods outside the village. As we went inside, her spaniel really did want to see who we were. It was shut in the kitchen and kept appearing in the upper portion of the half-glazed door as it jumped up to see through. Floppy ears followed the dog's Zebedee impressions in time-lapse mode.

Later, the pub in the village did us proud. It was big, comfortable, very villagey and not too busy, and the chef was trying out some new dishes on some regulars. There was a big discussion regarding mushrooms. Should they be in Stilton or not? He brought us some to try: Yum, Yum! He asked our opinion: Yum, Yum!

Finally, it really was Lesley's birthday. But it seemed like the apocalypse was coming! In the morning the sky was a strange eerie murky sepia colour. It was very windy and the air smelt faintly of smoke. The sea, when we got that far, was grey and angry. What could we do? Well, eat a Full English of course, and with an extra sausage for Paul as he was planning to cheat again and take a bus for part of the way (for the record, no ice!). Lesley messaged her Mum. A nice bright sunny day in Hertfordshire, she reported. Mary, who thought the burning smell might be coming from her car, drove us back to The Path, but the smell and the great sepia-yellow glow of the sun, low down over the sea, was still there when she left.

The walk started past a Sherman tank, a memorial to the American rehearsals for the D-day landings, and along the two-mile shingle ridge that separates the fresh-water lake, Slapton Ley from the sea. Then it headed inland and up, and we left Paul to follow on and to catch a bus from Strete. It turned out to be a double decker and so, it seemed, the extra sausage had been justified, especially when it overtook us as we negotiated Blackpool Sands and we could see him admiring the views from the upper deck.

The Path seemed to veer quite a way inland and we stopped at the war memorial in the churchyard in Stoke Fleming. It looked like the apocalypse had gone to look for a better place to start the destruction of the world, and the verger came out of the church and more or less insisted that we went in, visited, and presumably gave thanks, but only after we'd finished drinking tea of course. Lesley's mum messaged. She was worried. Her sky had gone all murky and a strange colour.

"Aha," we said, "it's the coming of the Apocalypse." But the TV knew better: Hurricane Ophelia, it reported, carrying dust from the Sahara and smoke from the wildfires in Spain and Portugal.

More inland paths eventually took us back to the coast again, where it was now hot and sunny but very, very windy. So much so, that the walking wardrobe became a bit of a handful (or should that be 'backfull'?). It was with some relief that we rounded the corner of the Dart estuary, full of boats moored up in safety, and started walking towards Dartmouth. Past Dartmouth castle and the adjacent old church we went, and then through woods, and actually through the ruins of another fortress, to the town itself.

It turned out to be rather nice, with some very interesting old buildings, places to see and very cheap out-of-date packets of crisps (we were Staaarving!). Paul had managed to get into the B&B soon after lunchtime and had spent the afternoon lying flat on the floor. But he did manage to get up and out to the oldest pub in town for the birthday meal.

Breakfast was on the first floor with a huge panoramic window looking out across the estuary. Two ferries were running. Two competing companies. Why couldn't one of them move round to one of the rivers we'd had to walk around, eh? The view was lovely, but Paul's back wasn't, so we left him drinking tea once again, and hatching a plan to use the steam train to get to Brixham.

On the other side of the estuary, a single lady walker seemed to be following us up the steep slope. We went faster; she matched us. A bit faster; the lady, the same. We stopped and greeted her. You won't believe it; her name turned out to be Sue! Fortunately, we'd had the advantage of a couple of moments rest and so were panting less than she was. She and her husband were walking the entire Coast Path, but in three- or four-day long bites. Her husband had developed a bad knee (she didn't seem convinced, but this was the story) and so she was continuing today, while he rested in Dartmouth, a town he very much liked. We walked together for a couple of hours, comparing notes, until we arrived at the boundary of the National Trust property of Coleton Fishacre. Apparently, she found it impossible to pass a place known to have a tea-shop without stopping. At the top of the next climb we found a bench and pulled out our Thermos flasks.

The book promised 'superb cliff scenery, tough in places' and with a rating of 'strenuous'. It was, and it continued to be so. Perhaps even 'severe' in places. As we got to the bottom of a deep dip, we met a chap of about thirty, with a giant-sized pack, coming the other way. He'd started at Lowestoft two months ago, planning to walk around the entire coastline of England, Wales and Scotland. However, his funds were being used up faster than expected, due to staying in too many B&Bs and hardly camping at all. He was contemplating doing just England and Wales, and cutting across the country at Hadrian's wall instead. We wished him well and watched him struggle up the steep incline, while we did the same on the other side.

Eventually, just before Berry Head, the path settled down a bit and the rain came. We arrived at Brixham harbour rather wet and to find Paul lurking in a bus shelter. It was still early afternoon, but for once I'd booked a small hotel and so we were let in and Paul went for a lie down, while Lesley and I dried out. Later we went for a stroll round the nice harbour town, but ended up in the Wetherspoon's nearby for a meal and perhaps the cheapest beer of the trip!

The following day started misty and later on the cloud came in so we could see hardly anything at all. But we did find a seal in Brixham harbour (until Lesley got her camera out, that is) as well as a big old-fashioned sailing galleon with lots of rigging.

The climb out of Brixham through woods had a lot of slippery steps and slippery wet leaves, covering slippery wet rocks and slippery wet roots. It was slippery. Up and down we went visiting small coves until we came out on a clear grassy promontory, where, in the distance we could see a steam train crossing a spectacular viaduct. Before long we were walking alongside the tracks taking photos whenever the train passed.

We approached the "English Riviera" of Paignton, Torbay and Torquay. There was a crocodile of colourful beach huts stretching along the shoreline in Paignton, where Paul went for the bus option again (Katie would have been proud of him). Even though we were walking on tarmac through an urban area, the Coast Path still managed to find ways to be very hilly. My feet started to ache and I changed into a pair of rather scruffy old running shoes. Just as I was feeling more comfortable, we re-entered slippery, steep woodland and the boots just had to go back on. Lesley's blisters were starting to give up and heal over. Or so she thought.

It was seriously steep down into Babbacombe, and we walked along the bottom of the cliffs by the sea over wooden walkways to the next bay, Oddicombe. Then it was seriously steep again, walking back up the cliff alongside the funicular railway. We were pleased to see that the acorn markers were still with us and we weren't just doing this to reach the B&B in the village at the top. We met Paul at the top, in the wide grassy 'park', and recovered for a while in the nearest pub.

Next day, the guide said 'Babbacombe to Teignmouth: strenuous'. It didn't lie. The roller-coaster path took us through woodland with no views. It was very humid and grey, but not actually raining. Lesley and I pressed on and we made good time in spite of tired legs and feet. She had renewed her blister bandages. I was wearing both neoprene knee supports. We were using a walking pole each; Cripples-R-us! Paul had generously offered to catch the bus home, so that when we got to Starcross we could call him and he could collect us in the car, saving us the five road-walking miles back to Kennford. No, that's not cheating! Honest! How could you suggest such a thing? Excuse: we'd done that section before on the Hare-Brained Hike and anyway it's not part of the Coast Path.

A rather pretty ferry took us over the river Teign. Other people, real people, not Coast Path people, were using it too. Ones without backpacks! And then the nature of the walk changed completely. We walked along Teignmouth sea-front alongside the sea wall and then out of town beside the (rather busy) railway line. As we left the shore to climb rich red cliffs of sandstone to go over a rather hilly bit, Portuguese Man o' War jellyfish were on display, washed inshore by the recent storm. Lesley insisted that they looked rather like used condoms. The (male) dog-walkers she imparted this information to looked somewhat surprised!

Dawlish: a repeat of Teignmouth; a sea-front by the sea wall and then out of town beside the (rather busy) railway line. It ended up at the out-of-season holiday resort town of Dawlish Warren. Roads, cycle tracks and rain took us onwards over flat ground the two-and-a-half miles to Starcross and the end point of our adventure. We hid in a bus shelter away from the rain and phoned Paul for rescue. We tried not to call him Sue. Warm, dry, and in the pub later on, thoughts turned to finishing the walk. Amazing really since the bodies had rather fallen apart on this one. The beer log contained bad news for Paul. He did approximately half the distance but, of course, all the beer. His Miles Per Gallon were down to almost nineteen, whilst mine was up above forty and Lesley won the Eco-award at almost ninety-eight. Perhaps Paul was keen to clock up some more miles and improve the overall economy.

10. The final POOsh (Starcross Poole October 2018)

October had arrived again and it seemed like time to try and finish what we'd started; to make the final POOsh, as it were. We'd been very pleased to find out that the railway station code for Poole is POO which gave many options for the title of this final expedition and, while the official walk ends at South Haven Point, unless you want to turn around and walk back to the start point again you really have to catch the ferry across the estuary and head on into Poole for your chosen escape route. Ours was the railway station near the old town, POO.

Strictly speaking we only needed to walk from Lyme Regis to Poole to finish, as we'd done the section from Exmouth to Lyme on the Hare-Brained Hike. However, Paul, who's responsible for start and end logistics, did some research into public transport from Exeter to Lyme Regis and back from Poole, and as a result floated an almost unthinkable idea.

"How about we start this one at Exmouth?" He ventured. "After all it's only a few days from there to Lyme, would make a better holiday and it's the only section we walked clockwise rather than in the 'proper' direction." What, Paul voting for extra helpings? Who were we to argue? Especially as last time we'd not seen it at its best, almost hermetically sealed, as we were, into our waterproofs for some of the days.

And so it was that we set off for Yeovil one Friday morning. 'Yeovil!' I hear you exclaim! Yes, you didn't see that coming did you. But just South of Yeovil is where Paul's friends Richard and Jenny live and they had promised to look after his dog, Suzy, for the duration, and their village is one of the places you can almost get to by train from Poole. The 'almost' is taken care of by a couple of footpaths. Complicated eh? Once there we separated Paul from his dog and took just one of them back to his house, although we did question whether we'd picked the one most likely to be able to finish the walk.

The weather gods were trying to put us off yet again, with heavy rain and strong winds. Storm Callum had arrived and was reported to be causing the worst flooding in Wales for thirty years. It claimed three lives. A 'danger to life' weather warning was in place for South Devon and the local news footage showed the sea breaching the coastal defences at Exmouth, just where the Coast Path runs. Why do we always get this just as we are about to start an expedition? Perhaps the BBC has it in for us.

It wasn't actually raining when we set off the next morning, but it was extremely blowy. Although the Starcross to Exmouth ferry was supposed to be running this late in the season, we didn't trust it and Paul's friend Teresa, who had volunteered to give us a lift to Starcross, now suggested that she took us all the way to Exmouth instead. It needs to be said that Teresa has featured already, as TBD in the last chapter. Since then she has accompanied Paul on various training trips by walking sections he cheated on last time. But now she seemed very keen that we, well Paul really, got going. It was a good job she did because when we arrived at the ferry point, a notice blamed the storm for giving the ferrymen some extra time off.

The instructions told us to examine the rock pools alongside the long promenade, but it was high tide and most of their contents, together with large amounts of sand, appeared to have been distributed on the road where we were trying to walk. Indeed, the sea was still shooting over the breakwater in places. Paul got a rather closer view than he would have liked, but amazingly, it was the only wetness of the day. Thank you, weather gods... or were they just playing with us?

When we were here last time on the Hare-Brained Hike, the landscape had also invaded the tarmac. Perhaps it's always like that. The difference this time was that there were people about, shops were open and so were the loos! At the far end we started to encounter Jurassic Coast World Heritage Site information boards. One helpfully told us that as we walked to Poole, we crossed geology from the start of the Triassic to the end of the Cretaceous periods, equivalent to 1,000 years per step!

After roughly 1,250,000 years, we came to the pyramid on Orcombe Point (posh name: geoneedle) and we started along the cliffs, along with what seemed to be everyone else. There were differences between them and us, we noticed. Firstly, they all seemed to have dogs that could run around on their own, while we had rucksacks that needed to be carried. Secondly, they were all properly dressed, while we'd felt the need to strip down to shorts.

All too soon, the eyesore of the enormous mobile home park near Sandy Bay encroached onto The Path and with it we found a few people sitting outside the café, trying to look like they were having a nice time and not being blown away at all. We continued; the going was easy and we were fresh. By lunchtime we'd reached Budleigh Salterton.

"Are you doing The Path?" an old gent asked. "I take my hat off to you".

We checked. The wind hadn't beaten him to it. But obviously he'd taken in the shorts, the rucksacks and the lack of dog, so what else could we possibly be doing? Several people told us that we 'looked the part' that afternoon. Strangely, we didn't get the same comments on future days. And I think we slightly disillusioned the gent by asking where there was a nearby pub, (for lunch, you understand, although Lesley did find some very nice beer too).

The next section should have been a walk inland alongside the river Otter, where beavers have taken up residence, but the path had been closed owing to an 'incident'. Unidentified flying heron perhaps? But the detour wasn't too far away and we ended up crossing the river on the correct bridge and heading back to the cliffs at the coast once more. Talk was of tea and cake as we carried on over the short turf and dropped down through trees to Ladram Bay, with its very red impressive collection of sea stacks. It also had another large mobile home park.

We'd had it easy up to now. Among the many people with dogs, we spotted a father and middle-aged son with rucksacks. They were doing a weekend of it: the same sections as us for today and tomorrow. Soon a very big, steep, intimidating sea-cliff faced us, our first big climb of the trip, and we left them behind. It was, of course, immediately followed by a huge drop and then another enormous climb before we started our descent into Sidmouth. Coming up the other way was a mother and daughter (probably in her fifties). She was walking in bare feet (pink toenails, for the record, or was that just blood?)

Paul had been very worried about his ability to complete the mission owing to the variety of system failures on the right side of his body that featured in the last chapter. Since then, lots of sessions with Katie the physio for his back and leg, and a support girdle thing to hold back the Alien (hernia) had finally convinced him to continue. Katie told him that he'd been walking wrongly for years and so he'd done lots of recent practice with the new silly walk, Suzy and the Berghaus bag, and was doing okay. In fact, much better than simply okay. As usual, Lesley and I seemed to have done absolutely no advance training whatsoever (except for eating pub food and drinking beer). When will we ever learn? So, as we walked along the promenade, made more difficult by the mounds of shingle and quite large pebbles covering the tarmac, Paul was fine, while Lesley and I were creaking rather at the knees and hips. After over fourteen miles, we felt that we'd done enough for the first day.

But the B&B was at the far end of town, up the High Street and beyond. I'd booked everything later than usual, as we waited for Katie and the Alien to give Paul the 'all clear'. Many of the B&B's were full: It turned out to be half term week for some schools. We rehearsed the potential conversation at the B&B.

"If she asks would you like tea and cake, what do you say?" Lesley, now not eating milk or eggs was rather inclined to say 'no thank you' rather than 'Ooh, yes please' and then secretly give her cake to her deserving husband. But it didn't matter. It was a guest house, so there was none on offer. But on the plus side it was very close to a useful curry house!

There was good news and bad, in the morning. The wind had dropped but the rain had come. The sea was a strange red-brown colour, rather like that of a good, strong cup of tea. As we started to tackle the first obstacles of the morning (we'd seen five very high hills and corresponding steep gullies ahead, on our approach to the town last night), we couldn't help but not notice people out walking, with or without dogs. There just weren't any.

The hills were exhausting and fully equipped with legions of killer-steps. Fortunately, we only had to climb three. The path detoured around two of the gullies, maintaining height. Eventually we dropped down to Branscombe Mouth and a big café, with heaters on full blast, and full of those missing people with dogs. It was Sunday lunchtime. The flapjacks were excellent. A thin couple came in with rucksacks but went to sit well away from us.

When we set off again, the rain had given it up as a bad job and the sun tried to come out, but it was distinctly cold. This time The Path didn't climb to the top of the nearest cliff, but instead picked a route along an old landslip between the cliff and the sea so we could admire the rocks: deep red rocks lower down, and white chalk with flints on top. All very striking, and Paul and Lesley had to suffer an impromptu geology lesson as we worked our way along and into the village of Beer.

Of course, Lesley had been promised some; beer, that is, and had been talking about it for some miles. We were doing well, well, Paul was. The creaky joints of the other team members were complaining again, but we had loads of time so we stopped in a busy pub. Soon after we settled down in a quiet corner, we noticed that the pub wasn't so busy anymore. In fact, it had almost emptied. Only day two, surely our clothes couldn't be that bad already.

It was about here that Paul made a confession. He'd added an extra secret column to my spreadsheet, which shows where we are walking each day, where our B&B is, and where we can find food in the evening. It turned out that Paul's version also had Lunchtime Pub Options. As a result, The Final POOsh turned out to be the booziest section of the entire walk, with forty-two different beers sampled between us in just ten days, coupled with a corresponding drop in our miles per gallon figures.

It was only a few of miles further on to our B&B in Seaton, but the path had been diverted around a cliff fall and so we ended up walking along a pebble beach for a long distance. It was slow and very tiring. Eventually we came to the promenade, with its colourful beach huts and people walking around all wrapped up in winter clothes. Some were even wearing woolly hats. We were still in shorts.

Tea, but no cake at the B&B and we also had trouble in the pub that night. The beer festival had finished some weeks ago, at the end of the summer season. The beer was poor, and the cider left over from the festival was not as fresh as it might have been. So, we went on to the Hat, a micro-pub in an old butchers' shop. It advertised good real beer without TV, sport or music, just old-fashioned pub chat, oh and hats, of course. Lots of them.

You know drizzle, the really wet sort? The type where you can pretend that it's not really raining, but where you are soon as wet as if you'd fallen into a river, and about as cold too? Well, as we left Seaton, crossing the estuary on the oldest concrete bridge in England (1877 if you are interested), that's what we got. We were heading for Lyme Regis and aiming to get there for Paul's choice of pub at lunchtime. It was this section of coast where we'd got completely drowned last time, on the Hare-Brained Hike.

After crossing a few fields, the path went down onto the great landslip of 1839. Once it was turnip fields, but now it's heavily wooded and, we noticed, has quite an array of damp-loving botany. As the narrow slippery path twisted and turned through what might possibly be the closest thing to real jungle in these parts, we gradually got wetter, if that was at all possible, and plodded on seeing no-one else at all. Pheasants ran along the path in front of us, just like small feathered dinosaurs. Well, this is the Jurassic Coast after all.

After about two-and-a-half hours, and still an hour or so from Lyme, we'd seen no-one, but just around a corner we found two couples who'd just stopped to talk to each other. As we chatted to them, yet another pair came out of the trees heading towards Seaton. These were the only people we saw on this entire section, so how come they were all just in this one place?

There were people in Lyme, of course, when we got there. Mostly they seemed to be hurrying between the car parks and the pubs and cafés. Paul's spreadsheet said that we were to go to the Pilot Boat, as we'd had a good evening there on the Hare-

191

Brained Hike. It had been ruined: changed into a fancy modern bistro, with prices to match and a mass-feeding, fast and furious service etiquette; the traditional fishing-village pub feel had been entirely exterminated.

And beyond there, there seemed to be no Coast Path signposts at all. We ended up in the tourist office and they had obviously been often asked where the route went. They even had a handout sketch-map to show the diversions, and the diversions on the diversions! In case you need to know, it now heads out of town along a brand-new section of promenade, some of which is cantilevered out over the sea, and then turns inland to climb a long set of steps to a car park and thus out to a road. After a while it leaves this to enter a very steep wood which, surprisingly and annoyingly after about twenty minutes of quite strenuous walking, loops around and brings you out again on the same road, some three hundred meters from where you left it! We weren't impressed!

So, when we eventually spotted a Coast Path sign, we followed it. It headed towards Charmouth, through the village and down to the sea. A mile or so later, back on the clifftops, we came to the place where the detour was supposed to emerge, having spent its time on roads and lanes. Golden Cap, the highest point on the South Coast of England, could just about be made out through the drizzle in the distance.

We sat for a rest on a bench. The creaky joints seemed to have self-healed, but now Lesley and I were both suffering from 'lead leg' syndrome whenever we encountered a decent hill. Any movement in the leg arena seemed to take an inordinate amount of effort. Paul, of course, was still doing well. Perhaps we had chosen the right Paul vs dog companion after all. He was doing well, that is, except for a bloody wound to his head, sustained from an aggressive low tree-branch in the pre-Lyme jungle and a cut on his hand due to an over-friendly encounter with a bramble. As carrier of the first aid kit, I was very disappointed that he refused several offers of large and spectacular plasters to make the wounds even more obvious than they already were.

A lone walker heading the other way joined us on the bench. It turned out that he was planning to do the entire Coast Path eventually, in day-trip sections. We gave him the tourist information handout, wished him luck and set off to tackle Golden Cap. We did reach the summit in the end, and even have pictures of us standing by the trig point in the drizzle to prove it.

Obviously from here, the only way was down. Down to Seatown, where I'd failed to find anywhere affordable to stay and so we had to head inland for a mile or so to a B&B at Chideock. Tea, and great showers, but no cake. It also had a large, friendly dog that got overexcited when it saw Paul and jumped up, head butting him in the mouth and causing more bleeding, just as we were about to go out. The family-run Clock pub was only a few metres from our B&B and had been recently rebuilt after a devastating fire. It was full of, well, clocks.

The luggage belonging to the 'thin couple' had been delivered to the B&B by a company that organises walking holidays. After the café we'd seen them a few times on The Path, but never close enough to talk to. Over breakfast, they revealed that they had started at Exmouth on the same day as us and had got just as wet as us. They admitted to having got lost on parts of the Great Lyme Regis Detours, but had only got to reach Portland to complete the entire Path, having done the final section some time previously. We set off before them in the now familiar drizzle back down the lane to Seatown, and never saw them again!

Looking at the map, I'd promised the others about three miles of up and down and then flattish for the rest of the day. Indeed, on reaching the coast, we were faced with a big up, straight into low cloud that pretty much obscured all the views. Back down again and we could admire Golden Cap, or at least its non golden foot. Then back up again we went, to Thorncombe Beacon. Well that was the plan. In the mist, we'd followed the most obvious path and had strayed too far inland and ended up on a bridleway. Fortunately, the cloud lifted just a bit as we realised we must have gone wrong and were wondering what to do about it. There it was, behind us but not too far away, and with two people on the top. It turned out that,

193

despite the weather, lots of dogs and their people were out today.

Three miles of ups and downs saw us in West Bay, with a nice little harbour, houses, a gravel (hard to walk on) beach and another big climb out. Not too high but very steep. The grassy clifftop settled down to mere undulations rather than epic inclines. Hurrah! The cloud lifted and the sun attempted to come out. A mile or so further and we'd dropped to sea level, to witness yet another mobile home site, at Burton Freshwater, and here we needed to follow the river inland to cross at a footbridge further up. A chap with a golden retriever told us that a mere half-mile detour would take us into the village where there were two pubs. Paul's spreadsheet revealed the same. As it was Lesley's birthday and as it was lunchtime, she insisted, so we had no choice really.

Yes, that's right, Lesley's birthday. Good news. It meant that her birthday present, a posh new fleece that had been weighing my pack down for days, could be extracted and handed over at breakfast so that she could carry it the rest of the way. That's fair isn't it? Don't you agree? Well, Lesley didn't. She insisted that I carried her grotty old fleece instead.

The pub had very strong, very black beer; Lesley's new favourite. Oh, and chips as well. Somewhat drier, warmer and merrier, we returned to the coast a little later and the turfy flat path continued for a while as we walked behind a shingle beach. Eventually the path gave up and we had to walk on the shingle itself. It was like the gravel you might put on your driveway, only much, much deeper and less compacted. It was exhausting walking, even if it was quite pretty! And it went on for some miles.

Eventually it turned into a tarmac track before veering inland and heading for our destination, Abbotsbury, with its nice old cottages, and St Catherine's chapel sitting on a small hill just outside the village. We stayed in the pub. No cake there! And Paul, supposedly experienced by now, made a schoolboy error: washing his clothes before the heating came on. It never did.

Abbotsbury is famous for its swannery. Originally it was set up to provide meat for the abbey, but now, of course, it is a tourist attraction. Attractive it was not, when we walked past the entrance. For a start it was closed, and secondly the weather gods seemed to be on a mission to outdo the badness of the TV forecast. Rain is what we got: some heavy, some drizzle, some low cloud, but all very wet, cold and rather miserable.

The path stayed inland for quite a while on leaving Abbotsbury, and we trudged through fields on what might have been a small ridge, in low clouds with nothing to see. Somewhere around here, the familiar wooden signposts of the Coast Path gave way to what looked like small gravestones! Eventually, we dropped down to the lakeside, below the clouds. What should have been a lovely walk, along the inland shore of the lake known as 'Fleet', was muddy, slippery and damp.

After five-and-a-half miles, we were pretty soaked. It was midday: time for a stop. The cell on the spreadsheet of possible lunchtime pubs was empty. Moonfleet Manor had a sign outside, offering morning coffee and afternoon teas, but it looked very posh. Later we found out that it advertises itself as a 'luxury family hotel and spa'. They claimed to welcome dogs, but for some reason didn't mention drowned rats. We were desperate and gave it a try anyway. A Polish lady greeted us warmly (warmth was what we needed!). She invited us in, seemed to have no problem with our damp muddiness, and insisted that we took up pole position in a very large, posh drawing-room right by a big fireplace. She then even lit the fire, so we could dry out.

We sat there, drinking tea/coffee for an hour, until really, we did have to move on. People, mostly rather plump middle-aged women if truth be known, kept walking through the room in twos and threes giggling and whispering when they saw us. We wondered if Ms Poland was using us as some sort of weird attraction for her 'normal' guests, or perhaps to encourage them not to escape to outside.

Outside hadn't improved. We plodded on. The army were busy shooting things at the rifle range near Charlestown and so we had a bit of extra diverted distance there too. Eventually, through the gloom, the bridge across to the causeway leading to Portland came into view. We noticed that, on the busy road, all the cars had their lights on and wipers going.

The official end point for this section was Ferrybridge, on the mainland end of the bridge. For almost all of this trip I'd stuck to the recommended stopping places. It gave us some shorter than normal distances, probably a good thing, but there were few other options, given the need to reach Lulworth Cove on a Friday or Saturday night. This was important. Failure to do so would mean exchanging what was promised to be an excellent section of coast walking through the Lulworth firing ranges, with a much longer day of inland road walking. But here, at Ferrybridge, the only place to stay (called, rather unsurprisingly, the Ferrybridge Inn) had closed. It was all boarded up and looked rather sad. A planning application had been made to convert the site into houses.

We continued, across the bridge and along the length of the causeway that is part of Chesil Beach, and then on another mile or so, around the marina and the site of the 2012 Olympic sailing events, until we reached our budget hotel in Castletown. There was a World War II torpedo outside and also an American Sherman tank. We left a trail of mud behind as we were shown to our rooms. Good job it was budget laminate flooring and not expensive carpet. But the receptionist didn't seem to mind and the rooms were okay. Importantly for Paul and his wet clothing and wet laundry, the heating was on!

I hadn't been worried about finding food for the evening until we suddenly realised that the pub over the street didn't have any real ale, and neither did our hotel or the one opposite. Google, and Lesley's phone came to the rescue and they took us to what seemed to be an old pub on Chesil Beach that had become run down and was being rescued by a very enthusiastic chef and barmaid. When Lesley started asking what was in the food so she could find something to eat, the chef eagerly shot out of the kitchen for a long chat and started making suggestions as to the specials he could cook just for her. She was impressed.

The official route undertakes a circumnavigation of Portland Island, so that no part of the coast is missed. We therefore had the novel experience of staying in the same place for two nights running, which meant not having to carry all our worldly possessions in the walking wardrobe and Berghaus bags.

Because we hadn't been able to stay at Ferrybridge Inn it was only eleven-and-a-half miles. The weather had broken. For the better. At last we had a lovely sunny day. And we had company; Richard had stopped off on his way to work and left us with Paul's dog, Suzy.

So, we headed back to the end of the causeway and followed the Southern part of Chesil beach towards Portland's cliffs, made of the famous limestone which has been used in the construction of many of London's important buildings. Yes, I used the 'cliff' word, and before long we were climbing steeply up the nearest one, straight towards an old quarry. Now it's also a sculpture park, with carvings on rocks still in place and other standalone sculptures that make excellent dog drinking bowls.

Onwards again, and around the cliffs to reach the tip of the island, Portland Bill. It boasts an obelisk, no less than three lighthouses, a car park, a visitors' centre and even tourists of the non-walking and non-dog-owning variety. The sea was deep blue with white-caps. We were taking it easy in the sunshine knowing that it was not a long day. It meant that we had plenty of time for a short detour to Paul's lunchtime pub. It was full of Halloween ghouls, spiders and bats, and, dare I say it, a barmaid who looked like she was already ready for the big night, even though it was still a couple of weeks away. Suzy enjoyed the beer.

Round we went, staying high on the cliffs and looking down on a couple of goats near a rifle range below. A dog-walker told us that a few, all billys, had been released to help keep the vegetation in check, but what good would a few goats be on an area this big? We admired the wall of a young offenders' Institute (from the outside!) and the walls of the Verne Citadel, an old defensive fortification and the headquarters of the coast artillery in both World Wars, but now a prison (also from the outside!) before dropping down an old railway track to emerge in Castletown, almost opposite the hotel.

It was still early, much too early for Richard to finish work and collect Suzy. The hotel was absolutely adamant that while wet, muddy people were okay, clean dogs were not. So, we took it in turns to sit outside in the sun with Suzy, while others showered and got clean. Eventually, as it started to get chilly, we did the decent thing. The thing that you'd totally expect by now. Of course, we convinced ourselves that we were just finding somewhere suitable for a rendezvous. It was a pub, of course. Right on the top of Chesil beach, it had windows facing West, straight out to sea to watch the fantastic sunset over the water. As well as beer, Suzy was given dog biscuits by the barmaid and so was very happy. Richard duly came and joined us for another beer, and then it was time once again to separate Paul from his dog. He was a bit miffed that Suzy seemed to go off with Richard without a fuss, though.

With Richard and Suzy's help, the beer log recorded that on this day we'd managed to visit four pubs and consume one and a half gallons of beer! Paul mainly blamed the dog!

We were back to normal the next day. Well, perhaps we weren't. The creakiness of the joints from the first few days had long since gone and yesterday had been better than a rest. Easy, interesting and it kept the muscles moving. We felt great and simply shot back over the causeway to the mainland to find that the path followed a nice, flat disused railway track towards the outskirts of Weymouth. We were soon there. The views back to Portland were lovely. The wind had dropped, the sun was out and shorts and t-shirts were the garments of choice. Down at the attractive harbour, the lifting bridge (similar in operation to Tower bridge in London) was, well, lifting and we watched the boats come through.

Beyond there was a very long section along the seafront, full of people promenading and out with their dogs. There did seem to be an awful lot of dogs in Dorset. We stopped for ice cream and tea/coffee at a simple seaside kiosk that was just opening. Elderly people started to come and join us. It became obvious that this was their daily routine. But what do you think they do when it's raining? No, I don't have an answer either.

We also met a surprising number of other Path walkers on the cliffs East of Weymouth. At least that's what they claimed to be. They were easy to spot by their big rucksacks and sparse clothing. There was the young couple who lived in Dorset, and so felt duty bound to do the Exmouth to Poole section. She seemed very keen indeed, although did confess to almost having a meltdown when it was very wet and when they had walked the section to Ferrybridge as well as the Portland circuit on the same day. He seemed less so, or perhaps that was because Lesley engaged them in conversation just as he was halfway through removing his trousers (to be clear, he was changing into shorts)!

There was the 'competitive dad' and his daughter. They were aiming to walk a hundred miles to raise money for her to go to Kenya. She went to dancing classes four times a week and so was much fitter than her dad (who looked more like he went to the pub four times a week). He was very enthusiastic, she less so. We met them again towards the end of the day. She still looked fine but dad was suffering rather and starting to wonder whether they should have planned day-trips, rather than consecutive days.

There was the old couple. He was 84 and she was 82, and we met them on a hilltop just West of Osmington Mills and they were still going strong. Strong in the walking department and strong in the talking department too.

Portland was still there, in the distance when we looked back.

At Osmington Mills, the path actually takes a route through the pub terrace, weaving its way between the picnic benches. It was lunchtime so we stopped of course, but when the young couple came through, she told us "If we stop for a pint we'll never get going again". And that was the last we saw of them.

By now the weather was absolutely gorgeous and the path started to get progressively tougher but even more spectacular. The sea was calm and deep blue, and the cliffs had turned from red sandstone to shining white chalk. There were three famous and impressive sights right at the end of this section: the great sea arch of Durdle Door, the folded rocks of Stairhole and the beautiful horseshoe-shaped Lulworth Cove.

The viewpoint overlooking Durdle Door is perhaps a mile from the visitors' centre and large car park at Lulworth Cove. A wide track leads from one to the other, and it was busy with sightseers on a lovely Friday afternoon. Many were shod in inappropriate footwear and, we noticed, the majority were speaking to each other in languages other than English. And what was that, visible in the distance? Oh yes, Portland. But it was towards the end of the day and, by the time we arrived in Lulworth and looked around a bit, the crowds had started to disperse. We headed on up the road towards West Lulworth and our B&B, searching as we went for the start of the path we needed in the morning. We found it. It had been blocked off.

Just as we pondered and looked at the map, a young chap on a bicycle stopped and offered to help. His job, he said, was directing lost tourists! We soon found out that yes, the path had been diverted again but, and here was some good news, if we took a different path almost opposite our B&B it would climb up to a long ridge that we could then walk along, rather than dropping back down to the sea again. It was even shown as an official variant of the Coast Path on my map. Finally, he revealed that the army ranges, closed all week and open most, but not all weekends at this time of year, would not unlock their gates until nine in the morning. There was no point in the very early start that I had been secretly planning.

The B&B was a surprise, and not just because it had drawings of dinosaurs riding bicycles on the walls. I'd phoned around just about everywhere, anywhere near Lulworth. Friday on a school holiday weekend when the firing ranges are open. Not a chance, until, that is, I was being turned away yet again and mentioned to the lady on the phone that we were walking The Path.

"Oh!" She said, "You could try my friend J., she'll do you proud!"

It turned out that J. doesn't advertise on the Internet and has a cottage on the main street through the village, just a few minutes from the absolutely heaving pub. We voted her 'biggest breakfast on the trip'. For example, Paul (no eggs or tomatoes) had a plate with three large sausages, extra bacon and a whole heap of mushrooms. Had we got one, we would also have given her the award for the most pillows and cushions on the bed. Paul had to remove no less than ten before there was room for him, and with rooms that were not overly large, the problem was where to put them all. So, why does a bed need ten soft cushions in addition to the normal pillows anyway?

The recommended walk is from Lulworth Cove to Worth Matravers, a village a little over a mile inland and at a distance of about fourteen miles. It is graded 'Severe', the highest possible rating. There is nowhere else really to stop before that. Unfortunately, I'd completely failed to find anywhere to stay anywhere near there. I'd been offered rooms a week later, or on days when the army range was closed, which were of course no use to us. So, I'd finally proposed a choice: postpone the whole holiday until the spring, or book a B&B in Swanage and either walk the whole way, twenty-one miles, or use taxis from where we give up and to return the next morning. Hence the idea of the early start.

So, we left the B&B, with as many Swanage taxi phone numbers as we could find and with breakfast weighing heavily inside us, at eight forty-five to climb the steep hill to the ridge and to the army firing-range gate. We arrived exactly at nine and it was already open. Ahead of us, a couple, all dressed in black, had just gone through. It turned out to be a great section. Yo-yo, yes but spectacular and almost like climbing some of the mountains in parts of the Brecon Beacons. It culminated in the large iron-age Binden Hill fort. Oh, so high and oh, so steep!

More severe walking and we came to the lovely Pondfield Cove: rather like Lulworth and horseshoe in shape, but without the crowds. There were two yachts anchored there; very picturesque. The weather was gorgeous. There were tanks hiding behind bushes, and all the time the black-clad couple strode on, about half-a-mile ahead.

We exited the ranges in Kimmeridge Bay. A visitors' centre and car park ensured that on a hot, sunny half-term Saturday there were lots of people about, but none who claimed to be doing The Path. The closest we got was a father, and son of about ten. They were going the other way and planned to camp for three days. The son was very excited. He'd been promised a cheeseburger in the pub that night – if they made it.

A signpost told us that Swanage was only another eleven miles distant. We didn't believe it! We could still see Portland behind us. At Chapman's Pool, yet another horseshoe shaped cove, but this one with exceptionally deep-blue water, we finally caught up with the black-clad couple. Mainly because they had stopped and turned around to go back the other way. They were South Africans, relocated to Dorset, out for a day trip. They'd planned a long walk! But, we reassured ourselves, they were at least thirty years younger than us.

Now we were onto the cliffs of St Aldhelm's Head. Short turf, easy walking, but then a sudden killer. Almost invisible until you were right up to it, it was so steep that it needed steps all the way down, and all the way back up the other side (Paul counted two-hundred-and-seventeen on the way back up). In the crevasse at the bottom, we met a couple going the other way. Once we gained the top we collapsed on a convenient bench, and noticed that they'd just done the same on the other side.

We managed to scrounge some water from the Coast-watch lookout station on the point. We'd drunk almost all of ours and had started rationing it. No-one was expecting these kinds of temperatures two weeks before bonfire night and, apparently, they'd been dishing it out all day.

We rounded the point and caught a glimpse of a lighthouse further along. It looked a long way off, but the distance was hard to judge. It soon disappeared again as the coastline curved round. It was decision time. We could see Worth Matravers inland. Was it time to head there for a rather late lunchtime pint and call for a taxi? But we were doing well and so, for once, the vote was to continue and bail out later on.

Looking at the map now, it seems as though the lighthouse was some four miles or so from where we first saw it, but well before we expected it, it showed up again, just in front of us. We'd gone beyond all the escape routes! Further on we could see The Needles off the Isle of Wight, gleaming in the sunlight, and, at last, looking back, Portland was no more. Durlston Head, with its ten-foot diameter stone globe, crowds of people and where the Coast Path heads North on its final approach to Swanage was not far away.

I'd booked us somewhere to stay, as close as I could to this end of town. Starting from West Lulworth and using the ridge path had saved us a little distance. We cut across Peveril Point and headed straight for the B&B, saving a bit more. And we made it. We rang the bell. They were surprised to see us. I'd suggested an arrival time of seven, but here we were and it was only five-thirty. We were surprised too. Amazed might be a better description. The distance had been nineteen-and-a-half miles. We agreed with the rating: Severe! It was among the top three longest walks that we'd completed on The Path, and the other two had been in the relative flatness around Plymouth.

And now came the final, final POOsh, as it were. From the B&B, we walked back to where we'd left the path, to 'do' Peveril Point, a mostly grassy section with dogs bounding about, before dropping down to walk along Swanage sea-front. It was packed. The weather was outstanding, just like a summer's day. The climb out of the town through New Swanage was not too hard, and was the last decent climb of the trip. We met a family halfway up the hill and hearing that we were due to complete the entire walk today, they repeated the phrase from the start of this adventure: 'Hats off to you'. Sadly, they weren't wearing any.

Easy clifftops and signposts to 'Old Harry' followed. The path entered a large turfed area, where there were masses of people, masses of dogs and a film crew lugging stuff up the slope. Offshore, 'Old Harry', a chalk sea-stack was being circled by canoeists. The path onto Studland was something like the London Marathon, but at walking pace and two-directional. There were just so many people (and dogs) of all shapes and sizes. One lady had her dog on a short lead. It tried to play with another and ran round and round her, spinning her like a top. About a hundred people laughed!

We went onto the beach and, although we left the crowds behind, it was still busy. The tide was quite high and so everyone was crammed into a small section between the dunes and the sea. We joined the procession by the water's edge, heading towards Poole, now easily visible in the distance. We tried walking in the dunes: too hard. Even the nudist area was busy. For the first time on the trip we felt overdressed.

It was a long slog and, if truth be known, rather dull. The walk finished, rather lamely, at South Haven Point by a giant, white car ferry. There was nothing spectacular, just a commemorative marker, standing about four metres high, to take some pictures with. It all felt rather an anti-climax. We took the ferry over to Poole with the aim of finding a pub for a celebratory drink.

It was not to be. The map shows the E9 European Long-Distance Route 2, also known as the Poole Harbour Trail at this point. It would take us to Poole old town and POO, the railway station. Surely it must pass some pubs on the way? But no, it walked past big, posh houses on hard, flat tarmac for about five miles. The tide was out and the fragrance had, perhaps, helped the planners decide on the railway station code. The traffic was considerable, and seemed to have more than its fair share of Aston Martins and Ferraris and the like.

We asked Google if there were any pubs nearby. It said no. We asked someone on a pavement. He directed us to a marina some miles ahead, which turned out to be a little off-route. The civilization was all a bit of an unwelcome shock. In the end, we abandoned the Poole Harbour Trail and cut across to our B&B in the old town. It was a café in the pedestrian area. Earlier, I'd received a text from Agent Fiona with the secret access code and the promise of further information in a sealed envelope when we arrived. Once we'd bravely entered the building, the further information turned out to be that the café was closed this week, but there were more secret codes to get into our rooms, secret Wi-Fi codes and an ever-so secret breakfast menu. Fortunately, the letter didn't self-destruct; we're not that good at remembering secret codes. Even though it was a café there was no cake!

We discarded our boots, set off from the safe-house and walked down to the harbour. It was lined with pubs. They were busy with people sitting outside in the sunshine. We joined them. We'd completed The South West Coast Path. What an achievement!

"What's next?" I was asked.

All the memories of the wet muddiness and the aches and pains seemed to have evaporated in the warm sunshine.

A follow-up to the Hare-Brained Hike maybe. "How about Return of the Hares?"

Perhaps.

Printed in Great Britain
by Amazon